HOLY TERROR

LIES THE CHRISTIAN RIGHT TELLS US TO DENY GAY EQUALITY

MEL WHITE

MAGNUS
BOOKS

Magnus Books
Cathedral Station
PO Box 1849
New York, NY 10025

Library of Congress cataloging-In-Publication Data available.
Printed in the United States of America on acid-free paper.

First Pulished by the Penquin Group 2007
First Magnus Edition 2012

Cover by: Wendy Bass

ISBN-13: 978-1-936833-09-2

www.magnusbooks.com

To Gary Nixon
Thank you for twenty-five amazing years!

Married in the eyes of God, our families, and friends,
but still denied the 1,047 rights and protections
that go automatically with civil marriage.

Also By Mel White

Stranger at the Gate:
To Be Gay and Christian in America

CONTENTS

Part Three
THE GREAT FUNDAMENTALIST HERESIES

Part Four
RESISTING FUNDAMENTALISM

PREFACE

"Those who cannot remember the past are condemned to repeat it."
—George Santayana

On July 1, 1999, Matthew and Tyler Williams broke into the country home of Gary Matson and Winfield Scott Mowder. The men's nude bodies were found the next day riddled with bullets. These two innocent men were murdered for one reason and one reason alone: they were gay. Sally Williams asked her son, Matthew, why he had killed "the two homos." Matthew replied, "I had to obey God's law rather than man's law...I just plan to defend myself from the Scriptures."[1]

This fear and loathing of homosexuals was shaped in William's mind—as it is currently being shaped in the minds of tens of millions of Americans—by the anti-homosexual teachings of the "religious right," Protestant and Catholic alike. To young Williams, if homosexuals are such a "threat to the family, to the church and to the nation," it only seemed natural to eliminate that threat.

At his trial, Williams made the connection between the "religious right" and the murder of two innocent gay men. "You obey a government of man until there is a conflict," he explained. "Then you obey a higher law. So many people claim to be Christians," Williams added. "They complain about all these things their religion says are a sin, but they're not willing to do anything about it. They don't have the guts."[2]

How long will it take for gay-bashing fundamentalists on the "religious right" to realize that their anti-homosexual campaigns lead directly to discrimination, bullying, suicide, torture and even death? During the trial of the young man who killed his brother, Mark Matson, who teaches at a Christian college, admitted to a reporter that "Gary saw the danger of the religious right...For him Christianity or at least a perverse segment of it was dangerous."[3]

Here's the really bad news. That "perverse segment" is back. In 2008, millions of Americans thought Barack Obama's election signaled the defeat and eventual disappearance of the "religious right." There was a collective sigh of relief that Christian fundamentalists had lost the war they were waging to create a nation ruled by biblical law (and to drive lesbian, gay, bisexual and transgender Americans back into their closets). Unfortunately fundamentalist Christianity didn't die that death. It simply went underground. On November 2, 2010 the "Christian right" returned in full strength.

Check out, for example, the demographics of the Tea Party movement and its allies across the U.S. It may be premature to say that the Tea Party movement is simply the "religious right" in disguise. But one recent survey reveals that nearly half of those who identify with the Tea Party consider themselves a part of the old "religious right." They believe the Bible is the literal word of God. They believe that America is a Christian nation and that public officials local, state and federal should pay more attention to [the Christian] religion.[4] Sixty-three percent believe that abortion should be illegal. Eighty-two percent oppose same-sex marriage.[5]

It's beginning to look like the goals and values of that "perverse segment" have been passed from the Moral Majority and the Christian Coalition to the Tea Party movement. Did you notice in the statistics above that Tea Partiers are almost united in their opposition to marriage equality? Think about it. At the very top of their social agenda is to deny lesbian and gay couples the rights and protections of marriage. And ending abortion rights is the second highest goal on their list. Homosexuality and abortion were the two hot button issues used by the old "religious right" to create fear, raise funds and motivate volunteers. How long before the Tea Party types do the same? It doesn't take much to conclude that the Tea Party movement represents a clear and present danger not just to the gay community but to all Americans who refuse to support their goals and values" or join them in making this "a Christian nation."

When I say "Tea Party movement" I am not describing the hardcore members of the Tea Party itself. I am describing a mentality, a set of goals, a hierarchy of values that is winning the minds and hearts of middle-America. Only that mentality, those goals and values are not new. They're just being packaged differently. If the Tea Party movement is in fact the old "religious right" in disguise, then the politicians and talk show hosts who lead the Tea Party movement have replaced televangelists and clergy as leaders of the "new religious right."

Listen carefully to Sarah Palin, Glenn Beck, Rush Limbaugh and their other comrades on the "right" and you'll hear the ghost of Jerry Falwell come back to haunt us. What the politicians and talk show hosts are saying about the nation, about the Bible, about abortion and homosexuality is exactly what Falwell and the other Christian fundamentalists on the "religious right" have been saying for decades.

Sarah Palin, for one example, believes that America is a christian nation and that it is "mind boggling" to suggest it isn't.[6] It is really frightening to think that the second most popular woman in America (after Hillary Clinton) believes that the nation's forefathers "...were quite clear that we should create law based on the God of the Bible," especially when she means a literal view of the Bible which would stone women caught in the act of adultery and execute men in same-sex relationships.[7] Palin told members of her congregation in Alaska that the Iraq war is "a task that is from God" and part of "God's plan." She also asked her fellow church members to pray for a $30 billion natural gas pipeline project she wants to build.[8]

Politicians, like former Governor Palin, who associate with (or try to please) the Tea Party movement are closely allied with the talk show hosts who drive the movement forward. For example, on August 17, 2010, politician Sarah Palin was a special guest of talk show host Glen Beck during his "Restoring Honor" rally on the steps of the Lincoln Memorial. Beck sounded so much like Falwell and the other leaders of the old "religious right" with his dangerous mix of politics and religion. "This day is a day that we can start the heart of America again," Beck began. "And it has nothing to do with politics. It has everything to do with God."[9]

It is ironic that in 1980 Jerry Falwell launched the Moral Majority with rallies on state capitol steps identical to Beck's rally thirty years later. In 1980, Falwell rallied Americans who still believed in "decency, the home, the family, morality, the free enterprise system."[10] The content of Beck's rally in 2010 was pure Falwell with a similar appeal to decency, the home, the family, morality, and the free enterprise system. In commenting on Beck's "Restoring Honor" rally, Robert Parham, Executive

Director of the Baptist Center for Ethics, described the politics of both men. "No amount of Bible reading, sermons masquerading as prayers and Christian hymns can cover up Beck's civil religion that slides back and forth between the Bible and nationalism, between authentic faith and patriotic religion."[11]

Leaders of the old "religious right" are happy to use the Tea Party movement to achieve their long-range goals for the nation. These antigay clergy are not gone. They're standing in the shadows applauding the politicians and talk show hosts who have taken up their cause. On September 7, 2010, just a few weeks after Beck's rally, Media Matters posted on AlterNet a list of 16 anti-gay religious extremists "in Glen Beck's creepy Christian army."[12] If you want to see the source of Glen Beck's power, look closely at the crowd of antigay biblical literalists gathered just behind Beck at the Lincoln Memorial. Consider these two examples.

Richard Land was there. Land is without doubt the most powerful man in the Southern Baptist Church and a major player in the antigay movement. As president of its Ethics & Religious Liberty Commission, Land has become the public face of the 16,000,000 member Southern Baptist Convention. Standing next to Land was John Hagee, the pastor of Cornerstone, the antigay mega church in San Antonio, Texas. Hagee is a charismatic who advocates speaking in tongues. Land is a Baptist who is wary of the charismatic movement and opposed to speaking in tongues. One of the primary reasons these two powerful preachers, with all their differences, stood behind a talk show host on the steps of the Lincoln Memorial is the fear they share about the gradual acceptance of homosexuality and homosexuals by the American public.

Land, a Bush White House favorite, sounded just like Falwell and Robertson after 9/11 when he warned that if the

U.S. continues to create policies which affirm homosexuals "...it will provide further impetus for God's judgment on the nation."[13] Hagee once described the antichrist as a "homosexual who is partially Jewish, as was Hitler, as was Karl Marx."[14] These men and the other antigay clergy on the "religious right" are standing behind Beck because he is the new face of the "religious right." Beck's values are their values. And they will support anyone who seems powerful enough to get their values superimposed on the rest of us.

With approximately 25,000,000 listeners ("Ditto Heads") Rush Limbaugh is the most popular and possibly most powerful leader of the "new religious right." Limbaugh announced that the Tea Party is "the first time" that "everyday citizens" have "risen up" "since the Civil War."[15] Jerry Falwell practically crowned Limbaugh as his successor in a televised sermon he preached on November 21, 1994. During this pre-Thanksgiving broadcast, America's leading fundamentalist told his nationwide audience: "I thank God now in the 21st century for talk radio." Then he praised Rush Limbaugh and other talk show hosts "who are telling the truth of what really is going on."[16]

On June 23, 1994, President Bill Clinton called the *Rush Limbaugh* show from Air Force One to condemn both Limbaugh and Falwell for their false charges against him. The President described fundamentalist leaders perfectly when he expressed his anger at those who "come into the political system and then say that anybody that doesn't agree with them is godless, anyone who doesn't agree with them is not a good Christian, anyone who doesn't agree with them is fair game for any wild charge, no matter how false, for any kind of personal, demeaning attack."[17]

In his rebuttal, Mr. Limbaugh laughed off the President's claim that Americans had no way to know whether what Limbaugh said was true. "There is no need for a truth detector,"[18] Limbaugh declared. "I am the truth detector." Even if he's joking, most supporters of the "religious right" are not that honest. If you have ever attempted to change a fundamentalist's mind you will discover first fundamentalists can't listen to new truth and second even if they do listen they will not change their views no matter what new truth they hear.

Limbaugh is a perfect example of a fundamentalist who refuses to be informed by new truth (and thus the perfect man to represent the fundamentalist "truths" of the "religious right.") And though he says it with tongue in cheek, it isn't really very funny when Limbaugh describes himself as one who does everything "...flawlessly with zero mistakes, doing this show with half my brain tied behind my back just to make it fair because I have talent on loan from...God."[19]

The self-acclaimed "truth detector" doesn't believe in climate change because his God "wouldn't have created humans with a capacity to destroy our own environment." He announced there was no need to clean up the BP oil spill in the Gulf of Mexico because, "The Ocean will take care of this on its own if it was left alone and left out there."[20] He claimed that God "revealed His opinion" about President Obama's health care bill by erupting a volcano in Iceland and shutting down air travel all across Europe.[21]

Limbaugh has equally ridiculous yet equally dangerous "truths" about homosexuality and homosexuals. When a high school teacher called his show to express her fears about gay bashing, the "truth detector" accused openly gay students of "trumpeting" their sexual orientation and "inviting dissent."[22] Limbaugh said that those who are working towards marriage equality "...seek to impose their perverted views, their depraved views on family and marriage...There's a definition of it [marriage]," Limbaugh added. "Marriage is a union of a man and a woman...This is about destroying an institution."[23] In his January 1, 2009, broadcast Limbaugh called Rep. Barney Frank, a gay man and a key member of the House Banking Committee, the "Banking Queen" and then went on to demean Frank with a comedian's rendition of a song written for the occasion: "The Banking Queen."[24]

Several gay bloggers thought Limbaugh's position on homosexuality had changed when he paid Elton John $1,000,000 to entertain at his fourth wedding. Elton John likes Limbaugh and is hoping to win him over. But Limbaugh's wedding was not a triumph for gay rights. Consider the man Limbaugh hired to conduct his wedding ceremony, the Rev. Ken Hutcherson.

Hutcherson, a fundamentalist pastor and notorious gay basher, has led campaigns to defeat the Matthew Shepherd Hate Crime bill; to defeat a ballot measure protecting workers from being fired on the basis of their sexual orientation; to stop the Day of Silence opposing "bullying" and harassment at his daughter's high school; and to defeat a bill for marriage equality. "Gay equality is not a civil rights issue," he said. "It is a moral and sexual preference issue...The gay community is not the new African American community...I've seen a lot of ex-gays," he said, "but I've never seen an ex-black."[25] The Rev. Hutcherson has been a very active spokesman for the values of the old "religious right." Now, as Rush Limbaugh's muse and monitor, Hutcherson is helping shape "the new "religious right" as well.

It is no coincidence that leaders of the new "religious right" are looking more and more like leaders of the old "religious right" with the Bible in one hand and the American flag in the other. On May 7, 2011, five potential Republican presidential candidates met for the first time to lay out their political agendas before 1,000 Iowa activists. An eyewitness described their meeting place as the "...star-spangled auditorium at Point of Grace Church outside Des Moines, Iowa."[26] The host pastor, Jeff Mullen, was a primary force in rallying the people of Iowa to recall the three Supreme Court judges whose unanimous decision in April 2009 legalized same-sex marriage.[27] And the host of that political forum was Ralph Reed, once President of Pat Robertson's Christian Coalition now President of the national Faith and Freedom Coalition.

"My message to the national Republican party tonight is real simple," Reed said. "If you turn your backs on the pro-family, pro-life constituents, and the values they stand for, you will be consigned to permanent minority status." In his opening remarks, former Louisiana Gov. Buddy Roemer responded to anyone who had doubts about his political agenda: "I'm a pro-life, traditional values man," he said and the other candidates rushed to show that they, too, were "pro-life, traditional values" men.

Is it necessary to remind ourselves that "pro-life" and "traditional values" were code words used by the old "religious right" to disguise their anti-abortion, anti-gay agenda? Put simply, the new "religious right" is as determined as the old "religious right" to repeal *Roe v. Wade*, the Supreme Court's decision to legalize abortion on demand (ending women's right to terminate an unwanted pregnancy) and to defend and enforce the Defense of Marriage Act (ending marriage equality for lesbian and gay Americans.) In Yogi Berra's oft-quoted words, "It's déjà vu all over again."

In a Christian church decorated in red, white, and blue (not a good sign if you believe in the separation of church and state) the potential Republican candidates also agreed in their far more dangerous agenda. Tim Pawlenty, the former governor of Minnesota, expressed it this way: "We need to be a country that turns toward God. Not a country that turns away from God." A reporter for the *Iowa Independent* summarized the "turn to God" theme expressed that night by five Republicans who would be President: "Each repeatedly referenced the country's founding fathers and the mention of God in the both federal and state founding documents. They all also made some mention of power not deriving from government, but rather from God or a creator."[28]

"God" is another code word especially popular these days with ultra-conservative politicians and talk show hosts. Invariably, the person who calls for the nation "to turn to God" (and is serious about it) is calling the nation to turn to "the Laws of God" as found in the inerrant Bible. And though it seems rather harmless when a politician or talk show hosts talks about turning to God, he or she is actually calling for the inerrant Bible to be used as the ultimate authority over the U.S. Constitution and all other state and federal laws.

According to the *Baltimore Sun*, on Wednesday, March 1st, 2006, in Annapolis, Maryland, at a hearing on the proposed Constitutional Amendment to prohibit gay marriage, Jamie Raskin, professor of law at AU, was requested to testify. At the end of his testimony, Republican Senator Nancy Jacobs said: "Mr. Raskin, my Bible says marriage is only between a man and a woman. What do you have to say about that?" Raskin replied: "Senator, when you took your oath of office, you placed your hand on the Bible and swore to uphold the Constitution. You did not place your hand on the Constitution and swear to uphold the Bible." The room erupted into applause.[29]

Unfortunately, too many Americans are no longer applauding. The Tea Party mentality supports Senator Jacobs when she insists that the "Laws of God" are the ultimate authority over laws and protections based on the U.S. Constitution. The "Laws of God"—as found in an inerrant or literal reading of the Bible—make it all too clear that men who sleep with other men must be put to death. Fortunately, only a few fundamentalist Christian extremists like R.J. Rushdooney and his fellow Reconstructionists still advocate the death penalty for practicing homosexuals. However, to understand what would happen to LGBT Americans if the new "religious right" comes into power we need to understand what the old "religious right" had planned for us.

Holy Terror exposes the long-term goals of Fundamentalist Christianity for lesbian, gay, bisexual and transgender Americans. The Tea Party Patriots, the Faith and Freedom Coalition and hundreds of other political organizations based on the "religious right" are united in their determination to strip us of our rights and drive us back into our closets. They believe that it is their sacred (holy) duty to wage war (terror) against LGBT people. To understand the ultimate goals of the new "religious right" is to understand the ultimate goals of the old "religious right."

I began this preface with Santayana's familiar quote: "Those who cannot remember the past are condemned to repeat it." *Holy Terror* is the past we must remember. This is the story of that rather terrifying and all too recent history of Christian fundamentalism and its war against LGBT people and a reminder that the civil and religious rights we have gained are easily reversed if fundamentalism has its way.

Mel White
May 2011

INTRODUCTION

FUNDAMENTALISM, CAUSE AND CURE

I am sixty-six years old, going on a hundred. I've spent my first dozen years as an out gay clergy bandaging and burying the victims of the false teachings and destructive actions of Protestant and Catholic church leaders against my gay sisters and brothers.* Unfortunately, most of these same religious leaders believe their antigay rhetoric. They don't know that most of what they say about us is untrue. Nor do they realize the tragic consequences of their untruths. These people are not evil, but we must resist the evil that they do.

I know from personal experience the tragic consequences of religion-based intolerance. In my autobiography, *Stranger at the Gate: To Be Gay and Christian in America*, I describe in painful detail how I wasted thirty-five years on useless ex-gay therapies, exorcism, and even electric shock to "overcome" my sexual orientation. Unfortunately, millions of my sisters and brothers are still victims of those six Bible verses that religious leaders misuse to condemn them. And now, those same religious leaders have elected a president, a Congress, governors, and legislators across the nation who are determined to turn those six Bible verses into laws—including a historic amendment to our U.S. Constitution—that will deny us the basic rights and protections that the Constitution guarantees.

Overall, I hope that *Holy Terror* will make it abundantly clear that this "culture war" is real and that fundamentalists will not be satisfied by denying homosexuals our rights. In fact, they are using their antihomosexual campaign to recruit volunteers, raise funds, mobilize voters, and eventually divide and conquer the nation. Their ultimate goal is to break down the wall that separates church and state, superimpose their "moral values" on the U.S. Constitution, replace democracy with theocratic rule, and create a new "Christian America" in their image.

I am not a Christian basher. My own roots are planted deep in evangelical Christianity. From childhood I have known and loved the evangelical church and its leaders. I have served the evangelical movement as pastor, professor, filmmaker, television producer, author, and ghostwriter for many of its most powerful leaders. But in the early 1970s, the evangelical church as I knew it began to fall under the influence of fundamentalist Christian leaders like Jerry Falwell, Pat Robertson, and James Dobson. With their powerful media voices, their call to "reclaim America for Christ" transformed the historic evangelical agenda from sharing freely the "good news" of Jesus' life, death, and resurrection to superimposing their "moral values" on the nation through a dangerous combination of bad religion and dirty politics.

While I was still a victim of fundamentalist lies about homosexuality—during those terrible decades when I thought my homosexuality was a "sickness" and a "sin"—I worked closely with many fundamentalist Christian leaders. Indeed, since I had a doctorate in religion and had already written for Billy Graham, I was asked to ghostwrite Jerry Falwell's "autobiography," *Strength for the Journey*, and eventually I worked on books, films, and TV specials with key players in the fundamentalist Christian movement: Francis Schaeffer, Pat Robertson, Jim and Tammy Bakker, D. James Kennedy, and W. A. Criswell (Billy Graham's pastor and, until his death, "Pope" of the Southern Baptist Convention). And though I've never worked with James Dobson, he and I lived in the same Southern California neighborhood and sat in the same bleachers at Maranatha High School while my daughter, Erinn, led cheers and his son, Ryan, played.

I learned about the rebirth of fundamentalism from the men who conceived it. I stayed in their homes, traveled in their private jets, and recorded endless hours of audiotape as they shared their life stories with me. Frankly, I learned to love these men and respect their sincerity. It drives my friends and allies crazy when I insist that these fundamentalists really do believe what they say about homosexuality and homosexuals. In fact, they are not just "using us" to raise money and volunteers.

My old friends and former clients believe sincerely that gay people are a "threat to children, to marriage and the family, to the nation and to western civilization itself." They are true believers, and we doubt their sincerity at our own peril. For the past decade, I have been an eyewitness on the front lines of the war the fundamentalists are waging against lesbian and gay Americans. In the process, I've come to realize that fundamentalist Christianity is not just a threat to lesbians and gays, but to all Americans who cherish democracy and the rights and protections guaranteed us by the U.S. Constitution.

At the beginning of this new millennium, religious leaders still ignore the mountain of scientific, psychological, historical, pastoral, personal, and even biblical evidence that homosexual orientation is just another mystery of creation. Their teachings and actions against us lead to wasted lives, divided families, ruined relationships, emotional suffering, physical violence, and even death. The hostile climate in which the suffering and death takes place is created in large part by the toxic misinformation of well-meaning Protestant clergy and laity, radio and television evangelists, seminary professors and Sunday school teachers. However, fundamentalist Christian Protestants aren't the only church leaders guilty of bearing false witness against gay people.

With Cardinal Ratzinger as his dark muse, Pope John Paul II called homosexual orientation "objectively disordered" and loving, intimate same-sex acts "intrinsically evil." He denounced the European Union's Charter of Fundamental Rights as "godless" because it would cause "moral and social destruction" by sanctioning gay unions and gay adoptions, which he called "deplorably dangerous." He demanded that governments deny lesbians and gays the right to parent, adopt, teach, coach, be ordained, or serve in the military. He refused to allow the "out" gay Catholics of Dignity/USA to meet on church property or even to be served the Eucharist by a priest. Now, his successor, Pope Benedict XVI, has declared outright war on homosexuality and homosexuals and launched an inquisition against gay priests and seminarians. And yet the U.S. Conference of Catholic Bishops denies angrily that their words and actions against us are acts of spiritual violence that lead to suffering and death. Worse, they refuse to even consider the evidence.

The suffering has gone on far too long. And though my old body is ready to retire, my heart says with Dylan Thomas, "Do not go gentle into that good night...Rage, rage against the dying of the light." I am angry. *Holy Terror* must begin, then, as did my first years out of the closet, with a kind of righteous rage against the lies and distortions and the religious leaders who tell them. But *Holy Terror* is not about anger alone. Fortunately, during the first years of my short, hectic life as a gay activist, Lynn Cothren, Coretta Scott King's longtime personal assistant and protégé, showed me how love can triumph over rage. Lynn introduced me to the "soul force" principles of relentless nonviolent resistance that were taught and lived not just by M. K. Gandhi, Martin Luther King, Jr., and Dorothy Day, the founder of the Catholic Worker movement, but by a host of nonviolent heroes and sheroes throughout the ages.

In 1999 Gary Nixon, my partner, and I founded Soulforce, Inc., and with a handful of generous friends set out to recruit, train, and equip volunteers who would join us in confronting the evil antigay words and actions by the fundamentalist Christians, Protestant and Catholic alike. During the past six years, we have trained an estimated ten thousand people in the "soul force" principles of truth, love, and voluntary redemptive suffering. Thousands of volunteers have joined us in elegant silent vigils and quiet, nonviolent protests at national conventions of the United Methodist, Southern Baptist, Presbyterian, Episcopal, Lutheran and Roman Catholic churches in the United States and at the Vatican. Over a thousand of us—gay and straight alike—have been arrested in nonviolent direct actions. And even while the general public is making huge strides toward understanding and fully accepting gay Americans, Protestant and Catholic churches continue their spiral downward into intolerance and discrimination.

HOLY TERROR IS MY RESPONSE TO THE SO-CALLED culture war that fundamentalist Christians are waging. Chapters one through three, "The Call to War," "The Warriors," and "The Spoils of War," document the slow, steady rise to power of fundamentalist Christians in American politics and religion. I show how they have used their war against homosexuality and homosexuals to recruit funds and mobilize volunteers for their much larger War against America. And I demonstrate how their antigay campaign—built on half-truth, hyperbole, and lies—has become the primary source of intolerance, discrimination, suffering, and even death for lesbian and gay Americans.

Thanks to recently discovered tape transcripts of a secret meeting in a castle in the Rocky Mountains of Colorado, chapters four and five, "The Secret Meeting at Glen Eyrie" and "The Glen Eyrie Protocol," detail the fundamentalist Christian solution for their "homosexual problem" and describe their carefully plotted plan to deny gay and lesbian Americans their civil rights, and end their "dangerous influence on culture."

Chapter six, "Idolatry: The Religion of Fundamentalism," describes the false gods fundamentalists call upon in their struggle to "reclaim America for Christ" and shows how badly fundamentalist Christians have veered off course from the life and teachings of Jesus.

Chapter seven, "Fascism: The Politics of Fundamentalism," illustrates the very real and just as frightening similarities of fascism under Hitler and fundamentalist Christianity under Falwell, Robertson, Dobson, D. James Kennedy, and the others.

Chapter eight, "Reclaiming Our Progressive Political Values," presents evidence that fundamentalist Christians are determined to make this a "Christian nation." Resistance means reclaiming the Constitution and its First Amendment, rejecting biblical law, reinforcing the wall of separation between church and state, and refusing fundamentalists the right to deny any American his or her civil rights.

Chapter nine, "Reclaiming Our Progressive Moral Values," takes a closer look at the "absolute moral values" of the Christian fundamentalists and suggests that it is long past time for progressives to claim "absolute values" of our own. I suggest that justice, mercy, and truth—the values of the Jewish prophets, of Jesus, and of thoughtful men and women throughout history—

would be a good place to start.

Chapter ten, "Discovering Soul Force," describes how the principles of relentless nonviolent resistance as shaped by M. K. Gandhi and Martin Luther King, Jr., can bring new power to our individual lives and new direction to our struggle for justice. Jesus said, "Love your enemies." Love demands that we quit cooperating with those who oppress us. It is time for a campaign of relentless nonviolent resistance that will convince our adversaries to do justice at last. They have assumed that we are infinitely patient or too comfortable to call for revolution. For their sake, and for the sake of the nation, we must prove them wrong.

Part One

MY FRIENDS, THE ENEMY

ONE

THE CALL TO WAR:
BILLY GRAHAM, FRANCIS SCHAEFFER,
AND W. A. CRISWELL

A fundamentalist is just an evangelical who is mad about something.[1]

—*JERRY FALWELL*

*W*ho are these fundamentalist Christians who are polluting the nation with their toxic rhetoric against lesbian and gay Americans? What is a fundamentalist anyway? Perhaps the simplest definition I've heard was stated off the cuff during a History Channel interview of Sir Jonathan Sacks, chief rabbi of the United Hebrew Congregations of the Commonwealth. "I define fundamentalism," he said, "as the attempt to impose a single truth on a plural world." In the face of fundamentalist aggression by Jewish, Christian, and Muslim fundamentalists, the chief rabbi explained: "What really lies behind fundamentalism is fear, a profound insecurity that makes you feel when you meet someone who doesn't like you or who doesn't agree with you that that challenges and threatens your very being. Aggression," he added, "is always a sign of insecurity, and insecurity is always at bottom a lack of faith, not the presence of it."[2]

If you want the very best scholarly definition of fundamentalism, read Karen Armstrong's *The Battle for God*. Her description of the twentieth-century rise to power of Christian, Muslim, and Jewish fundamentalists is as exciting to read as an international thriller by Dan Brown or John le Carré. Armstrong defines fundamentalism as "militant piety," and in three rather frightening sentences she gives us these insights into what that means:

"It is only a small minority of fundamentalists who commit acts of terror," Armstrong explains, "but even the most peaceful and law-abiding are perplexing, because they seem so adamantly opposed to many of the most positive values of modern society. Fundamentalists have no time for democracy, pluralism, religious tolerance, peacekeeping, free speech, or the separation of church and state. Christian fundamentalists," she adds, "reject the discoveries of biology and physics about the origins of life and insist that the Book of Genesis is scientifically sound in every detail."[3]

If you want a seasoned theologian's definition of fundamentalist Christianity, read John Shelby Spong's *Rescuing the Bible from Fundamentalism*. This former Episcopal bishop of Newark, New Jersey, is spending his retirement years yanking on the fundamentalists' chains. He writes passionately about the dangers he sees in the current rise of fundamentalist Christianity for church and state alike.

Spong defines fundamentalist Christians as "those whose religious security is rooted in a literal Bible." And he adds, "...they do not want that security disturbed. Fundamentalists," he continues, "are not happy when facts challenge their biblical understanding or when nuances in the text are introduced or when they are forced to deal with either contradictions or changing insights...For biblical literalists," he warns, "there is always an enemy to be defeated in mortal combat."[4]

If you want a skilled apologist's definition of fundamentalism, Edward John Carnell's three-word summary is the clearest yet. "Fundamentalism," he writes, "is orthodoxy gone cultic." In his *The Case for Orthodoxy*, an invaluable resource that is sadly out of print, Carnell, a former professor and president of Fuller Theological Seminary, defines fundamentalism with the perspective of an evangelical who was desperate to keep his seminary from falling into the hands of militant fundamentalists.

Writing in 1959, Carnell described contemporary fundamentalism twenty years before Jerry Falwell launched his Moral Majority campaign "to return America to its Christian roots." "The mentality of fundamentalism is dominated by ideological thinking," Carnell writes. "Ideological thinking is rigid, intolerant, and doctrinaire; it sees principles everywhere, and all principles come in clear tones of black and white; it exempts itself from the limits that original sin places on history; it wages holy wars without acknowledging the elements of pride and personal interest that prompt the call to battle; it creates new evils while trying to correct old ones."[5]

And if you want a media prophet's definition of fundamentalism and a frightening description of the fundamentalists' successful forty-year campaign to "take back the White House, the Congress, and the Courts," read Bill Moyers's "Armageddon and the Environment." Lyndon Johnson's former press secretary (until they excommunicated him, a lifetime Southern Baptist himself), Moyers is using his considerable media skills to alert his fellow Americans that while we were sleeping, fundamentalists have taken power over the executive, legislative, and judicial branches of our government.

While accepting an award from the Harvard Medical School, Moyers warns us of the tragic consequences of our apathy.

"One of the biggest changes in politics in my lifetime is that the delusional is no longer marginal. It has come in from the fringe, to sit in the seat of power in the Oval Office and in Congress. For the first time in our history, ideology and theology hold a monopoly of power in Washington. Theology asserts propositions that cannot be proven true; ideologues hold stoutly to a worldview despite being contradicted by what is generally accepted as reality. When ideology and theology couple, their offspring are not always bad but they are always blind. And there is the danger: voters and politicians alike, oblivious to the facts."[6]

Bill Moyers speaks with a prophetic voice that leaves those of us who hear him on our feet cheering. "Let me assure you," he said at a National Conference for Media Reform, "that I take in stride attacks by the radical right-wingers who have not given up demonizing me although I retired over six months ago. They've been after me for years now, and I suspect they will be stomping on my grave to make sure I don't come back from the dead. I should remind them, however, that one of our boys pulled it off some two thousand years ago—after the Pharisees, Sadducees and Caesar's surrogates thought they had shut him up for good. Of course I won't be expecting that kind of miracle, but I should put my detractors on notice: They might just compel me out of the rocking chair and back into the anchor chair."[7]

I am not a rabbi, historian, theologian, apologist, or media prophet, but I did spend a good part of my lifetime rubbing shoulders with fundamentalist Christians and their gurus. My son, filmmaker Mike White, says I might be a fundamentalist myself if I hadn't been born gay. I hope he's wrong, but I do know for certain that without my homosexual orientation my position of white, male, Protestant privilege would have protected me from ever understanding what it means to be an outcast of any kind, let alone what it means to be a gay Christian in America under attack by church and state alike.

During those years when I still believed that homosexuality was both a "sickness" and a "sin," my literary agent, Irving "Swifty" Lazar, hired me out as a ghostwriter to powerful fundamentalist Christians who had fascinating stories to tell but neither time nor energy to tell them. My personal definition of fundamentalism was shaped by these fundamentalist leaders during the considerable interview time we had together, but even more by those off hours when I was simply a member of their entourage looking on from the shadows as they lived their complex and often chaotic lives.

BILLY GRAHAM

Billy Graham was without a doubt my favorite ghostwriting client. In his life we see the difference between a fundamentalist Christian and an evangelical. I want to show through Billy's example that in spite of the fact that all fundamentalist Christians are evangelical, all evangelicals are definitely not fundamentalists. Born in 1918 to a dairy farmer turned businessman, William Franklin Graham, Jr., is known to the world as "Billy." In high school he was converted, or "born again," during a revival meeting held in Charlotte, North Carolina, Billy's hometown, by Mordecai Ham, a fiery young evangelist. As a boy, Billy felt called to preach and, according to a well-established myth, delivered his first practice sermons to cows in the pasture of his father's dairy farm.

Billy began preaching to people on street corners, at rescue missions, and in small churches even while attending Florida Bible Institute and Wheaton College. He enrolled first at Bob

Jones University, a rigid fundamentalist stronghold, but "could not adjust to campus life."[8] (Just off the farm and Billy was already at odds with fundamentalist Christianity.) After leaving Bob Jones, Billy transferred to Wheaton College, an evangelical center, and at Wheaton he met, fell in love with, and married Ruth Bell, the daughter of a Southern Presbyterian missionary surgeon in China.

In 1945 Billy was hired as vice president of Youth for Christ International and spent the next four years launching YFC Bible Clubs in high schools across the United States and Canada. At the same time Billy was holding his own evangelistic meetings organized by his boyhood friends the brothers Grady and T. W. Wilson, accompanied by two other life members of his evangelistic team: baritone soloist George Beverly Shea (who must have sung "How Great Thou Art" a million times during the next fifty years) and Cliff Barrow, Billy's song leader, whose choirs in the larger crusades often numbered in the thousands.

During a 1949 crusade in Los Angeles, William Randolph Hearst got word that Billy's preaching had led to the conversion of a well-known crime boss and several Hollywood celebrities. Captivated by the gangly young preacher who stood six feet four inches in his white shoes and brightly colored jackets, Hearst ordered the editors of his papers across the United States to "puff Graham." Henry Luce, cofounder of *Time* magazine, often called "the giant of twentieth-century journalism," followed suit. Suddenly a darling of the media, masses of people rushed to hear Billy preach, and the Los Angeles Evangelistic Crusade was extended for seven long weeks.

In a very short time millions of people were listening to Billy's "Hour of Decision" radio broadcasts on 1,200 stations across the United States. His evangelistic crusades filled the largest public arenas and athletic fields in the United States, Europe, South America, and Asia. In the 1950s and 1960s, during my high-school and college years, I watched Billy's regular television specials and the full-length movies produced by Billy Graham's World Wide Pictures—*For Pete's Sake, Mr. Texas, The Restless Ones, The Hiding Place*—and I dreamed that one day I would produce motion pictures of my own. My feelings about Billy Graham shaped in my childhood and youth are rather biased in his favor. Everyone does not agree. While President G. H. W. Bush called Graham "America's Pastor," Harry Truman labeled Graham a "counterfeit" and a "publicity seeker."[9]

Whatever history will call Billy Graham there is no question that this young evangelist was a primary influence in shaping my earliest Christian beliefs. So you can imagine my surprise in 1982 when Billy Graham himself called me from Acapulco, Mexico, to see if I would be interested in helping him write his next book. In *Stranger at the Gate* I tell the story of the sudden chaos Billy's call brought into my life, of the way it led to the end of my relationship with Thomas Montgomery, my first gay love, and of the way it might have contributed to Tom's tragic death. I won't repeat that story here, even though my stomach still churns from those not-so-happy memories.

The same night Billy Graham called me, I flew from Seattle to Acapulco. To my surprise, Billy was waiting for me at curbside driving an open jeep. Billy and Ruth were taking a few days off in a beachfront condo loaned them by a supporter. During the next week, Billy walked in the sand while I recorded his rather passionate feelings about the four horsemen of the apocalypse described by John in Revelation 6: war, famine, pestilence, and death.

Before that walk on the beach, I saw Billy Graham as an evangelist, nothing more. He had just one sermon, really, centered in the story of a Pharisee named Nicodemus, who came to Jesus by night seeking the way to heaven. Jesus answered simply: "You must be born again." The young ruler was confused and asked again, "But how can you enter into your mother's womb the second time?" Jesus' reply to that closeted young seeker is the essence of almost every sermon Billy Graham ever preached. "You must be born of water and of Spirit to enter God's kingdom," Jesus explained. "That which is born of flesh is flesh and that which is born of the Spirit is spirit." Billy Graham invited people to come down to the front of the arena to be born again, and looking up at Billy from the front row in the San Francisco Cow Palace, my life changed forever. As an adolescent I was a Billy Graham evangelical and proud to be.

Evangelical has its roots in the beautiful Greek word "evangel," or good news. Billy Graham and the evangelicals of my past were bearers of the good news that "God so loved the world that He gave his only begotten son that whosoever believes in him shall not perish but have everlasting life." I first memorized those words from John 3:16 when I was five years old. When asked to describe history's most profound theological truth, Karl Barth, perhaps the most influential theologian of the twentieth century, replied with the first song I sang in Sunday school: "Jesus loves me this I know for the Bible tells me so." In just twelve words, Barth described what it means to be an evangelical.

Evangelical Christians believe that the Bible is our trustworthy guide to faith (what we believe about God) and practice (how we live out those beliefs in the world). They believe that Jesus' death on the cross provides humankind the way to be reconciled with our Creator. They believe that reconciliation comes through a personal conversion experience when we acknowledge Jesus as "Savior and Lord." They believe that from the moment of our conversion we are called to share the good news (evangelize) and to join God in redeeming and renewing the world by seeking justice for the outcast and showing mercy to the poor (Christian service).

For most of his ministry, sharing the Good News was Billy Graham's primary goal. He was often criticized for not raising his powerful voice against war, famine, pestilence, and death. Until walking that beach in Mexico, I had no idea that Billy Graham was determined to speak prophetically on those issues as well. In this new book, Billy would confront the powers. He would call Christian believers to "do justice; love mercy; and walk humbly." In Acapulco I listened to a man being called by the Spirit of God to remind the world that being "born again" is not enough. God's spirit calls us to work for peace as well, to feed the hungry, care for the sick, and confront the powers that lead to death for our planet and for all those who live upon it. I'll never forget the stories he told me from his own life that illustrated his change of heart.

Shortly after his first visit to India, Billy was invited to the White House by President Eisenhower. After a few minutes of "mindless chatter," Billy told the president about children and old people he had seen lying in the streets of Calcutta, malnourished, sick, and dying. Being a farmer's kid himself, Billy knew that the year's harvest of wheat, oats, and barley had been plentiful and that the nation's grain elevators were full to overflowing.

"We must send tons of grain to feed the hungry people," Billy told Ike, apparently with the same enthusiasm he called people to "come forward and be born again." Ike admitted that he, too, had felt that way after seeing starvation across Europe—that is, until he had a conversation with John Foster Dulles, his Secretary of State. Eisenhower summoned Dulles to give Billy a lesson in world trade.

"The Secretary of State told me," Billy remembers, "that if we donated tons of grain to feed the starving, the price of grain would drop and American farmers would suffer. He told me that in the long run more good would be done if grain prices remained stabilized and the American farmer out of harm's way." Billy paused and then said quietly, "I believed him then. I don't believe him now. We are followers of Jesus, who commanded that we feed the hungry, and if obeying that command causes prices to fall and profit margins to narrow, so be it."

When finished, Billy's book, *Approaching Hoofbeats*, was rich in personal stories that illustrated what must be done if we are to stop the four horsemen: war, famine, plague, and death. "Even in Eisenhower's time we could hear the hoofbeats," Billy said. "But now they are upon us, and when we don't answer Christ's call to justice and mercy," he added, "we sin and the Bible promises that we will be judged for that sin."

Then he opened his Bible to Matthew 25 and read that story of the last judgment when the sheep are separated from the goats by a King. Those who were sent into everlasting fire asked the King, "When did we see you hungry and not give you anything to eat? When did we see you thirsty and gave you nothing to drink? When did we see you naked and didn't put clothes on your back or a stranger and didn't take you in or a prisoner and didn't visit you?" And the King answered, "When you did it *not* unto one of the least of these my children, you did it *not* unto me."

Coming from Billy Graham, this new sermon was strong stuff, especially since the stories came directly out of the life and experiences of an evangelist with a prophet's heart. But when galleys of the book came back from the editors and the all-too-protective members of Billy's team, those stories were missing. I was sick thinking Billy had been pressured to remove them. After a few days, Billy called and said, "I respect your judgment, Mel, but why did you take out all those stories?" Neither of us had removed them. It seemed fairly clear that somewhere along the line Billy's handlers were softening the message so that Billy wouldn't be drawn into political or economic controversy. Billy explained to me that his Evangelistic Association had suffered when, during the Watergate scandal, he had admitted his close, personal friendship with Richard Nixon. They didn't want it to happen again.

I understood why it was risky to condemn the rich for neglecting the poor when the Billy Graham Evangelistic Association had to raise $100 million or more a year, much of it from wealthy businessmen and women. I knew it was dangerous to confront the politicians who sat on the stage at Billy's crusades for ignoring the world's needs, and I realized that the more fundamentalist pastors in Billy's camp would accuse the evangelist of getting off track with his sudden interest in "the social gospel." But it was exciting for me to see Billy Graham raising his powerful voice on behalf of people who were hungry, thirsty, sick, naked, homeless, outcast, and in prison. And it broke my heart to see Billy's people—for whatever reason—force him to focus on saving souls and in the process silence the prophet in our midst.

From childhood I identified myself as a Billy Graham Evangelical. In my work as a gay Soulforce activist, I stand proudly (and without reservation) with people of other faiths and of no faith at all, but I still see myself as an evangelical. My desire to seek justice for God's lesbian and gay children comes directly out of my evangelical heritage. And though Billy's influence on my life had more to do with the inward journey, experiencing the presence of God in my life, I had plenty of evangelical models who were heroes of the outward journey, who gave their lives on behalf of justice, serving the poor, the homeless, and the outcast.

As a high-school senior, I was fortunate to be chosen by the American Friends Service Committee to spend a week with Martin Luther King, Jr., and his wife, Coretta Scott King, in

Carmel, California, along with a dozen or so other students from across the United States. Dr. King was an evangelical and obviously committed to sharing the same Good News that Billy shared, but in Dr. King I heard that Good News put into practice in a whole new way. "The Gospel at its best," King declared, "deals with the whole man, not only his soul but his body...Any religion that professes to be concerned about the souls of men and is not concerned about the slums that damn them, the economic conditions that strangle them and the social conditions that cripple them is a spiritually moribund religion awaiting burial."[10]

William Sloan Coffin, "Freedom Rider," Yale chaplain, and courageous spokesman against the Vietnam War, is another of my evangelical heroes. "To know God," he wrote, "is to do justice...To believe you can approach God without drawing nearer in compassion to suffering humanity is to fool yourself. There can be no genuine personal religious conversion without a change in social attitude."[11]

Sharing the Good News (Graham) and seeking justice in the world (King and Coffin) have come to represent the two sides of my evangelical faith. I became a fan of Billy Graham in my adolescent years when the inward journey was everything. Then I discovered Bonhoeffer, King, Coffin, and other evangelicals who risked their lives on behalf of justice, mercy, and truth and inherited from their lives my own dream of doing justice as they did. That's why time with Billy Graham on that beach in Acapulco was so important to me. I discovered that Billy, my evangelical hero, was not interested just in saving souls. He also felt passionately about doing justice. That's why I was so angry and disappointed when Billy's editors eliminated the stories that illustrated his concerns.

Now, looking back, I can understand why Billy's handlers didn't want their man to get into more trouble. He was already under fire by supporters for taking his stand against the arrogant and dangerous spirit of fundamentalism in newspaper interviews, press conferences, and talk shows. Billy was using his own quiet voice to show the difference between an evangelical and a fundamentalist, and the fundamentalists, once his most loyal friends, were howling.

Fundamentalist Christian leaders accused Graham of "breaking down the walls of biblical separation between sound and apostate churches," and for "sending thousands of converts back into Roman Catholic and modernistic churches that preach heretical gospels," and for "claiming that Pope John Paul II was a moral and spiritual leader and that when he died surely went to heaven," and for "accepting an honorary degree from a Catholic university" and for "inviting Catholic bishops, Jewish Rabbis, and even Muslim clerics to sit with him on the platform of his citywide evangelistic campaigns."[12]

Perhaps fundamentalists were most angry at Billy Graham because he dared to imply that people could find God through other religions. They claimed that in a 1985 newspaper interview, Graham expressed the belief that those outside of Christ might be saved. In fact, he just left the judgment in God's hands when Los Angeles reporter David Colker asked Graham: "What about people of other faiths who live good lives but don't profess a belief in Christ?" Graham replied, "I'm going to leave that to the Lord. He'll decide that."[13]

Graham infuriated fundamentalist Christians when he said, "I used to think that pagans in far-off countries were lost— were going to hell—if they did not have the Gospel of Jesus Christ preached to them. I no longer believe that....I believe there are other ways of recognizing the existence of God— through nature, for instance—and plenty of other opportunities, therefore, of saying yes to God."[14]

Equally infuriating to fundamentalist Christians was

Graham's stand on biblical inerrancy, the cornerstone that holds the entire fundamentalist superstructure together. "I believe the Bible is the inspired, authoritative word of God," Graham says, "but I don't use the word 'inerrant' because it's become a brittle divisive word."[15]

At the same time Jerry Falwell, Pat Robertson, James Dobson, and other fundamentalist Christians were vilifying President Clinton for his infidelity and calling for his impeachment, Billy Graham said: "I forgive him because I know the frailty of human nature and I know how hard it is, and especially a strong vigorous young man like he is—he has such a tremendous personality. I think the ladies just go wild over him."[16]

When asked about abortion in a *TV Guide* interview, Graham said simply: "I don't get involved in the abortion thing."[17] On ABC's *Good Morning America* Graham said he agreed with John Paul II but added: "…there is a Christian position [on abortion], I think. But I'm not prepared to say what it is."[18] Two weeks later on the same program Graham added, "There are occasions when abortion is the only alternative." At the same time fundamentalist media gurus were raising millions to end a woman's right to choose, Billy Graham, the nation's foremost evangelical, refused to be drawn into the fight.

He handled the controversy around homosexuality in exactly the same way. When asked about it on a *20/20* television interview, Graham answered, "I think that the Bible teaches that homosexuality is a sin, but the Bible also teaches that pride is a sin, jealousy is a sin, and hate is a sin, evil thoughts are a sin, and so I don't think that homosexuality should be chosen as the overwhelming sin that we are doing today."[19]

During the contentious battle over Oregon's Proposition 9, Graham was asked by a chairman of his evangelistic crusade in Portland to endorse the measure that would require the state of Oregon to declare homosexuality a condition that was "abnormal, wrong, unnatural and perverse." Graham replied, "I find it emotional with strong arguments on both sides of the issue. I intend to stay out of national and local politics while here. God loves all people whatever their ethnic or political background or their sexual orientation...Christians take opposing views on many issues...Those on both sides of the issue must love each other."[20]

I don't mean to suggest that Billy Graham or his evangelical colleagues are accepting of gay and lesbian people (although more and more evangelical leaders live out acceptance in their daily lives while still unable to make up their minds about the meaning of those pesky Bible verses). But I am saying that a handful of my evangelical friends have never given up on me. They have difficulty knowing how to apply those ancient biblical texts to my life, but they accept me without reservation and simply hold judgment on the larger issue, demonstrating Billy Graham's words, "I'm going to leave that to the Lord. He'll decide that."[21]

In June 1994, shortly after the release of *Stranger at the Gate*, Billy Graham sat down to answer questions from America's leading newspaper publishers. That Q&A session was taped live by C-SPAN. Mike Pride, editor of the *Concord Monitor*, asked Dr. Graham a question about a letter I had written asking Billy to meet with me to discuss the tragic consequences of the fundamentalist antihomosexual campaign: "Dr. White has expressed frustration that after such a long and close professional relationship, you've spurned his attempts to speak with you since his coming out."

Graham, obviously unaware that I had written, faxed, and phoned his headquarters trying to schedule a meeting, answered, "If I saw him today, I'd gladly put my arms around him and hug him. I believe we should love homosexuals. God loves homosexuals. Homosexuality is called a sin in the Bible in the

Old Testament. It's not mentioned in the New Testament except in the first chapter of Romans...But I love them and welcome them to our meetings. [Mel is] welcome to come and see me, have lunch with me, whatever...I didn't know of any instigation on his part to get to me. Perhaps he did. But I'm surrounded by a lot of people who try to protect me."

Twelve years after that invitation, they're still protecting Billy. They ignore my requests for a meeting, but I still hope that one day I will see my friend again, throw my arms around him, and ask him respectfully to raise his powerful prophetic voice to condemn the fundamentalists' war against my gay sisters and brothers. I believe in his heart that Billy Graham knows enough gay and lesbian people to be assured that homosexual orientation is not a sickness, nor a sin, but a gift from God to be accepted, celebrated, and lived with integrity. I'm still hoping that Billy Graham will step to the microphone one last time and use his booming Southern baritone to speak in no uncertain terms directly to Pat Robertson, Jerry Falwell, James Dobson, Benedict XVI, and the rest of them: "Stop it!" I hear him say. "You're killing God's gay and lesbian children and it must end!" In the meantime, Billy is almost ninety years old. His Parkinson's disease is growing more severe. Soon my friend will die, and the Billy Graham Evangelistic Association will be left in the hands of Billy's son, Franklin, who, unlike his father, is a fundamentalist Christian to the core, and the evangelical world as a whole is in imminent danger of continuing its downward spiral into militant fundamentalism.

I have a very personal way of deciding who is an evangelical Christian and who is a fundamentalist. An evangelical loves and accepts me in spite of what the Bible says or doesn't say about homosexuality. A fundamentalist cannot. Fundamentalist Christians may share many basic beliefs with evangelicals, but they hold tightly to their beliefs with the grip of the Pharisees, who knew the law by heart but forgot the heart of the law: "Love God and love your neighbor as yourself."

Jerry Falwell states the difference perfectly. "Fundamentalists," he says, are evangelicals who are angry about something." And no one contributed to the origins of that fundamentalist anger in modern times more than the little man from Indiana who gave up on his fellow evangelicals and exiled himself and his family to a tiny Alpine village in Switzerland.

FRANCIS SCHAEFFER

Francis Schaeffer, a small man whose lederhosen (alpine leather pants) became a kind of trademark, was my first client as a "ghost." Dr. Schaeffer and his wife, Edith, were fundamentalist Christian expatriates who moved from St. Louis, Missouri, to the village of Huemoz in the Swiss Alps high above Geneva. History may teach us that the rise to power of fundamentalist Christianity in our time began in L'Abri, the Schaeffer home in Switzerland, where a very loving Francis and Edith welcomed anyone "seeking the meaning of life."

Beginning in 1955, the always expanding, never quite large enough Schaeffer compound offered hospitality to literally thousands of young, dissatisfied Americans who visited L'Abri ("the shelter") to study, pray, dialogue, and debate with Francis, who taught "with a Bible in one hand and *Time* magazine in the other." Anyone who visited L'Abri during the next three decades will remember Edith Schaeffer's amazing gift of hospitality and the delicious orange rolls she served to the young people sitting at Francis's feet.

In 1976, Schaeffer's book *How Should We Then Live?* became a best seller in Christian bookstores across the United States. Film and television producers from the United States, Italy, England,

and the Netherlands signed a contract with Francis to turn the book into a twelve-part series for television and film release. Francis insisted on hiring the director, a convert from L'Abri whose specialty was one-minute commercials. The results were catastrophic, and I was called in to "make some sense of it" by the frustrated producers. As a result, I commuted to Switzerland for approximately eight weeks and spent a summer interviewing Schaeffer and reediting the series with my friend and colleague Heinz Fussle while my wife, Lyla, and I were co-pastoring First Covenant Church in Pasadena, California.

During those long hours with Francis Schaeffer, I was reminded that fundamentalist Christians are people, too, that they are our brothers and sisters with whom we need to be reconciled, and that we must not caricature and condemn them as they often do us. I went to Switzerland with real fears about working with Schaeffer, a major fundamentalist with whom my theological friends had done battle, and during the first day there I thought my fears were justified.

Billy Zeoli, president of Gospel Films, the American partner in the production of Schaeffer's series, warned me as we entered a screening room in Bern, Switzerland, that I should not question Schaeffer's views, at least not during this first meeting. "Just watch the film," he said, "and share your thoughts with us after Francis has gone."

Apparently when Dr. Schaeffer learned that I was from Fuller Theological Seminary, he had worried that I would "be too liberal" for the project and almost vetoed my participation. After the various producers were seated, Francis and his entourage entered the room and took their places without acknowledging my presence. They would make their decision about hiring me after hearing my response to the rough cut of the first hour-long program.

When the rough cut ended and the lights came on, Francis

himself said, "Well, what do you think?" I looked at the producers. Their eyes said it all. "Don't think. Compliment. We'll talk later." Knowing that I couldn't help Schaeffer or these filmmakers from four different nations to finish a several-million-dollar series without being open and completely frank, I asked one small question.

"Dr. Schaeffer, do you want to talk about the film's production values or its content?"

"Both!" Schaeffer answered. "Feel free."

My friend Zeoli slumped slowly into the screening room chair. But I had noticed a rather glaring error in Schaeffer's content and I needed to see how he would react to a public critique.

"Dr. Schaeffer, there is a lot of fascinating content in this first hour of your series, but did you mean to say that Karl Barth's *Commentary on Romans* was an example of the influence of Schleirmacher and the other liberals who didn't take the Bible seriously?"

The German Protestant theologian Friedrich Schleirmacher has been referred to as the "father of modern theology." To oversimplify his position, Schleirmacher believed that our final authority was not found in scripture, creeds, or dogma but in the heart of the believer. Needless to say, that idea makes a fundamentalist's blood boil. To them, the Bible is inerrant (without error), infallible (foolproof), the ultimate authority, the only trustworthy source of truth not just about faith (what we believe) and practice (how we live out that belief in the world) but about all things.

"As I remember it," I added softly, "Karl Barth's *Commentary on Romans* was in fact his effort to rescue the Bible from the influence of Schleirmacher and his friends."

After an awkward silence, Schaeffer left the room without saying a word, his entourage in tow. When the door closed, Billy

Zeoli groaned; others whispered and looked away. I knew that before the day was over I'd be back on that Swiss Air 747 flight to Chicago and the American Airline connection to Los Angeles. Nobody moved. After five or six minutes, Schaeffer walked back into the room, looked me in the eye, and said, "Okay. I'll give you Barth. What else?"

Francis Schaeffer turned out to be the kind of fundamentalist Christian I could work with, even when we disagreed. (Of course, at the time he didn't know I was gay, but neither did I.) Although he was absolutely committed to his belief that the Bible is without error, he was also humble enough to admit that fundamentalist Christians can't say the same for themselves. I find the spirit of Francis Schaeffer rather rare in the fundamentalist Christian leaders who have succeeded him.

A month after the premiere of Schaeffer's film series "How Should We Then Live?," I received a package shipped from Huemoz, Switzerland. In it was a framed photo of Karl Barth and across the broken glass in black marker pen Francis had written, "You like him. You can have him." I treasure that photo and honor the memory of the fundamentalist Christian who had a sense of humor and became my friend (even though I'm still trying to figure out exactly what Francis was trying to say in that convoluted twelve-part video series).

Although Dr. Schaeffer died in 1984, his idea of giving shelter to spiritually hungry young people did not die with him. L'Abri shelters have opened in Australia, Canada, England, Germany, Korea, the Netherlands, and the United States (in Southborough, Massachusetts, and Rochester, Minnesota). During our months together in Huemoz, I learned to love the Schaeffers. Unfortunately, what Francis taught his guests and how his teachings have evolved in their hands now threaten the rest of us.

One afternoon in L'Abri, while we were filming his on-camera narration, I asked Dr. Schaeffer rather playfully, "Besides yourself, what twentieth-century theologian do you trust?" "None of them," he answered without a pause, "except the Princeton Group, of course."

All right, I confess. At the time I had no idea that "the Princeton Group" were three fiery Presbyterian theologians (long dead) who literally laid the foundations for fundamentalist Christianity in the twentieth century on the principle of biblical inerrancy. Everything rises or falls on that belief. Actually it's Charles Darwin we can thank (or blame) not just for his *Origin of Species* but for the origin of biblical inerrancy and for "The Princeton Group"—Hodge, Warfield, and Machen—three of its earliest and most eloquent defenders.

In 1858, twenty-two years after he circumnavigated the globe in the sturdy little HMS *Beagle*, Darwin stunned the world with his belief that all things come from a common source by way of natural selection. Until that time most people just assumed that God had created the world and all the creatures it sustains in just six days. Darwin's notion that we've all evolved from a single cell was a blatant attack on that Christian belief and on the inerrant view of Scripture, the source of that belief.

Charles Hodge (1797-1878), a distinguished theology professor at Princeton Seminary, rushed to denounce Darwin's "godless theory." To Hodge, because evolution did not include any mention of God's design, it contradicted the Genesis stories of creation and seriously undermined the inerrancy of Scripture. Hodge's successors at Princeton, Benjamin Warfield (1851-1921) and J. Gresham Machen (1871-1939), joined their mentor in taking an unqualified stand against evolution and for biblical inerrancy even when a majority of Presbyterians no longer supported the belief that the Bible was without error in the whole and in the part.

For Francis Schaeffer, Hodge, Warfield, and Machen were

the ultimate theological authority. He was as committed to biblical inerrancy as "The Princeton Group." In fact, Machen, after being defrocked by the Presbyterians, started Westminster Seminary in Philadelphia to train men who could defend inerrancy in the face of growing opposition. Francis Schaeffer enrolled there one year later because the new seminary was committed to a literal reading of an inerrant Bible.

The first decades of the twentieth century were a bad time for fundamentalist Christians. H. L. Mencken, America's favorite columnist at the time, voiced the growing trend to condemn the church: "I believe," he said, "that religion…has been a curse to mankind—that its modest and greatly overestimated services on the ethical side have been more than overcome by the damage it has done to clear and honest thinking."[22] In his novel *The Job*, Sinclair Lewis captured the mood of those who ignored the church in the description of his hero: "His entire system of theology was comprised in the Bible, which he never read, and the Methodist Church, which he rarely attended."[23]

Unnerved by secular forces at work undermining Christian tradition, conservative Christians united around five fundamentals of the faith. You would think that this new Christian credo or confession would begin with something about Jesus. Instead, biblical inerrancy is the first of the five fundamentals. The old Princeton list of "five essential and necessary articles" were: "the inerrancy of the Bible; Christ's virgin birth; Christ's death to satisfy divine justice, and reconcile us to God; Christ's bodily resurrection; and the authenticity of Christ's mighty miracles that made changes in the order of nature."

The nondenominational fundamentalists changed the virgin birth to the deity of Christ, and changed the mighty miracles to the pre-millennial return of Christ, to create these five fundamentals: "the inerrancy of the Bible; the deity of Christ; Christ's death to satisfy divine justice, and reconcile us to God; Christ's bodily resurrection; and the pre-millennial return of Christ."

These five fundamentals were constructed as a kind of Iron Curtain against the changes sweeping America during the Industrial Revolution, World War I, and the "Roaring Twenties." Their origins can be traced to *The Fundamentals*, a series of essays published in twelve volumes between 1910 and 1915 by approximately sixty conservative Christian pastors and teachers from the United States and England. Fundamentalists were those who defended these fundamentals of the faith.

Fundamentalists like Schaeffer were afraid that the values of a secular society were rapidly displacing Christian values as they understood them. They believed that the very existence of their conservative churches was threatened by "modernism" or "secular humanism." They were terrified that scholars using linguistic and historic analysis of the biblical texts were finding "errors" in God's "holy inerrant word." They feared that Christianity as they knew it would not survive. The strict and literal religion they had inherited directly from their Pilgrim Fathers was being replaced by a watered-down version of the Christian faith.

Fundamentalists also feared that the nation, too, was losing its spiritual moorings. God, who had blessed America and made it the world's hope, could not continue to bless a nation that no longer honored Him. By calling the American people back to "true belief" (as described in their five fundamentals of the faith), fundamentalists were waging a war to save both church and state alike. It is the same war that fundamentalist Christians are waging in our time. And it is the same infallible, inerrant, literal understanding of the Bible that guides them (with no consideration of the linguistic or historic context of each verse, let alone what we have learned through empirical data and personal experience over the centuries).

However, it isn't Schaeffer's inerrant view of Scriptures that makes him the father of modern fundamentalism. It is his call to overthrow the "tyranny of secular humanism" that helped mobilize millions of fundamentalist Christians to become political activists for the first time. Fundamentalists hadn't come roaring out of their churches into the public square since they fought to amend the U.S. Constitution to prohibit the public sale and consumption of alcoholic beverages (Eighteenth Amendment, 1920) and fought equally hard to end the teaching of evolution in the public schools (Scopes trial, 1925).

Fundamentalism rises and falls in almost predictable cycles. When I was growing up in the 1940s and '50s, Schaeffer's call to political action would have left most evangelicals cold. For the most part, evangelicals didn't participate in politics. When my dad ran for election as a member of the Santa Cruz, California, City Council and then went on to serve as mayor, our friends at church couldn't believe it. "Carl," they said, "if God wanted something changed in Santa Cruz, God would do it. Our job is to bear witness to the change Christ has made in our lives, not to mess with government."

For African-American Christians that kind of thinking ended in the fifties and sixties with Martin Luther King, Jr.'s call to relentless nonviolent resistance. There were white evangelical Christians who joined King in seeing the Good News as a call not just to announce God's love to the world but to live out that love in the world. And evangelicals had shown for centuries their missionary zeal to bring hope and healing to the world. But most white, evangelical Christians were not involved in politics until Francis Schaeffer's call to take direct, nonviolent action against any government that strays from our "Judeo-Christian heritage."

Schaeffer's book *A Christian Manifesto (1981)* sold more than two million copies and mobilized masses of conservative

Christians to become politically active. Sitting with him in
L'Abri, interviewing him for his film series, and listening to
him speak at film premiers all across the country, Schaeffer
repeated his call for Christians to reclaim America for Christ,
and his words echoed across the nation through fundamentalist
preachers and televangelists.

Schaeffer and his fellow fundamentalists clipped articles
from *Time* and other national newsmagazines that illustrated
their fears that this "once great Christian nation" was under
siege by secular forces. There was a kind of terror in the air
that Christian values as they understood them were being
undermined in church and state alike. Schaeffer and his cronies
were especially concerned about the "anti-Christian" decisions
being made by justices on the U.S. Supreme Court. It was their
1963 decision against mandatory reading of Bible verses or
prayers in the classroom that motivated Schaeffer to declare
war on the highest court in the land. Not since Carry Nation
attacked her local saloon with a hatchet on June 1, 1900, had
a fundamentalist Christian gone to war with the tenacity of a
Francis Schaeffer.

"It's illegal, in many places," Schaeffer warned, "for
youngsters to merely meet and pray on the geographical
location of the public schools. We are not only immoral," he
added, "we are stupid for the place we have allowed ourselves to
come to without noticing. There is no other word we can use
for our present situation that I have just been describing, except
the word TYRANNY! TYRANNY! That's what we face!"[24]

There is no doubt in my mind that Francis Schaeffer
was sincere in his beliefs, but he was sincerely wrong in his
interpretation of that Supreme Court decision on prayer
in public schools and in his understanding of America as a
fundamentalist Christian nation. To save that nation, Francis
Schaeffer used half-truth and hyperbole to rally the troops. He

never lied. He was sincerely afraid that America was doomed unless it returned to its Christian roots, but his rather biased interpretation of the daily news, seeing secular humanists under every bed and behind every bush, sounded very much like the anticommunist crusade of Joseph McCarthy. Our current fundamentalist Christian gurus have followed directly in Francis Schaeffer's footsteps. Hyperbole, half-truth, and even lies are all acceptable in the battle "to reclaim America for Christ."

Schaeffer warned his fellow Christians that the Supreme Court had made it impossible for students to pray. In fact, the court's decision that public schools could not require students to recite prayers from a specific religion each morning was hardly an example of "judicial tyranny." Even after the court's decision, students had the right to pray alone or in student-led groups at the flagpole, before lunch, in the school bus, or on the playground and in Bible clubs or prayer groups that met on campus before or after the school day. Students could carry their Bibles to school, dress in T-shirts inscribed with Bible verses, and wear Jesus jewelry. They could share their faith with other students outside class. They could even distribute religious literature. But the Supreme Court decided that students could not be forced by their teachers to pray in the classroom.

Schaeffer used the court's decision to illustrate (in fiery language) the end of "the Christian consensus" that guided the founding fathers in the establishment of this so-called Christian nation. "We must absolutely set out to smash the lie of the new and novel concept of the separation of religion from the state," Schaeffer exclaimed, "which most people now hold and which Christians have just bought a bill of goods. This concept [separation of church and state] is new," Schaeffer added, "and novel. It has no relationship to the meaning of the First Amendment."

Schaeffer was calling for a revolution, but unlike those who followed him he didn't attempt to fund that revolution by creating fear and loathing of homosexuals through mass-mail fund-raising appeals. Schaeffer's take on homosexuality and homosexuals was far more gentle and loving than that of the fundamentalists who followed. Although he made it clear that homosexuality was "a part of the abnormality of the fallen world," I can't find one example of Francis exploiting the fear of homosexuals to raise funds or recruit followers.

In a letter dated 1968, Francis Schaeffer wrote: "If a person who has homophile tendencies, or even has practiced homosexuality, is helped in a deep way, then they may marry. On the other hand, there are a certain number of cases who are real homophiles. In this case they must face the dilemma of a life without sexual fulfillment. We may cry with them concerning this, but we must not let the self-pity get too deep, because the unmarried girl who has strong sexual desires, and no one asks her to marry has the same problem. In both cases this is surely a part of the abnormality of the fallen world. And in both cases what is needed is people's understanding while the church, in compassion and understanding, helps the individual in every way possible."[25]

Schaeffer's number one social concern was abortion, not homosexuality, and he repeated endlessly his angry condemnation of the Supreme Court's decision on *Roe v. Wade* supporting a woman's right to end an unwanted pregnancy. "This thing [abortion] has been presented under the hypocritical name of choice. What does choice equal? Choice means the right to kill for your own selfish desires. To kill human life! That's what the choice is that we're being presented with."

From Switzerland, in his quiet, angry voice, Francis Schaeffer sounded the alarm to his fellow Christians in the United States. He called his brothers and sisters to wage war against the secular forces that were "undermining the spiritual foundations of this once great Christian nation" Schaeffer saw abortion as the primary example of secular forces at work. It was his call to do battle with evil in high places that helped launch the thirty-five-year struggle by Christian fundamentalists to gain political power, and, thanks to Francis Schaeffer, "stop the killing of a million unborn babies every year" became the battle cry of fundamentalist Christian leaders across America.

Francis Schaeffer was also the first fundamentalist in our time to call Christians to acts of civil disobedience if the political process failed. "At a certain point," he exclaimed, "it is not only the privilege but it is the duty of the Christian to disobey the government...You heard it from the Scripture: 'Should we obey man rather than God.'"...There was not a single place... where the Reformation was successful, where there wasn't civil disobedience and disobedience to the state...If there is no place for disobeying a human government, that government has been made GOD...We have lots of room to move yet with our court cases, with the people we elect—all the things that we can do in this country. If, unhappily, we come to that place, the appropriate level must also include a disobedience to the state... We must save this country from utter tragedy."[26]

In this one paragraph, Schaeffer sets out the first-stage tactics in the fundamentalist strategy to reclaim America for Christ: winning court cases that support fundamentalist Christian goals for the country and electing people into political office (local, state, and national) who will introduce legislation that will turn fundamentalist Christian values into law. The fundamentalists who succeeded Schaeffer have been so successful at those tactics that they haven't needed to follow his call to civil disobedience... at least not very often.

However, fundamentalist Christians have experimented in new forms of civil disobedience that impress and frighten me. When their leaders called Christians across America to use their phones to stop Bill Clinton from ending the ban on gays in the military, they generated literally millions of calls, enough to close down phone systems in the White House, the Congress, the State Department, and the Pentagon. The fundamentalist Christian troops made it impossible for the president to govern until he broke his promise and left the ban in place. There is no telling what they will do next.

During those months in Switzerland, I never dreamed that Francis Schaeffer was launching a political revolution that would gain fundamentalist Christians such frightening power over my life, let alone the life of this nation. And it happened in large part through the ministries of thousands of young men and women who spent long evenings at L'Abri, eating Edith's orange rolls and listening to Francis's dreams of fundamentalist Christians making this a Christian nation once again.

W. A. CRISWELL

At the same time that Francis Schaeffer was calling for a fundamentalist Christian army to "take back the government," W. A. Criswell, the senior pastor of the First Baptist Church in Dallas, Texas, was raising up a fundamentalist Christian army to "take back the church." While ghostwriting his autobiography, *Standing on the Promises*, I learned that Southern Baptists consider Criswell, not Francis Schaeffer, the father of modern fundamentalism.

Born in 1909 in Eldorado, Oklahoma, the son of a barber, Wallie Amos Criswell fought his way out of poverty to become the most powerful preacher in the Southern Baptist Convention, the largest and most influential Protestant denomination in the United States. With twenty-eight thousand members, Dallas's First Baptist became the nation's first mega-church during W. A. Criswell's fifty-year term as senior pastor.

During a tour of Criswell's First Baptist campus in the heart of downtown Dallas, I was not surprised to see that a man billed as "America's leading fundamentalist" would be such a creative and compassionate pastor. Fundamentalist Christians are not ogres who live in smoky caves casting spells on the nation, pushing pins into little effigies of Uncle Sam stuffed with hay. Fundamentalist Christians are my sisters and brothers, my family and friends, my oldest colleagues and coworkers. From childhood I have witnessed their commitment to the poor, the hungry, the homeless, and the outcast. I don't doubt for a minute their genuine concern for this nation and for the people of this nation. But I fear their love for the nation has become an obsession to reshape it in their own image.

Criswell was a raging fundamentalist determined to reshape the Southern Baptist Church in his image, but at the same time he was concerned about the people of Dallas. Besides the massive sanctuary and dozens of offices, conference rooms, and classrooms at Dallas First Baptist, he provided the city a large take-out library, a gym, a jogging track, a skating rink, several basketball courts, and even a bowling alley. Also housed in their huge facility was an innovative family life program, ministries to the homeless and unemployed, a food bank, and a counseling center.

From Criswell's "secret second office" in a modern glass-and-steel high-rise across the street from his First Baptist Church, an office decorated with very thick carpets, original oil paintings of the western frontier, and a collection of Remington bronzes depicting scenes from the wild west, Jack Pogue, Criswell's lifetime friend and investment broker, pointed out the six square blocks of downtown Dallas real estate owned by First Baptist, a source of revenue for a growing congregation with an annual budget that averaged over $11 million in the early 1980s.

Like Schaeffer, Criswell was revered as a loving pastor and a powerful preacher. When I interviewed Criswell in 1990, he was eighty-one years old, just five years from retirement (actually from becoming the very active, some say obstructively active, "Pastor Emeritus"). I was really impressed with the gentle, self-effacing way Criswell handled conflict both in public and in private, and the very loving way he treated people who approached him nonstop, day and night.

"The Pastor," as people called him, was in great health, due in no small part to his practice of swimming in the nearby YMCA pool almost every day. Always dressed in a dark suit, white shirt, a conservative power broker tie, and matching silk pocket handkerchief, Criswell was a formidable presence, with a thick head of perfectly white hair, dark blue eyes, and an almost constant grin.

Like Schaeffer, Criswell was transformed before a crowd from loving pastor to fiery preacher. You could still sense his Oklahoma, circuit-riding, "holy roller" background from the passion in his presentations that spilled over the pulpit and into the pews. His sermons were peppered with Greek references, sometimes dozens of them, and he seemed to have an endless supply of new stories in the tradition of O. Henry and Will Rogers that illustrated his points perfectly. A master of surprise endings and funny punch lines, Criswell could hold an audience in the palm of his hand. His sermon manuscripts were read and reused in their own congregations by Southern Baptist pastors across the country.

Greatly respected by clergy and laity alike, Criswell was considered "the Pope" of Baptist fundamentalists, and like a pope he spoke ex-cathedra, literally "from a throne" (First Baptist Dallas), with a kind of infallible authority. Of course, having Billy Graham as a member of your church, even a long-distance, seldom-in-attendance member, helped develop the

W. A. Criswell myth.

Francis Schaeffer may have been the first to call evangelical Christians to wage war, against the forces of secular humanism in government, but it was W A. Criswell who fired the first shots in the fundamentalists' war to purge "moderates" and "progressives" from their churches. Southern Baptists trace the origins of this Southern Baptist purge to a sermon Criswell delivered during his first term as president of the Southern Baptist Convention in 1969. That sermon, "Why I Preach That the Bible Is Literally True," was in civil war language, the shot heard round the denomination.

The essence of that sermon—that the Bible is inerrant and anyone who disagrees cannot be trusted theologically—spread like wildfire across the denomination by manuscript, audiotape, and word of mouth. And though I can't find that 1969 sermon in the Criswell archives, other sermons just like it demonstrate why Criswell's position on biblical inerrancy divided pastors, seminary professors, and laypeople in the pews.

"If this Bible, which is supposed to be written by God," Criswell announced, "who knows all of history and who knows all the facts of His creation—if this Bible, which is supposed to be written by the Lord God, the Holy Spirit of God, is full of historical and scientific errors, it is a work of men. It is not a work of God. Period. It's that plain."[27]

Or consider the fury these three sentences provoked among moderates in the denomination. "The Bible," said Criswell, "has been written by something like forty men, over fifteen hundred years, and, for two thousand years, has remained unchanged... God, who wrote that Book, wrote it all down according to the truth of the omniscient, infallible mind of the Almighty Lord. And, when I read it, every syllable of it is truth. It's God's Word and there are no errors and no mistakes in it."[28]

Southern Baptist fundamentalists—and there were then and

there are now Southern Baptists who are not fundamentalists—began to use a person's views on biblical inerrancy as a litmus test for "orthodoxy." When anyone questioned (let alone opposed) inerrancy in the pulpit or the classroom, in a book or magazine article, they were charged in the court of public opinion and declared guilty of aiding and abetting the denomination's "slide down the slippery slope of liberalism." When Criswell warned that the SBC seminaries were a hotbed of liberals who opposed inerrancy and were teaching generations of young preachers to do the same, the witch hunt began.

By the early 1990s, fundamentalists had won control of all the national boards, committees, and agencies of the Southern Baptist Convention. Seminary presidents, deans, and even tenured seminary professors were fired and replaced by fundamentalists. Missionaries were interrogated and recalled. Ordained women (including Billy Graham's daughter) were denied the right to preach. Gay pastors, teachers, organists, and choirmasters were hunted down and hounded out of the SBC. Local congregations were divided and whole state conventions either withdrew or were purged from the denomination. The lives and careers of many of the best and brightest of Southern Baptist leadership were sacrificed by fundamentalists determined to purge the moderate's influence and firmly establish their own.

Jimmy Carter's very public resignation of his lifelong membership in the Southern Baptist Convention came as a direct result of the fundamentalist purge of his beloved denomination. "I have finally decided that, after sixty-five years," Carter said, "I can no longer be associated with the Southern Baptist Convention." Then he carefully listed his objections to the fundamentalist takeover that violated "the basic premises of my Christian faith." He was disturbed by the SBC decision to prohibit women clergy, and by a statement asking women "to be submissive to their husbands." The most offensive reason for both Carters was the elimination of language that identifies Jesus as "the criterion by which the Bible is interpreted."[29]

Although "I believe in biblical inerrancy" has become a kind of creed or confession for fundamentalists, they also have another test to see if you are really a Bible-believing Christian. The test goes something like this. Are you a "post-," "a-," or a "pre-millennialist"? If you don't have a clue what the question means, or if you have never used the word "millenarianism" (Christ's thousand-year reign) in a sentence, you are probably not a fundamentalist and you've certainly not read the books or viewed the films of Tim LaHaye's popular "Left Behind" series. In the book of Revelation, John describes what will happen at the end of history, or as the fundamentalists say, "at the end of this church dispensation." John's description of the end of time in the book of Revelation is pure poetry, creating unforgettable images of men and angels, heaven and hell, death and redemption.

Criswell understands John's apocalyptic vision literally. The Pastor's "pre-millennialist" position declares that when time as we know it runs out, Christ will return temporarily to rapture his saints to heaven. Almost immediately Jesus will depart again, leaving the world and those men, women, and children who remain on earth to suffer through seven years of tribulation. This is Dante at his best, complete with beasts rising from the sea and the four horsemen of the apocalypse bringing war, famine, plague, and death to the earth. During this terrible time of suffering, humankind is given one last chance to repent and confess that Jesus is God's only son. When the tribulation ends, Christ returns and sets up his thousand-year reign on earth.

To the majority of fundamentalists, "pre-millennialists" are the true Christians. "They are literalists," Criswell declares. "They believe the Word of God, syllable by syllable, verse by verse. And according to the Word of God, they believe that sin is dark, and the only hope we have is in the intervention of God from heaven, the second coming of Christ."[30]

Criswell mocks "post-millennialists" by caricaturing their position that Christ will come after the world has been saved in these words: "[They say] we're going to preach the millennium in," Criswell claimed. "[They say] we're going to evolve. We're going to breed out of the human race, the fang and the tooth and the claw and the ape. We are going to bring in the kingdom. And then, at the end of the millennium, Jesus will come." Criswell made it very clear that post-millennialists are wrong.

Criswell defines "a-millennialists" as those who don't think there will be a tribulation or a thousand-year reign of Christ on the earth. "They take all of the endless words in the Bible and spiritualize them," he said. "They give them meanings that appeal to them, but they don't reveal, don't stand by, don't preach the literal meaning of the Word of God."

In sermon after sermon, Criswell reminds Southern Baptists that "Jesus was a pre-millennialist…," that "the Apostle Paul was a pre-millennialist…," that "without exception every saint of God, for the first three hundred years of the Christian faith, was a pre-millennialist." He usually ends the list of pre-millennial saints with "…and Billy Graham is a pre-millennialist." It is interesting to note that Billy Graham hired me to help him write Approaching Hoofbeats, his personal take on the book of Revelation, and not once in the entire 236 pages does he even pick up this divisive debate.

Several times in Sunday morning worship at Thomas Road Baptist Church, I've heard Jerry Falwell introduce a guest preacher or performer with these words. "He's pre-mill," Jerry exclaims with a knowing grin, "and pre-trib." Having passed the primary fundamentalist test, the people smile and nod their approval. It isn't difficult to draw the conclusion from Criswell,

Falwell, and the rest of them that anyone who is not a pre-millennialist is not really an authentic Bible-believing Christian.

Criswell's certainty about biblical inerrancy and pre-millennialismand his demand that everyone agree with him or else—led to terrible suffering in the Southern Baptist Convention. Now fundamentalist Christians are using those two issues to divide and conquer once again. Before his death on January 10, 2002, W. A. Criswell realized how many people have been wounded by this debate. "I wish that the people who believed the most about the Bible had the most loving spirit about what they believed, me included," Criswell said. "The war of words must have grieved our loving Father, for it certainly broke my heart."[31]

On September 21, 1980, Criswell preached his first sermon on homosexuality and inadvertently launched another war of words with far greater significance to the lives of my sisters and brothers than any end-times debate could ever have. At the outset, Criswell admits his ignorance. "I didn't know what it [homosexuality] was until I came to the city," he said at the beginning of that Sunday night sermon broadcast live across the nation. "And I certainly wasn't introduced into its ramifications and intimacies," he added, "until I began to study for this message several months ago."

Maybe so. Maybe not. While I was digging through boxes that Dr. Criswell had contributed to his personal archives, I found a handful of old letters bound together by a black ribbon. Because Criswell had given me permission to rummage through these personal treasures, I untied the ribbon and began to read. If I remember correctly, the letters were dated 1927 or 1928, when Criswell was in his late teens. They were written by another youth who had known W. A. since childhood.

The letters often responded directly to questions young Criswell asked his friend, giving me a clearer picture of their significant friendship. There was no talk of love, let alone sexual intimacy. No clear picture could be drawn to describe their relationship more than that they were intimate friends who shared each other's hopes and dreams. After reading the letters several times, I was certain that theirs was a Jonathan-David kind of friendship with absolutely no clear evidence that either man was homosexual or even had sexual feelings toward the other.

The Reverend Nancy Wilson, who replaced Troy Perry as the moderator of our Metropolitan Community Churches, has a perfect right to say, "King David, as a young warrior, was the love of Prince Jonathan's life. Centuries of homophobic Bible commentaries have kept them in the closet too long! But just in case you still have any doubt, here is the clearest evidence." Then Reverend Wilson quotes the words of David's lament upon hearing of Jonathan's death: "I am distressed for you, my brother Jonathan; greatly beloved were you to me; your love to me was wonderful, passing the love of women" (II Samuel 2:26).[32]

Those letters bound with a black ribbon echoed with that kind of sentiment. They were clear evidence that W. A. Criswell had truly loved another man. And though I would not presume for a moment even to suggest that Dr. Criswell was gay or bisexual, in the late 1920s there would be no way for one man to even admit his love for another. The last letter in the pile was from the mother of Criswell's young friend with the sad news that the boy had drowned while swimming in a water hole near the oil derrick in Oklahoma where he was working for the summer. More than sixty years later, when I asked Dr. Criswell about the letters, he just looked at the old envelopes and folded sheets of writing paper in my hand. Then slowly he reached out, took the letters from me, placed them in his desk, and said quietly, "Those letters should not have been given to the archives." It was the one and only time he spoke of them.

Dr. Criswell began that first sermon he ever preached on homosexuality by referring back to his ultimate authority on this and every issue. "We're going to begin," he said, "with a look at the words that are used in these Holy Scriptures concerning this subject." Criswell could read the Greek text, but he never read it in its historical or linguistic context. And he was equally uninterested in the scientific, psychological, and historical evidence that homosexuality is neither a sickness nor a sin. This sermon, from the Southern Baptist "pope," helped launch a war of words that twenty-five years later still has tragic consequences in the lives of America's gay people. And in that historic sermon, Criswell modeled how the case against us would be framed by all the generations that followed.

First, he refers to the story of Sodom, suggesting that all the men and boys of that ancient city of approximately one thousand to three thousand people[33] were homosexuals and that if God hadn't intervened they would have "…violated [the angels] with all that could be imagined of dignity and virtue." Too polite to say "rape," Criswell still made it clear that all five hundred to fifteen hundred men and boys who lived in Sodom were homosexuals and that they had all come to rape the strangers in their midst. [34]

In the process of misusing this story to condemn homosexuals, Criswell ignored the real sin of Sodom as described by Jesus and five Old Testament prophets: "This is the sin of Sodom," says the prophet Ezekiel. "She and her suburbs had pride, excess of food, and prosperous ease but did not help or encourage the poor and needy. They were arrogant and this was abominable in God's eyes" (Ezekiel 16:48-49).

Criswell goes on to misquote the six other "clobber passages" in the Old and New Testament that are still being used to condemn homosexuality and homosexuals. He ignored the fact that Jewish and Christian scholars all agree that the holiness passages in the Torah have nothing to do with homosexuality or homosexuals. He ignored the reality that biblical authors knew nothing of homosexual orientation as we understand it today and therefore said nothing to support or condemn homosexuals. He ignored the fact that Jesus and the Jewish prophets were entirely silent on the subject. And he ignored the growing scientific, psychological, historical, pastoral, personal, and even biblical evidence that homosexuality is neither a sickness nor a sin. And in the process, W. A. Criswell helped launch the war that fundamentalists still wage against us.

Criswell also demonstrated the various ways homosexuals can be caricatured and condemned. For example, he led the way in using pseudoscience to "prove" that homosexuality was a sickness. In his first antihomosexual sermon, Criswell quotes a Dr. Reuben, M.D., to prove his point that "...in psychology it is definitely proven that homosexuality is not inherited. It is an acquired characteristic. It is a learned sin, an act of perversion." Then they were quoting Reuben. Now it's Paul Cameron, Joseph Nicolosi, and his National Association for Research and Therapy of Homosexuality. Every generation finds a fundamentalist pseudoscientist they can use to create "empirical" data that supports their ignorance and fear.

In that same sermon, Criswell also stereotypes the gay community in ways that raised more fear and loathing in the hearts of those who heard him. "In San Francisco," he declares, "one-third of the population is homosexual. That means that in that one city alone there are something like two hundred thousand sodomites and lesbians....This year there was a march of over a hundred thousand of them. What are they marching for? They are marching for the right to have lesbian or homosexual relationships with children and with young people, if they so desire. Freedom of expression. This is the gay rights movement." Here Criswell is almost inventing a terror tactic that continues to this day with fundamentalist preachers, radio and television talk show hosts endlessly exploiting a few X-rated scenes of leather men and dykes on bikes to caricature and condemn millions of lesbian and gay Americans.

In his first sermon on homosexuality, Criswell also caricatured sex education in the public schools. "What frightens me to death," he said, "what scares me no end, is what is developing in the public school systems of America with regard to what they call sex education. Sex education favors homosexuality, intimacy, masturbation, and sex. 'It is healthy,' they say, that's what the teacher is supposed to teach. You stand aghast, overwhelmed, by what is happening in the culture of America." Does that technique sound equally familiar?

Criswell also used dramatic stories that show, in his words, "Gay might not be so gay." "I had an associate here," Criswell said, "a minister here, my first associate. He went to the cemetery and blew his brains out, killed himself. He was found molesting little boys, and rather than face the judgment, he destroyed his own life."

Twenty-five years later, fundamentalist preachers and televangelists still follow Criswell's lead. They misuse the Bible to prove that homosexuality is a sin. They use pseudoscience to prove that homosexuality is a sickness. And like Criswell, they caricature the gay rights movement, condemn sex education programs, and conclude their attacks with dramatic stories meant to prove that homosexuals live miserable lives that always end in tragedy.

Of course Criswell, like those who follow him, tried to end his sermon on a positive, loving note. It didn't work then. It doesn't work now. "Do you notice that this sin of homosexuality is not set aside as a special or an unusual sin?" Criswell concludes. "It is one out of a whole list of them...thieves, the covetous, drunkards, revilers and extortioners...Homosexuality...is one out of many, many, many sins...What Jesus is able to do is deliver us."

It is sad to see how fundamentalist Christians want it both ways. After spending forty-five minutes demeaning, dehumanizing, and demonizing lesbian and gay people, they add our names to a list of criminals and perverts that makes us look even worse. Then they try to soften their false and inflammatory attacks by tacking on an invitation to accept God's grace (and their ex-gay therapies)...or else.

When we demonstrate clearly how the false and inflammatory attacks on gay people—then and now—lead to ruined lives, broken families, divided churches, physical and spiritual suffering, and even give license for others to kill us and for us to kill ourselves, they justify themselves with this idiotic excuse: "We love the sinner but we hate the sin." In practical terms that means "we hate the sinner and the sin alike." When you hate what I am and whom I love, you hate me.

Francis Schaeffer hardly mentions homosexuality in his vast collection of books, pamphlets, articles, videotapes, and film. Criswell develops the basic fundamentalist Christian case against homosexual practice but never uses it to raise money or recruit volunteers. It was Criswell's friend Jerry Falwell, pastor of the Thomas Road Baptist Church in Lynchburg, Virginia, who elevated gay bashing to an art form and in the process raised up an army to take back America.

TWO

THE WARRIORS:
JERRY FALWELL AND PAT ROBERTSON

*I*n 1986, I was hired to write Jerry Falwell's autobiography, *Strength for the Journey*. As a result, I became a member of Jerry's traveling entourage off and on for almost a year. During that time I witnessed the powerful influence of this man in the lives of fundamentalist Christians, clergy and laity alike. In 2003, my partner, Gary Nixon, and I moved from our home in Laguna Beach, California, to a four-room cottage across the street from Jerry Falwell's massive church in Lynchburg, Virginia, to be eyewitnesses on the front lines of the war Jerry and his fundamentalist Christian friends are waging not just against gay and lesbian Americans but against women's rights, against the rights of Muslim, Hindu, Buddhist, agnostic, and atheist Americans, against national and international measures that would preserve and protect the environment, against sex education that includes safe-sex information, against stem-cell research, against affirmative action, against entitlement programs even if designed to help the poor, the homeless, and the retired.

I wish you could spend one weekend with us in Lynchburg, just long enough to visit Falwell's Liberty University, according to Jerry one of the fastest-growing schools in America where this year he claims the registrar turned away 13,500 qualified freshmen for lack of space while building three thousand new dorm rooms trying to keep up. I wish you could hear him preach on Sundays to his congregation broadcast live across the United States and to seventy or so other countries.

It is rumored that Jerry wears TV makeup all day to be available as a last-minute guest on network television through a satellite uplink on his Liberty University campus. Larry King told me that Jerry has been on his program something like five times more than the next most popular guest "because he stirs things up," and hardly a day goes by that his startling sound bites are not broadcast to the nation on the evening news, talk programs, radio and television specials, and even showbiz reports.

On Sunday mornings when we're in town, we still attend early service at Jerry's Thomas Road Baptist Church. Actually, when I'm in town I visit Jerry's church. Gary finally had his fill and now is happy for me to go alone. Early on we decided that whenever Pastor Falwell misused Scripture to caricature and condemn God's gay children, we'd stand and bow our heads in silent protest. Sometimes others stood with me. I thought this public witness might help Jerry's congregation to realize there is another side to the issue. But Jerry took my public witness and used it for his own advantage. In a gathering of more than six thousand ministers in his campus arena, one of Jerry's associates encouraged the clergy from across the United States to preach a stronger gospel like the Gospel Jerry preaches "until you, too, have visitors standing in protest." Now if we stand in protest the people applaud Jerry. Oh, well!

Jerry is a media genius who can turn almost any criticism into a compliment, almost any loss into victory. And though too many of my friends and allies have written him off as a kind of nutcase, Jerry Falwell continues to be the folksy, down-home, good-old-boy spokesman for a movement that is threatening to rip out the very heart of democracy.

In *The Battle for God*, Karen Armstrong's magnificent study of Christian, Muslim, and Jewish fundamentalism, the author credits Jerry Falwell and his Moral Majority as the father of this round of fundamentalist Christianity in America. In a ride to the Houston, Texas, airport after we had both given keynote addresses to a large gathering of justice seekers gathered in that city, Dr. Armstrong commented on our move to Lynchburg. "I spent years studying and writing about fundamentalism," she said, "but I can't imagine living that close to a fundamentalist like Falwell."

It was Francis Schaeffer who called for a militant fundamentalism that would "take back America," but Jerry Falwell was the first to recruit and train the troops. Before his Moral Majority took the field, Falwell had demonstrated his skills at mobilizing people as founding pastor of the Thomas Road Baptist Church.

In 1952, eighteen-year-old Jerry was converted in a Sunday evening service at the Park Avenue Baptist Church in Lynchburg. Four years later, he graduated from a Bible college in Springfield, Missouri, and shortly after accepted the invitation to pastor thirty-five disgruntled members from Park Avenue Baptist who were determined to start a church of their own.

In 1956, that handful of dissenting Baptists found a home in the empty Donald Duck Bottling Company on Thomas Road. By 1986, thirty years later, Thomas Road Baptist Church had eighteen thousand members with a budget of more than $60 million annually, and Jerry's Sunday morning sermons were heard weekly in one of every four homes in America, broadcast "live" on 392 television channels and six hundred radio stations. This year, Jerry's budget for Thomas Road Baptist Church, Liberty University, his *Old Time Gospel Hour,* and his various other educational and media ministries including his already accredited law school will reach $200 million for the very first time.

In 1986, Irving Lazar, my literary agent, arranged for me to meet in New York City with Michael Korda, best-selling author and editor in chief of Simon & Schuster, one of America's largest publishers. Mr. Korda was looking for a ghost to write Jerry Falwell's autobiography. Convinced by Lazar that Falwell had a huge following across the country, Korda had given Falwell a million-dollar advance for his story.

I was stunned by the first question Mr. Korda asked as we stood together in his high-rise office overlooking the New York City skyline. "Who the hell is Jerry Falwell?" and it was fairly obvious by the tone of his voice that he was serious. "Irving Lazar convinced me to give this Falwell guy a million-dollar advance for his autobiography and I've never even heard of the man."

Mr. Korda's question illustrates the very deep chasm that separates the two Americas. On the one hand Michael Korda is a highly respected author and publisher with deep roots in British and American history. Michael's uncle, Alexander Korda, was the film director credited with modernizing the British film industry, and his aunt, actress Merle Oberon, was an international star of stage and screen.

For more than four decades, Michael Korda has written his own bestselling fiction and nonfiction while also editing and publishing best-selling authors including Graham Greene, Larry McMurtry, Carlos Castaneda, Jackie Susann, Harold Robbins, and Irving Wallace. Michael Korda is the editor of two presidential memoirs—Ronald Reagan's and Richard Nixon's—and the author of *Ulysses S. Grant: The Unlikely Hero*. Yet this distinguished American liberal had never even heard of the fundamentalist Jerry Falwell whose Sunday morning sermons were heard weekly in one of every four American homes and who was organizing an army of Christian fundamentalists whose ultimate goal was to end the influence of people like Michael Korda on this country's "declining moral values."

Falwell, of course, was delighted to cooperate with a liberal New York publisher to get his story to the nation. However, until Falwell began the Moral Majority in the late 1970s, it was not common for fundamentalists including Falwell to collaborate with their friends, let alone to collaborate with their enemies. At the time, there were approximately twenty-three thousand different Protestant denominations in the United States, adequate proof that Protestants, especially fundamentalist Protestants, have a serious separatist streak.[1] Falwell says, "Baptists multiply because we divide." Jerry's own church on Thomas Road was formed by thirty-five members of the Park Avenue Baptist Church in Lynchburg who disagreed with their pastor about some now-forgotten issue.

This separatist streak may originate in the apostle Paul's second letter to the Christians at Corinth, where the gigantic Temple to Apollo cast a dark shadow over the little band of Christians trying to grow a church in that busy Roman city. It must have been a very difficult concept for people who grew up worshipping idols made of gold, silver, bronze, wood, and clay to understand that the Spirit of God was alive and living within the human temple made of flesh and blood.

From Paul's letter urging the new Christians in Corinth to separate themselves from all things pagan, modern fundamentalists have inherited two favorite verses: "Be ye not unequally yoked with unbelievers," and "come out from among them and be ye separate saith the Lord" (II Corinthians 6:14-18).

In the past fundamentalist Christians didn't use these texts exclusively to support their isolation from agnostics, atheists, and people of other faith traditions. They also applied them to other Christians with whom they disagreed. In high school I was convinced that my Presbyterian friend Joel Van Gorder (who went on to distinguish himself as a Presbyterian pastor) was not a real Christian and that it was my job to "lead him to the Lord." And though I joined my other classmates in a moment of silent respect as we were bused past Catholic churches on the way to a football game, I could never understand why we did it since Catholics weren't "real Christians," either. In the seventh grade, my teacher claimed that one reason priests traveled with Columbus to America was to Christianize the Native Americans. "How could they?" I asked. "Catholics aren't Christians." Fifty years later, I am still embarrassed by that memory.

This kind of separatism practiced by Christian fundamentalists until the 1970s ended with Jerry Falwell's Moral Majority. In order to get their president elected, their legislation passed, and their nominees to the Supreme Court confirmed, fundamentalist Christians decided to work closely with one another and with mainstream Protestants, Roman Catholics, Jews, agnostics, and even atheists. That new reality can be traced at least in part to a conversation Jerry Falwell had late in the 1970s with Francis Schaeffer.

"When I began considering how to put together a political organization that included all Americans," Jerry told me, "I was faced with a terrific problem: my own personal psychological barrier. All of my background from Baptist Bible College and other places and persons providing my religious training made it difficult for me to consider such a prospect. And yet I was convinced that there was a moral majority out there among those 200 million Americans sufficient in number to turn back the flood tide of moral permissiveness, family breakdown, and general capitulation to evil."[2]

Not knowing exactly how he could (or even if he should) build bridges between himself and his enemies to accomplish his fundamentalist Christian goals, Falwell took his dilemma to Francis Schaeffer, the man *Time* magazine had just labeled the "guru of evangelicals." Schaeffer reminded Jerry that the Bible has many stories "of the yoking together of persons from various philosophical backgrounds for the purpose of carrying out a cause that was good for humanity and pleasing to God…as long as there is no compromise of theological integrity."[3] Actually, in our interview, Jerry said it in stronger and far more revealing language. "Francis Schaeffer told me," he said, "that in the past God used pagans to accomplish His will. Why shouldn't we?"

At the meeting with Schaeffer, Falwell heard for the first time the word *cobelligerent*. "Belligerent" is defined as someone who is "hostile, ready to start a fight, or ready to go to war." Jerry and his fundamentalist friends were ready to go to war. They were convinced that the Christian church was under attack by secular humanists. They were afraid that easy access to porn, drugs, and alcohol would ruin their children. They were angry at the authorities for not cracking down on violence in the streets. They were stunned when abortion was made legal and really frightened by homosexuals and their pride parades. Jerry and his fundamentalist friends were ready to go to war. Remember, Jerry still defines a fundamentalist as "an evangelical who is mad about something." All he needed to do was find mainline Protestants, Catholics, Jews, even atheists and agnostics who shared his anger.

Many of his fellow fundamentalists were furious when Jerry Falwell entered into his working agreement with non-fundamentalists. At the time, Bob Jones, a powerful fundamentalist leader, called Jerry the "most dangerous man in America."[4] Falwell didn't even blink. When his fundamentalist critics attacked him for "being unequally yoked with unbelievers," Jerry answered: "It isn't necessary to be born again to hate abortion, the drug traffic, pornography, child abuse, and immorality in all its ugly, life-destroying forms. Whatever plan God had for this free nation was being threatened, and we needed to draw together millions of people who agreed on these basic issues to take a stand with us and to turn the nation around."[5]

With the help of Robert Billings, Paul Weyrich, Richard Viguerie, Howard Phillips, and Ed McAteer, Jerry Falwell launched the Moral Majority in 1979. The original board of directors included Charles Stanley of the First Baptist Church of Atlanta; Greg Dixon of Indianapolis's Baptist Temple; Tim LaHaye from San Diego, California; and James Kennedy from Coral Gables, Florida. Falwell was the president, Ronald Godwin was the initial vice president, and Robert Billings was the first executive director. Roy Jones was the legislative director of the Moral Majority. In 1981, Cal Thomas was appointed the Moral Majority's vice president for communications.[6]

Immediately, Jerry announced the Moral Majority's fourfold platform. For twenty-six years that platform has been the battle plan of fundamentalist Christian leaders and their cobelligerents in the war to "take back America for Christ." In our interviews, Jerry summarized his platform as pro-life, pro-traditional family, pro-moral, and pro-American. Already Jerry Falwell was showing his skill as a master of spin.

By "pro-life," Jerry meant he opposed *Roe v. Wade* and would do everything in his power to deny women the right to choose how they would exercise their reproductive rights.

By "pro-family," Jerry meant he opposed granting all civil rights or protections to lesbian and gay Americans, including the right to serve in the military, to marry, to adopt, or to provide foster care for children.

By "pro-moral," Jerry meant he opposed "drug traffic, pornography, child abuse, and immorality in all its ugly, life-destroying forms." It also meant that Jerry would register millions of new "pro-moral" voters to elect "pro-moral" candidates who would pass "pro-moral" legislation that would superimpose Jerry's "pro-moral" values on the nation.

And by "pro-American," Jerry meant "making this a Christian nation once again" by ending the separation of church and state, by electing "righteous men" to every important local, state, or national office, and by using those men to create a new kind of democracy that is de facto a theocratic state with a strong commitment to free enterprise, to keeping the military strong, and to limiting the government's role over business and the national economy. He also supported prayer in the schools, display of Judeo-Christian symbols in public places, and keeping "One nation under God" in the pledge.

From the beginning Paul Weyrich and Richard Viguerie were responsible for selling Falwell and his ideas to the masses. Weyrich, a Jew, and Viguerie, a Roman Catholic, had proven their genius in mass-mail marketing. Tired of seeing the politicians they had helped elect go soft on core conservative issues, Weyrich and Viguerie saw in Falwell and his Moral Majority a powerful source of money and volunteer activists for a whole new Republican Party.

Weyrich and Viguerie were scientists when it came to understanding the hot buttons that raised money and mobilized volunteers. They studied the entire country, zip code by zip code, to determine what cobelligerency issues would mobilize masses of people to support Jerry's Moral Majority. Understanding that "the enemy of my enemy is my friend" (or should be), Weyrich, Viguerie, and Falwell began by exploiting people's fear of the "godless Soviet empire" and its threat to the American way. That "threat to democracy" mobilized millions of people who would never agree with Falwell's theology. When the Soviet empire collapsed in 1990, Falwell's mass-mailing mavens switched to two other issues that had proven equally successful at raising funds and recruiting volunteers: the threat of abortion to millions of unborn babies and the threat of the "gay agenda" to children, the family, and the nation.

By 1991, Falwell and his development team had launched a full-scale war on homosexuality and homosexuals. In October of that year, Falwell sent a letter to millions on his Moral Majority list that began: "Last Wednesday, I was threatened by a mob of homosexuals. This convinced me that our nation has become a modern-day Sodom and Gomorrah...Please send your $35 gift today...Please pray also that God will protect me as I serve Christ."

For the last fifteen years, loyal volunteers, especially my friend Daryl Lach, have helped us collect and archive Jerry's antigay rhetoric in his fundraising letters, books, pamphlets, magazines, tapes, sermons, and guest appearances on radio and television networks. Our rather massive collection of Falwell's half-truth, hyperbole, and lies about lesbian and gay Americans demonstrates how Falwell turned gay bashing into a very successful art form.

My favorite example of Jerry's bogus fund-raising letters was mailed in April 1993, again to nobody knows how many million people, in an oversized envelope (4x12-inch) with A DECLARATION OF WAR written across the back in bright red block letters. In the letter enclosed, Jerry asks in another bold headline: "Will You Join Me in a Declaration of War?" He goes on to explain that homosexuals "...have a godless, humanistic scheme for our nation—a plan which will destroy America's traditional moral values...Complete elimination of

God and Christianity from American society is being designed right now…" In that letter Jerry's handlers also added abortion to the mix. "Already the hands of America drip with the blood of millions of innocent little unborn babies. Who will defend them?" and all that overstatement just to motivate an "Emergency Gift to help cover the tremendous cost of national television." The enclosure card says "YES JERRY! I join you in declaring war against the godless forces that will spread across America. You must keep *The Old Time Gospel Hour* on the air nationwide."

Apparently it worked. Jerry's broadcast is now seen live in all fifty states and simultaneously in seventy nations around the globe, and he financed this development of his own worldwide satellite network largely with lies about gay Americans who in Jerry's mind "are a threat to Jerry, to the military, to the church, to the nation's values, to children, and to the family." How many of Jerry's millions believed his lies that homosexuals "recruit children through scouting and the schools, that we want to eliminate God and the Christian church, that we want to control society, politics, schools, and free speech, and that we are determined to destroy morality and religion, pervert the arts, and murder America's soul."

November 14, 2004, just days after fundamentalist Christians reelected their president and established their rather firm hold on majorities in the House and the Senate, Jerry Falwell announced the creation of a Moral Majority Coalition. Using *The Old Time Gospel Hour* (television program), Liberty Network, the *National Liberty Journal*, and an amazingly effective Internet campaign, Falwell announced that the first million members had signed on several weeks later.

Falwell's goals have not changed. On the surface he is determined to see "strict constructionist" pro-life judges confirmed to the Supreme Court, to pass a constitutional Federal

Marriage Amendment, and to elect another fundamentalist or fundamentalist-friendly president in 2008. And if he continues to maintain the six days on the road by private jet, returning on Sunday to preach a sermon someone else has written, as he did during the last presidential campaign, he just may reach his goal to inspire 40 million "faith and values" voters to go to the polls in 2008. However, beneath the surface, Jerry Falwell wants to accomplish this one thing: to see our "Christian nation" become "Christian" once again.

PAT ROBERTSON

Jerry Falwell was the first fundamentalist to exploit (and he continues to exploit) the fear and loathing of homosexuals to raise hundreds of millions of dollars and add millions of new donors to his mailing list. On a regular basis he spews his antihomosexual venom to scare people into supporting Liberty University, Liberty University School of Law, Liberty Baptist Theological Seminary, Thomas Road Baptist Church, the Liberty Channel, Liberty Godparent Home, the *National Liberty Journal*, Liberty Alliance, Liberty Counsel, and the Moral Majority (now the Moral Majority Coalition).

Pat Robertson continues bashing gays in the Falwell tradition to raise funds, add millions to his mailing list, and build his own billion-dollar media, educational, legal, and political empire: the Christian Broadcasting Network (CBN), the world's largest noncommercial television network; CBN's flagship program, *The 700 Club*; Operation Blessing International Relief and Development Corporation; Regent University; the American Center for Law and Justice, now headed by Jay Sekulow; and until 2001 the Christian Coalition. Robertson quit the Christian Coalition that year not because it had failed, but because it had succeeded in reaching Pat's primary goals. In an article nominating President George W. Bush to take Robertson's place as president of the Christian Coalition, a writer for the *Washington Post* describes the extent of that success:

> Pat Robertson's resignation this month as president of the Christian Coalition confirmed the ascendance of a new leader of the religious right in America: George W. Bush. For the first time since religious conservatives became a modern political movement, the president of the United States has become the movement's de facto leader...Christian publications, radio and television shower Bush with praise, while preachers from the pulpit treat his leadership as an act of providence. A procession of religious leaders who have met with him testify to his faith, while Web sites encourage people to fast and pray for the president.[7]

Late in 1985, I met Pat Robertson for the first time in the Nashville offices of Thomas Nelson Publishers. Pat had decided to run for president and he wanted a campaign book that would reveal his agenda for the nation. I was just beginning to accept my sexual orientation as a gift from God and was living in Laguna Beach with Gary when I was called by one of America's largest religious publishing houses to ghostwrite the book that Pat Robertson would use in his presidential campaign. I was still in the closet, afraid that being honest would alienate the religious publishers and end my career as a ghostwriter, and though it doesn't justify my writing for the enemy, I was determined to get my daughter and my son through college so they would graduate without a mountain of student loan debt. For that reason, I compromised my integrity and accepted the invitation to write for Pat Robertson, a man whose political and religious views I despised.

I'm sorry now that I wasn't honest sooner. No amount

of money could justify my decision. However, looking back, the guilt I still feel is mitigated somewhat by the fact that my ghostwriting projects were primarily biographical. I had not been forced to ghostwrite propaganda against my gay sisters and brothers. However, accepting Pat Robertson's invitation to help him write a campaign book, titled *America's Date with Destiny*, would have forced me to compromise almost everything I believed as a Christian and as an American.

Fortunately, I discovered that most presidential candidates who had written books committing themselves in advance on complex and controversial issues ended up losing the election. I persuaded Pat that he, too, should avoid that risk. When we realized that the publisher had already sent out the announcement of a new Pat Robertson book titled *America's Date with Destiny*, I suggested we just make it *America's Dates with Destiny* and choose extraordinary but little-known people and events in our nation's history, each representing an important crossroad for the world's oldest democracy.

"Okay," Pat said, "you choose the dates." And with those four words to guide me in writing a three-hundred-page book that would have his name on the front cover, not mine, Robertson and his entourage headed out the door of his hotel suite toward the airport and another campaign trip across the country. The next six months of writing and research provided me the rare opportunity to read American history seriously and to discover the role people of faith played in the development of this great nation. I am proud of that little book and the stories it tells, and I was delighted to find it still on sale in the lobby bookstore of Robertson's headquarters ten years later when Pat had me arrested there and dragged off to jail.

Thanks to Pat Robertson, during my research for his *Dates with Destiny* I rediscovered Pat's favorite evangelist, Charles Grandison Finney, the self-taught lawyer-preacher whose sermons led to what church historians call America's "Second Great Spiritual Awakening." Starting shortly after his ordination in 1824, the spirit of Finney's revival preaching swept first through New England among Congregationalists, Presbyterians, Methodists, and especially the Baptists. Then it moved down to the Mid-Atlantic states, into the South, and out across the Appalachian Mountains to the frontier farms and settlements.[8]

The "Second Great Spiritual Awakening" changed our country in many different ways. For example, Charles Finney's preaching led to the conversion of Thomas Weld, a man unknown and unrecognized by American history who played a large part in both the emancipation and woman's suffrage movements. Finney taught Weld that sin was "anything that was destructive or dehumanizing to human life, and sin, whether personal or corporate, must be confronted and overthrown whatever the price." Finney labeled slavery a sin and called evangelicals to fight the sin of slavery. Finney also labeled the second-class citizenship of women a sin and called evangelicals to end all discrimination against them.

Feeling his own call to ministry, Weld enrolled at Lane Seminary, where the Reverend Lyman Beecher, an evangelical and an abolitionist, was president. Beecher was no coward. He even enrolled an ex-slave as an official student at Lane, but Beecher believed in gradual emancipation. His student, Thomas Weld, disagreed and without president Beecher's approval made the Lane campus a station on the Underground Railroad where slaves escaping to the North were housed, trained, and equipped for their journey.

President Beecher's daughter, Harriet Beecher Stowe, was caught up in the debate led by Thomas Weld. That debate divided and eventually destroyed Lane Seminary, but Harriet Beecher Stowe, though loyal to her father, had been convinced that Thomas Weld was right about slavery. The nation should take steps to end it immediately, and according to Abraham Lincoln, her book *Uncle Tom's Cabin* was a primary influence in his decision to write the Emancipation Proclamation.

Thomas Weld married Angelina Grimke, one of his students. Motivated by her teacher and husband, Angelina joined him as an outspoken enemy of slavery and a powerful champion of women's rights. Impressed by the courage and commitment Thomas and Angelina Weld showed in their struggle against slavery and for woman's suffrage, Lucy Stone enrolled at Oberlin, insisted on taking "the men's classes and not just home economics," and in the following years became one of the truly powerful voices in the suffragette movement. Elizabeth Cady Stanton called Lucy Stone "the first person by whom the heart of the American public was deeply stirred on the woman question."

By ghostwriting for Pat Robertson, I learned again that my evangelical heritage includes generations of men and women committed in Christ's name to bring justice to the world. Thomas Weld, Harriet Beecher Stowe, and Lucy Stone were all children of the Second Great Spiritual Awakening and of the preaching of Charles Grandison Finney, whose revivals led to personal spiritual change in the hearts of those who heard him and also to significant social changes at the heart of American culture, as well.

Just a word about the current "ghostwriting" practices of leading fundamentalist Christians. These powerful men have multimillion-dollar organizations to run. They have no time to sit and write a book. So ghostwriters are hired to interview the "author" and then produce a book that is as close as possible to the "author's" desired style and content. And though I tried to reflect each "author's" views, looking back I realize that I was part of a very unethical and somewhat dangerous practice. I say "dangerous" because those who shop in Christian bookstores and read Christian books may be reading the writings of a ghost who spent little or no time with the "author," who may or may not have even read the book he supposedly authored.

When I had finished Robertson's *America's Dates with Destiny*, I tried to get Pat to sit down long enough to read the 120,000 words I had written in his name (with "You choose the dates" as my only guide). I wanted him to approve what I had written before "his book" was released by Thomas Nelson Publishers. He promised to read it, flew me to various cities to make changes with him, and then didn't even have time to read or discuss it. With the release deadline long past, Pat promised to read (or at least scan) "his newest book" and asked me to fly to New Orleans to discuss any changes he wanted made.

For two days I sat in my hotel room (the same hotel where Pat and his entourage were encamped) waiting to be summoned. Finally, he called and asked that I come to his hotel room for our long-awaited discussion. When I got there the room was filled with staffers, friends, and a reporter. He didn't even recognize me at first until I reminded him that I had written *America's Dates with Destiny* and that the publisher was really anxious to print and release the book.

After waiting several hours, Pat walked me into his personal suite, sat down beside me, opened the book, and said, "I've not had time to read it, Mel, so I thought we could read it aloud together." I was stunned. At roughly two minutes per page, reading more than three hundred pages aloud would have taken six hundred minutes or ten hours, and that doesn't include time to consider any suggestions or changes Pat might have made. When I explained that, he stood up, said he would read it that night in his room and phone me if he had any suggestions. He didn't call. In fact, early the next morning when I called his suite, Pat and his entourage were gone.

At the Christian Booksellers' Convention that year where hundreds of people had lined up to get Pat's autograph on "his latest best seller," I was embarrassed for both of us (though I still think the book is a wonderful read). Pat signed my hardback copy, "To Mel White, a magnificent writer, best wishes, Pat." So now when people ask how much does a ghostwriter contribute to the content of "the newest book" by a fundamentalist Christian "author," I can say for certain that in my copy of *America's Dates with Destiny* there are nine words that Pat Robertson wrote.

One last comment on ghostwriting. In 1999, when I showed Jerry Falwell a collection of his various fund-raising letters filled with false and inflammatory comments about homosexuals and homosexuality, he looked rather surprised at what he had written and admitted to the press that he had gone too far. Now I know that Jerry and the rest of them don't write their own fund-raising letters. They don't have time for it. There are skilled advertising agencies hired to exploit those subjects that motivate people to fear and then to make a donation, and it's all too easy to become their victim.

Although he was unsuccessful in his 1988 presidential bid, Pat Robertson still had politics in his genes. Born on March 22, 1930, Marion Gordon "Pat" Robertson is the son of a powerful and privileged southern family with political roots deep in olde Virginia. Pat's father, Absalom Willis Robertson, served in the U.S. House of Representatives from 1933 to 1946 and in the Senate from 1946 to 1967. He is remembered by his critics as one of the nineteen senators who signed the Southern Manifesto opposing racial integration in public places in 1956. The manifesto's primary goal was to counter *Brown v. Board of Education*, the landmark Supreme Court decision in 1954 integrating public schools.

It is fascinating to read the Southern Manifesto on "legislative tyranny," a phrase that Robertson and his fundamentalist

Christian colleagues use regularly more than fifty years later to expose a "threat to the nation" almost as dangerous as their so-called "gay agenda." The Southern Manifesto opens with these words: "We regard the decision of the Supreme Court in the school cases as a clear abuse of judicial power. It climaxes a trend in the Federal judiciary undertaking to legislate, in derogation of the authority of Congress, and to encroach upon the reserved rights of the States and the people."[9] It is highly probable that even a one-time viewer of Pat Robertson's *700 Club* would have heard the Senator's rhetoric of the confederacy repeated by the Senator's son in one of his daily attacks on the U.S. Supreme Court and on the nation's judicial system at almost every level.

Besides a father who served in Washington, D.C., for thirty-four years, Pat claims as distant kin both Winston Churchill and Captain A. Robertson, one of George Washington's officers in the Revolutionary War. Pat's Virginia ancestry also includes Benjamin Harrison, a signer of the Declaration of Independence and governor of Virginia, and two U.S. presidents, William Henry Harrison and Benjamin Harrison.

After graduating Phi Beta Kappa from Washington and Lee University, Pat served in the U.S. Marine Corps before receiving his law degree from Yale University Law School (1955) and his divinity degree from New York Theological Seminary (1959). That same year, while Pat's father, the senior senator from Virginia, was taking his seat on the powerful U.S. Senate Committee on Banking, Housing, and Urban Affairs, Pat was moving his wife, Dede, and their three children to Tidewater, Virginia. Shortly after their arrival, Pat began raising money to buy a bankrupt UHF television station in Portsmouth.

During a private dinner at the Commander's Palace in New Orleans, Pat told me the story behind his sudden urge to buy and begin broadcasting from WYAH (the Y stands for Yahweh, the Hebrew name for God). During those early years, Sunday morning was a dead spot for commercial television. The former owners of the then-almost-bankrupt UHF station filled the dead spot with a panel of local Christian clergy. When Pat asked to be included on the panel, he was rejected.

I often wonder how history might have changed if these liberal clergy had welcomed the charismatic evangelical ("He speaks in tongues!") as a colleague and a friend. Instead, they turned their backs on Pat Robertson, who bought the station, silenced the liberal clergy, and went on to build a media empire.

Pat's Christian Broadcasting Network (CBN) was launched on October 1, 1961, with live, thirty-minute programs and old travelogues on the air from 7 to 10 P.M. Because Pat refused to sell airtime for commercial ads, in 1963 he announced a telethon to raise the $7,000 per month needed for the 1964 budget. Pat's *700 Club*, still the daily anchor for CBN, began during that first telethon when he told viewers that a "club" of seven hundred contributors, each giving $10 a month, would enable CBN to meet its expenses. Today, Pat's Christian Broadcasting Network is available to 1.6 billion viewers in two hundred countries.[10]

In the mid-1980s, just twenty years after arriving in Virginia Beach with $70 in his pocket, estimates of CBN's annual budget ranged from $101 million[11] to $230 million.[12] Today, CBN produces programming seen in two hundred nations in seventy languages, including Russian, Arabic, Spanish, French, and Chinese. It is very possible that Robertson is not exaggerating when he claims that his *700 Club*, now one of America's longest-running television shows, reaches an average of one million Americans daily.

In 1977, just sixteen years after graduating from seminary himself, Robertson founded Regent University in Virginia Beach. Now Robertson is president and chancellor of a fully accredited graduate university offering to its more than three thousand students bachelor's, master's, and doctor's degrees in business, communication and the arts, divinity, education, government, law, organizational leadership, psychology, and counseling. Thousands of students have enrolled online to attend Regent's virtual educational programs, as well. Regent recently established in the Washington, D.C./Northern Virginia area a Graduate Center training men and women for political careers.

Don't let Pat's biblical definition of the word *regent* escape you. A regent is a person who rules a kingdom in place of the king until the king returns. When you're driving through Virginia Beach South on Highway 64, just before you cross Indian River Road you will see the sign pointing to Regent University. The name Pat has chosen for his educational programs may seem benign on the surface, and Pat would certainly scoff at my paranoia, but given Pat's long-range goals to make this a "Christian nation" once again, I still can't help but feel uneasy when I think about this powerful fundamentalist Christian training tens of thousands of young fundamentalists as Christ's regents to take political power "until the king returns."

Pat Robertson's success as a broadcast mogul stunned a lot of us in 1997 when just one of Pat's spin-off media ventures, The Family Channel (a satellite-delivered cable-television network Pat had helped sign on 63 million U.S. subscribers), was sold to Rupert Murdoch's News Corporation for $1.9 billion. The sale had one condition: that Robertson's *700 Club* be broadcast three times daily on the new Fox Family Channel.

The sale of Pat Robertson's Family Network netted Pat $400 million. He donated $148 million to Regent University, $136 million to CBN, and $109 million to the Robertson Charitable Trust—which pays out to CBN in 2010 or upon the death of Robertson or his wife, Dede, whichever comes later. Robertson himself banked $19 million profit.[13] Not bad when you realize that continuing to broadcast Pat's *700 Club* was included in the deal.

For six months, Fox Family officials ignored my urgent requests for a meeting to discuss why it was totally inappropriate to show Pat Robertson's *700 Club* three times daily on any commercial network, let alone a network dedicated to children's programming. On February 12, 1999, I gathered together forty clergy colleagues from across the ecumenical spectrum to sign a letter to Richard Cronin, president and CEO, and Eytan Keller, vice president, of the Fox Family Channel asking for a meeting to discuss our concerns about exposing children to *The 700 Club*, "a major source of misinformation that leads to intolerance, especially towards Gay, Lesbian, Bisexual and Transgender Americans."

For eighteen months, Fox Family officials refused to meet with us. Finally, on February 23, 2000, our Clergy Committee organized "to bring truth to Pat Robertson and the Fox Family Channel" marched on Fox Family headquarters in Beverly Hills, California. Although our numbers were decreased by a rare winter thunderstorm, twenty-six Christian ministers and Jewish rabbis waded through the flooded streets of West Los Angeles carrying "Beware the Fox" signs and singing songs of the civil rights movement. Notified well in advance that clergy would protest that day, Fox Network officials simply locked up their multistoried headquarters, refusing to let anyone in or out of the building, including all the other tenants who had offices there.

Police were in place to arrest us. The media covered our protest from every angle. Police vans arrived to carry us away. But Fox Family officials decided to leave the building closed rather than suffer the negative publicity that would follow the arrest of two dozen respected pastors, priests, and rabbis protesting Pat Robertson's antifamily rhetoric on their "family" channel. After the protest, Fox Family officials met with us and agreed that Pat Robertson's *700 Club* was entirely inappropriate for a children's network, but they showed us the contract they had signed with Pat, a contract their lawyers found unbreakable.

Just one year later, Fox Family was sold to ABC/Disney for $3 billion cash and $2.3 billion in assumed debt, a $5.3 billion investment for just one of Pat Robertson's media enterprises, and once again the contract stipulated that Pat Robertson's *700 Club* would be broadcast on the new ABC Family Channel three times daily. After Robertson called for the United States government to assassinate Venezuelan President Hugo Chávez on *The 700 Club*, August 22, 2005, Media Matters for America urged ABC Family to stop showing Pat Robertson's show.

The Media Matters for America press release illustrates briefly Robertson's "...history of vitriolic and false statements." In addition to urging the assassination of a foreign leader, Robertson has "blamed gays for divorce, abortion, and [the] September 11th [terrorist attack], claimed that a gay-oriented event [Gay Day at Disney World] would bring about 'terrorist bombs, earthquakes, tornadoes, and possibly a meteor,' and stated that liberal judges 'are a bigger threat to society than Al Qaeda'"[14] "Robertson's vitriol is not appropriate for children, or for anyone else for that matter," added David Brock, Media Matters's president and CEO. "His calls for the killing of a foreign leader certainly do not belong on a television channel that purports to offer family-friendly programming."[15] Like Fox, ABC/Disney feels compelled by their contract to continue showing *The 700 Club* whatever the cost to its viewers. Maybe it's time for another public protest.

It is tragic when we underestimate the political, financial, or public relation skills of these new fundamentalist leaders. For example, Pat Robertson's failed run for the presidency was not a failure at all. When he announced his candidacy in September 1986, Robertson made it clear that he would run only if three million people signed up to support him in the next twelve months. That "failed presidential campaign" added millions of dollars to his political treasury and at least three million names and addresses to Pat's fund-raising list.

It is a regular ploy used by fundamentalist Christian broadcasters to launch various campaigns that offer listeners (of their TV and radio programs) or readers (of their newspapers, magazines, and fund-raising letters) a practical way to respond to "an urgent personal or national threat." Perhaps the most famous (or infamous) example is the plea from Oral Roberts to ask the Lord "to call me home" unless sufficient funds were mailed in to save his City of Faith Medical Center. As I write, in 2005, Jerry Falwell is now launching a totally phony "friend or foe" campaign "to protect Christmas in America." Just last year, he made millions with his "One Man One Woman" campaign to "save traditional marriage from homosexual activists."

Using hyperbole, half-truth, and lies to scare people silly, the fundamentalist Christian leader then offers a very practical way viewers can respond by signing a "Petition to the President" or an "Appeal to Congress" or a "Letter of Complaint" to the Attorney General or a "Letter of Support" to the new chairman of the FCC. Fundamentalist Christians and others eager to help support or help defeat this, that, or the other return the petition along with a small check and a new active donor name or address. Thanks to modern technology, the names and addresses of millions of new supporters who want to "sign on" can be collected by e-mail in just hours and millions of dollars can be donated by credit card through the Internet. One week after launching his ONEMANONEWOMAN campaign (to deny lesbian and gay couples the 1,047 civil rights and protections that go automatically with heterosexual marriage), Jerry announced from his pulpit that "...already one million people have signed on."

Pat lost his presidential bid, but another consolation prize was millions of new names and addresses on his mailing list and millions of unspent dollars in his campaign fund, enough to launch his new grassroots political movement, the "Christian Coalition." Schaeffer called for evangelicals to take back the nation. Jerry Falwell's Moral Majority called for an army of Christian warriors. But Pat Robertson's Christian Coalition recruited, trained, and equipped that army for political action.

From 1989 to 1997, Robertson shared the spotlight with Ralph Reed, the coalition's first executive director. The other side of Ralph Reed's boyish charm was his ruthless political ambition. "I want to be invisible," he said. "I do guerrilla warfare. I paint my face and travel at night. You don't know it's over until you're in a body bag."[6] On May 15, 1995, Reed was even featured on the cover of *Time* with this headline: "The Right Hand of God: Ralph Reed and the Christian Coalition."

By 1995, Reed had been able to recruit, train, and mobilize what Francis Schaeffer had dreamed: a powerful fundamentalist Christian political force. During Reed's leadership, the Christian Coalition claimed to have nearly two million members and 1,500 local chapters in all fifty U.S. states. The coalition was committed to recruiting, training, and mobilizing millions of "people of faith" to influence local, state, and national government. And though Bill Clinton defeated George Bush in 1992, during the off-year congressional elections of 1994 Gary and I saw the power of the Christian Coalition in our small Texas precinct and across the entire state.

Ralph Reed had determined that the Christian Coalition would take power over the Republican Party, precinct by precinct in every state, before the next presidential election. He recruited Christian Coalition volunteers to return to their polling places across the United States just as the polls closed. Precinct chairmen and women were voted into office at that time, and in Texas and at least a dozen other states, Christian

Coalition members were elected to head their local precincts. In Texas, during the very next meeting of the State's Republican Party, these new precinct leaders defeated the old guard Republicans and took control of the Republican Party in Texas.

And though their candidate lost the election, the Christian Coalition continued to take direct action against President Clinton in such a way as to make it almost impossible for him to govern. With their phone trees that could mobilize thousands of phone calls to the president or members of Congress; with their calls for protest or support letters to be sent they could fill up every mailbox on Capitol Hill; with their online and direct-mail petition drives they could enlist and deliver a million signatures in a day; with their radio and television networks, their books, magazines, and pamphlets, with their films and videos, the Christian Coalition had more muscle in Washington, D.C., and in state capitals all across the country than any lobby in history.

In 1997, Ralph Reed resigned as the Christian Coalition's executive director and moved to Atlanta to work as a political consultant and organizer. In 2006, he is actively preparing to run for lieutenant governor of Georgia while being investigated along with a consulting associate, Jack Abramoff, for bilking their own clients in an Indian gambling scheme. In 2000, even without Ralph at the helm, the Christian Coalition played a large part in getting George W. Bush elected president. During that closely fought presidential race, the Christian Coalition claims to have distributed more than 70 million voter guides (English and Spanish) in churches all across America.

Although Pat Robertson resigned its leadership and severed all connections with the Christian Coalition in 2001, what a run he had. Under Ralph Reed, the coalition became *the* major fundamentalist political force in America, with 1.7 million members, 1,700 chapters in all fifty states, full-time staff in twenty states, fifty thousand precinct leaders, twenty-five thousand church liaison leaders, and an annual national budget exceeding $25 million.[17]

In 2005, Roberta Combs, the Christian Coalition's executive director, denied the rumors that the organization was in legal and financial trouble. She assured supporters that the Christian Coalition was alive and well with ten full-time employees in Washington, extension offices in Charleston, South Carolina, and Chesapeake, Virginia, and thousands of Christian volunteers lobbying in their states and on Capitol Hill pushing the 109th Congress among other things to make abortion illegal, to deny lesbian and gay couples their civil rights, and to eliminate all restrictions on politics in the pulpit.[18]

It is a mistake to say that the Christian Coalition (or the Moral Majority, for that matter) failed or collapsed just because they aren't what they used to be. In 2000 and 2004, fundamentalist Christians achieved their goals. They placed a fundamentalist Christian in the White House and elected enough fundamentalists (or pro-fundamentalists) to achieve their majority in the U.S. House and Senate alike. Now, together the executive and legislative branches of our national government are reshaping the U.S. Supreme Court in their own fundamentalist Christian image.

During his Christian Coalition years, we monitored Pat Robertson's inflammatory rhetoric rewriting American history, calling this a "Christian nation" that only Christians should rule, condemning the separation of church and state, accusing Muslim Americans of supporting Qaddafi and Khomeini, trashing those on his Enemy List, including the United Nations, especially its Conferences for Women, Planned Parenthood, People for the American Way, the ACLU, People for the Separation of Church and State, the National Council of Churches, the Metropolitan Community Churches, the United Church of Christ, and dozens of other individuals and organizations.

Year after year, Robertson grew more shrill in his rhetoric against lesbian and gay Americans particularly. He liked to summarize the quality of our lives in just three words— "disease, despair, and decadence." Consistently he used the phrase "sexual preference" rather than "sexual orientation" to support his notion that homosexuality is a choice. He quoted the pseudoscience of Charles Socarides and Joseph Nicolosi to prove that homosexuality was a pathology based on "the abdicating father and the over binding mother." He quoted the totally discredited Paul Cameron to demonstrate that homosexuality was a "sickness" with terrible physical consequences, and he misused those same old clobber passages from the Old and New Testaments to "prove" that homosexuality was a sin.

Pat and his *700 Club* guests insisted that lesbian and gay Americans were demanding "special rights" when in fact all we want are the same rights every American is entitled to. Pat warned against granting us the rights and protections of marriage because that mistake would "destroy traditional marriage," open up similar demands "by those involved in pedophilia, bestiality, sado-masochism and even snuff films," and eventually cause God "to take His hand of blessing off our nation…leading to its ultimate destruction."

Robertson claimed that lesbians were leaders in the pro-choice movement "because lesbians will never be mothers naturally so they don't want anybody else to have that privilege either." He praised White House guards for wearing rubber gloves when escorting a group of gay leaders to meet the president. He explained HIV/AIDS as "the judgment of God" and declared that "from a biblical standpoint, the rise of homosexuality is a sign that society is in the last stages of decay."[19] I wonder if he realizes the tragic consequences of his antihomosexual rhetoric. In the meantime, using the fear and loathing of homosexuals to raise funds and mobilize volunteers,

Pat Robertson has become a major political and economic force in America and around the world.

During my twenty-one-day incarceration in a Virginia Beach jail (after being arrested on the CBN campus for trespassing during a protest of his antigay vitriol), I was visited by one of Pat's former employees who got past the warden by claiming he was my attorney. It was obvious that this person, who shall remain nameless, knew in great detail the business dealings of his former employer. He begged me to widen my criticism of Pat Robertson while the news media were still interested in my story. He wanted me to condemn Pat for his business enterprises. He warned me that Pat was an example of fundamentalist Christians at work amassing huge fortunes to bankroll their "takeover of America," and that unless we realize the financial power of this new generation of fundamentalists we will "wake up one morning without a country." I declined the invitation, believing with Gandhi and King that it is very unwise to switch issues in midstream.

Now, however, the world knows about Pat Robertson's financial enterprises besides the Family Entertainment Network, which he sold to Fox for $1.9 billion. There was CENCO, the company Robertson formed to purchase a defunct offshore oil refinery near Huntington Beach, California. American Benefits Plus/Kalo Vita was Pat's failed multilevel marketing scheme. Also failed was Robertson's contract with the Bank of Scotland giving him 25 percent ownership in a phone-based U.S. consumer bank they failed to launch in the United States with Pat's help. His appointment to the board of Laura Ashley, a U.K.-based retail firm specializing in fabrics and fashions, didn't last much longer. However, it seems that Robertson's African Development Company succeeded in digging up gold and diamonds in Zaire (now the Congo) by creating a working relationship with Mobutu Sese Seko, the country's dictator.

No one knows yet if Freedom Gold Limited, the company Pat formed to go into business with the terrorist president of Liberia, has succeeded equally in finding and exporting gold from that West Africa nation. [20]

Pat Robertson is a capitalist and a Christian. It is his business to decide how much time and money he spends on building a financial empire versus building what he calls "The Kingdom of God." He says—and I don't doubt him—that the profits from his capitalist ventures are or will be plowed back into his work for Christ. It is not my right to judge. But it is my responsibility to point out that my old friends, the enemy, are willing to take huge risks to accumulate the resources they need to "reclaim America for Christ." It is a fatal mistake to see Falwell, Robertson, and the others as "kooks" and "crazies" when in fact they have recruited, trained, equipped, financed, and mobilized millions of American who are also willing to take great risks to get the job done.

THREE

THE SPOILS OF WAR:
JAMES DOBSON (THE ENFORCER) AND
D. JAMES KENNEDY (THE EXTREMIST)

JAMES DOBSON

*T*he fundamentalist Christian leader Dr. James Dobson, founder and chairman of Focus on the Family, has become the primary source of misinformation about homosexuality and homosexuals in this country and around the world. But even worse, backed by millions of his loyal listeners, Dobson has developed enough political muscle to begin persuading the executive and legislative branches of our government (national and state alike) to pass his bogus "Marriage Protection Amendment" and to force his long list of fundamentalist Christian values on the rest of us.

Dobson's influence in Washington, D.C., and in statehouses and state legislatures across the United States is a sign that fundamentalist Christians are winning their war to make this a "Christian nation once again," and Dobson has appointed himself the "Enforcer," seeing that politicians keep their promises to the fundamentalists and their allies who "got them elected."

Never underestimate the power of Dobson's media empire. Besides his weekly column carried in roughly five hundred American newspapers, Arbitron estimates that Dobson's *Focus on the Family* broadcast is heard by approximately 25.6 million listeners in the United States every week or five million people a day. Focus on the Family surveys estimate that every day Dobson is heard by 220 million people in seventeen languages through four thousand radio facilities in 122 nations.

Okay, so cut Dobson's estimates in half (110 million people a day who hear him) or downsize Dobson's numbers by 90 percent (that's still 22 million people who just might hear him in 122 countries every day). Arbitron also estimates that the percentage of African-Americans who hear Dobson regularly (14 percent) is slightly larger than the African-American representation in the general population, and that his Spanish-language program *Enfoque a la Familia* is also heard by millions throughout the Americas.[1]

My first very personal experience of Dobson's skill at using the media to support his friends or chastise his enemies was on Sunday, July 17, 1994. During our first protest of Dobson's antigay rhetoric, I awakened in a trailer parked in front of his Focus on the Family headquarters in Colorado Springs to find that James Dobson had bought a full page in Colorado Springs's *Gazette Telegraph* to reprint a letter he had written responding to my charges against his obsessive antihomosexual campaign. You can imagine how I felt as I sat down on the curb to read the first (and, I hoped, last) full-page ad anyone has taken out to shame me personally:

I've never tried to hurt you or anyone else [Dobson writes]. In fact, I have not uttered a word about you publicly even though you've been attacking me unjustly for almost a year. You appear to be a very angry man who is looking for someone to blame for the pain in your life and I'm a convenient scapegoat. So be it. I just ask that you fight fair. When you make an accusation of me, please be man enough to document it with quotations and circumstances. And especially, I ask that you not tell the world that we are close friends or that we have worked together in the past. You know that is a baseless claim.[2]

"Baseless claim" is a gentle way of calling me a liar. He is referring to a mistake made by a newspaper reporter who included Dobson's name on a list of my ghostwriting clients. The reporter published a retraction and an apology, but Dobson ignored the reporter's mea culpa and accused me of lying about our relationship anyway. So let's make it clear one more time. James Dobson and I have never worked together. As Dr. Dobson pointed out in his "Open Letter," "The most lengthy conversation between us occurred in the lobby of the Amway Grand Hotel, January, 1993, when we shook hands and talked for about two minutes." How he remembered that still amazes me.

However, Jim Dobson and his family were our neighbors in Pasadena, California, when my former wife, Lyla, and I were co-pastoring the Evangelical Covenant Church on Lake Avenue. Dr. Dobson attended the Nazarene Church in nearby Sierra Madre. His son, Ryan, a member of the Minutemen football team, and my daughter, Erinn, a cheerleader, were classmates at Maranatha High School, and though I've never claimed to have a professional let alone a personal relationship with Dobson, I spent a lot of time in his general vicinity, sitting on the football bleachers at Maranatha High, watching our kids grow up.[3]

In 1977, the year Focus on the Family was launched, I visited their little redbrick headquarters in Arcadia, California, just minutes from our family home. I was stunned at how quickly Dobson's ministry outgrew the Arcadia location and almost as rapidly his massive new complex in nearby Pomona. Less than twenty years after it began, Dobson's Focus on the Family accepted a large gift of land in Colorado Springs, and today the various headquarters buildings on their forty-nine acres provide FOF more than five hundred thousand square feet of office room, barely enough to house Dobson's more than one thousand employees. Dobson's headquarters is so large it has its own zip code.

With an annual budget approaching $150 million and a formidable national and even international radio presence, Dobson has developed considerable political clout. A Washington insider told me off the record that when Dobson comes to D.C., "all three branches of government stand at attention," and the president "dives under his desk." A feature article in the *Boston Globe* said this about Dobson's political power:

> Dobson stands in the vanguard of a crusade by evangelical Christians to place their agenda at the forefront of public debate over presidential and congressional elections, judicial appointments, gay marriage, and the "life issues" of abortion, euthanasia, and embryonic stem-cell research. Dobson, 69, is arguably the dominant ideologist of the movement. His influence is so considerable among conservatives that, before President Bush nominated Harriet E. Miers for the Supreme Court, White House adviser Karl Rove reportedly called Dobson with private assurances about Miers' judicial philosophy.[4]

One example of Dobson's political clout was his invitation to the White House Correspondents Association Annual

Award Dinner, April 30, 2005. Dobson was included on that prestigious guest list headed by President George and Laura Bush, Vice President Dick and Lynne Cheney, the Secretary of State Condoleezza Rice, other members of the president's cabinet, the Congress, the courts, and entertainment and sport celebrities Richard Gere, Goldie Hawn, Dennis Hopper, Venus and Serena Williams, fashion designer Roberto Cavalli, and a roomful of radio and television personalities whose names and faces are recognized by most Americans.

It was Laura Bush who brought down the house with her hilarious remark about the president. "At nine o'clock," she said, "Mr. Excitement here is sound asleep and I'm watching *Desperate Housewives* with Lynne Cheney." Then she added, "Ladies and gentlemen, I am a desperate housewife." After that glamorous evening with a lineup of celebrities roasting and toasting the president, Al Franken, the liberal political satirist, was most impressed by an informal encounter he had with James Dobson.

Apparently Franken spotted Dobson in the crowd and tried to goad him into some kind of angry response with an opening remark that would have angered a saint: "It must be great to always know the absolute truth," he said, "because, for me, you know, it's such a burden not to." Dobson just smiled. "He knew it was a joke," Franken recalled, "and he didn't bite." In fact, according to MSNBC columnist Howard Fineman, they spent the rest of their time together debating the morals of abortion "in what apparently was a civil manner." In his MSNBC column, Fineman went on to explain why he was writing about this chance encounter of liberal national comic Al Franken (who is seriously considering running for the seat in the U.S. Senate once held by Paul Wellstone) and fundamentalist Christian power broker James Dobson, who is using his considerable political power to use the Senate to superimpose his moral values on the nation. Fineman writes:

Dobson is, arguably, the most powerful social conservative in the country, central to the battle over federal judges—and a danger to the people who would oppose him. He has built an empire—Focus on the Family—by projecting an avuncular, unflappable image. Unlike evangelical Christian provocateurs such as Jerry Falwell or Pat Robertson, Dobson isn't a minister. He wants to convert souls to Christ, and denounce the evils of society, but there is no fire or brimstone in sight and no sound of doom in his voice...He is plunging into politics headlong after a lifetime of staying away from it, convinced that he must use all of his accumulated good will and power as a family counselor to render a harsh message of judgment against political leaders— federal judges and members of congress—he thinks are allowing the country to sink into a hellhole of relativism and licentiousness.[5]

Just three months before the annual Correspondents Dinner, Dobson was the keynote speaker at a pre-inaugural black-tie dinner with senators and members of Congress present. During his speech he warned that a film about to be released to sixty-one thousand American schools supporting tolerance and diversity would be a bad influence on children because it featured SpongeBob SquarePants, the animated character who held hands with his sidekick, Patrick. The audience and millions of his supporters took Dobson's remark seriously while the rest of the country shook their heads in disbelief.

The man who wrote the video's featured song and founded the We Are Family Foundation (WAFF), which released the new video, says it is intended to help teach children the values of cooperation and unity. "We believe that this is the essential first step to loving thy neighbor," he said. "And the fun and exciting format makes it a lesson that's easy for children to learn."[6]

Dobson's spokesman, Paul Batura, told the *New York Times*, "We see the video as an insidious means by which the organization is manipulating and potentially brainwashing kids." Mark Barondeso, spokesman for We Are Family, replied that anyone who thought the video promoted homosexuality "needs to visit their doctor and get their medication increased."[7]

Immediately, Don Wildmon, founder of the American Family Association and a powerful Dobson ally, joined the debate. "It is as unprecedented as it is cunning, using all the right words and happiest faces in an attempt to speak directly to the nation's children about 'tolerance and diversity.' Once again, of course, those ideas include homosexual advocacy."[8] The Reverend John H. Thomas, an outspoken Dobson critic and president of the United Church of Christ, the only Protestant denomination that has adopted a national policy extending to gays and lesbians the right to marry and be ordained, replied, "The UCC extends an unequivocal welcome to SpongeBob," he said. "Jesus didn't turn people away. Neither do we."[9]

Hearing that a Dobson spokesman had accused We Are Family of "crossing the moral line" with their video featuring SpongeBob, Reverend Thomas replied, "On the contrary, it is Dobson who is crossing the moral line for sending the mistaken message that Christians do not value tolerance and diversity as important religious values...While Dobson's silly accusation makes headlines, it's also one more concrete example of how religion is misused over and over to promote intolerance over inclusion. This is why we believe it is so important that the UCC speak the Gospel in an accent not often heard in our culture, because far too many experience the cross only as judgment, never as embrace."[10]

Once again, a few words from James Dobson and the whole

country explodes into debate. The United Church of Christ's J. Bennett Guess adds his voice to the growing number of Americans concerned about James Dobson's growing national clout. "Dobson, despite his often-outrageous viewpoints, is arguably one of the most oft-heard religious voices in popular culture today. Through his Focus on the Family media empire, Dobson produces daily commentaries that appear widely on television and radio stations across the United States, often times as 'public service announcements.'"[11]

Using his media empire, Jim Dobson has become the "Enforcer" for millions of fundamentalist Christians who believe that they placed George W. Bush in the White House and Republican majorities in both the House and Senate. And there are good reasons to believe that without Dobson and his fundamentalist voting bloc (and the anti-same-sex marriage amendments they managed to get on the ballot of thirteen states), Mr. Bush might not have won the election. Dobson didn't waste a minute cashing in his chips. The new president was still moving into the Oval Office when Dobson demanded that he be more aggressive about supporting the fundamentalist Christian pro-life, anti-gay-rights agenda. Or, Dobson warned, the president and his party would "pay a price in four years."

The president knows he owes Dobson a debt and is working hard to pay it back. Even before the presidential election in November 2004, it is widely reported that the Bush reelection campaign included Dobson in weekly telephone strategy sessions. Saying that he "rarely endorsed political candidates" and that he was speaking "as an individual and not for the organization he leads," Dobson endorsed George W Bush because "this year the issues were so profound that I felt I simply could not sit it out."

During those preelection months, Dobson also endorsed several statewide candidates, including Patrick Toomey, a Republican Representative running for the U.S. Senate in

Pennsylvania. In his Toomey endorsement letter, Dobson claims that Toomey's opponent, the incumbent Republican Senator Arlen Specter, has "opposed almost everything we hold dear." Then Dobson named the three crimes that Republican Specter had committed, including blocking the confirmation of conservative pro-family judges to the federal courts, opposing the Federal Marriage Amendment, and helping defeat "...one of the strongest conservative thinkers ever to be nominated to the Supreme Court, Robert Bork." Dobson ended the letter with "The defeat of Arlen Specter would send a mighty signal that the days of waffling devious, anti-family Republicans who are liberals in disguise is finally over."[12]

With Dobson's powerful support, Toomey almost defeated a distinguished four-term Republican with powerful seniority that would benefit the people of Pennsylvania. Dobson didn't care about seniority or the people of Pennsylvania. He cared about packing the Senate with fundamentalist Christians and their allies. Specter squeaked by with a 52 percent majority and went on to become the only five-term senator in Pennsylvania history. However, even when his candidate lost the election, Dobson had demonstrated to all Republicans, candidates and incumbents alike, that he was determined to drive moderates and progressives from the Republican Party.

Mark Kittel, a moderate Republican himself, called James Dobson's determination "chilling" because in his campaign to defeat Arlen Specter, Dobson had made it clear that "at least for that fundamentalist Christian [James Dobson], there is no room in the Republican party for anyone that does not follow the fundamentalist agenda...Dobson clearly means to state that any Republican that does not oppose gay rights and gay marriage, does not support repealing abortion rights, and generally does not support fundamentalist stances, is not really a Republican."[13]

Even worse, it's beginning to feel like there is no room in

America for anyone who is not a fundamentalist Christian. While the Iraqi prisoner-abuse scandal unfolded in the press, President Bush participated in the National Day of Prayer, which excluded Muslim-American clerics. James Dobson's wife, Shirley, is chairperson of the National Day of Prayer Task Force that plans this annual event. When asked why Muslim-American clergy and other clergy outside the "Judeo-Christian" tradition were excluded, Vonette Bright, Mrs. Dobson's predecessor, answered, "They are free to have their own national day of prayer if they want to. We are a Christian task force."[14] Or you might say it this way: *They're Muslims. They can live in any Muslim country they want to, but not in ours.*

Dobson and his friends are undermining the principles of tolerance and inclusion upon which our democracy is built. Enjoying their new political power, fundamentalist Christians are flexing their religious muscles, as well. After converting to Christianity in the late fifth century, the Frankish King Clovis gave his subjects two choices: become a Christian or die. Fundamentalist Christians seem equally determined to turn every American into a fundamentalist Christian through conversion, and those who do not convert will simply be excluded, or worse.

During the opening ceremonies of Dobson's headquarters in Colorado Springs, the Air Force Academy's parachute team, the Wings of Blue, delivered "the keys of heaven" literally from the sky. From that day, Dobson and his fundamentalist Christian colleagues in Colorado Springs have had an ever-increasing influence on the Air Force cadets.

According to an extensive report by Devlin Buckley for the *Online Journal*, Focus on the Family leaders are regularly invited to Bible study programs on the academy campus. A former coach of the academy football team was appointed executive director of Dobson's Family Ministries. Focus on the Family helped promote *For God and Country*, a book written by another academy football coach who hung a banner in the team's locker room to motivate the players, saying, "I am a Christian first and last..." Protestant cadets were commonly told that Jesus had "called" them to the academy as part of God's plan for their lives.[15]

"The evangelicals want to subvert the system," complained Captain MeLinda Morton, the academy's chief chaplain. "They have a very clear social and political agenda. The evangelical tone is pervasive at the academy and it's aimed at converting these young people who are under intense pressure anyway."[16] Immediately after accusing evangelical officers, staff members, and senior cadets of using their positions inappropriately to push their evangelical Christian beliefs on cadets, Captain Morton was fired. A Dobson spokesman brushed off the chaplain's concerns, claiming that once again evangelicals were being victimized by a "witch hunt."[17]

In the months following the reelection of George W. Bush, James Dobson stormed back and forth between Colorado Springs and Washington, D.C., determined to see that both the executive and legislative branches of government stayed in lockstep with the fundamentalist "value voting" Christians who elected them. Before the election, Bush had tasted Dobson's anger when the fundamentalist kingmaker refused to attend the Republican National Convention because the president was ignoring his fundamentalist Christian base.

It's no wonder that the Republican National Committee was wary about giving the fundamentalists a significant place on the convention agenda. They had reason to be afraid that Dobson might scandalize the general public with his reckless rhetoric. For example, in August 2004, Dobson used one of his Focus on the Family broadcasts to compare the ethics of embryonic stem-cell research to "Nazi medical experiments on prisoners."

Following the election, Dobson's rhetoric got even worse.

When Terri Schiavo died on March 31, 2005, Dobson claimed that "this pitiful forty-one-year-old mentally disabled woman was condemned to death by an immoral Florida court judge named George Greer, who never came to visit her, yet ordered that she be dehydrated and starved to death at the insistence of her 'husband' Michael. Mr. Schiavo lives with another woman with whom he fathered two babies, and yet he was designated as the 'guardian' of Terri's welfare to the moment of death."

On April 11, 2005, Dobson compared the members of the US. Supreme Court to the KKK: "I heard a minister the other day talking about the great injustice and evil of the men in white robes, the Ku Klux Klan, that roamed the country in the South, and they did great wrong to civil rights and to morality. And now we have black-robed men, and that's what you're talking about."

In May 2005, Dobson scolded Republican senators for defeating his efforts to get an "up-or-down" vote on the president's Supreme Court nominees, leaving the filibuster in place. "This Senate agreement represents a complete bailout and betrayal by a cabal of Republicans and a great victory for united Democrats...The unconstitutional filibuster survives in the arsenal of Senate liberals...We share the disappointment, outrage and sense of abandonment felt by millions of conservative Americans who helped put Republicans in power last November. I am certain that these voters will remember both Democrats and Republicans who betrayed their trust."

In June 2005, Dobson met with a handful of the most powerful fundamentalist Christians in the United States— Tony Perkins of Family Research Council, Reverend Donald Wildmon of American Family Association, Gary Bauer of American Values, and Paul Weyrich of Free Congress

Foundation—to announce that starting after the 2006 midterm elections, a team of fundamentalist Christian leaders would hold personal interviews with all the candidates lining up to succeed George W. Bush to see if they would support unequivocally the fundamentalist Christian values they espouse.

In October 2005, Dobson let it slip that he had private "conversations" with Karl Rove about Harriet Miers, the woman nominated to replace retiring Justice Sandra Day O'Connor, and that during the conversation he was trusted with information "...that I probably shouldn't know." The media had a field day. The Democrats and even some Republicans demanded to know why Dobson had more information about the president's nominee than they did.

When the U.S. Senate refused to support the Federal Marriage Amendment that would deny gay and lesbian couples the rights and protections of marriage, Dobson took out full-page ads condemning the six senators who blocked support. "As our ads say," Dobson explains, "the votes of these six senators were a slap in the face of every American child."

MSNBC columnist Howard Fineman witnessed the very personal, fullpage-ad attack on six senators who had the temerity to disagree with the Dobson doctrine and wondered where this new fundamentalist approach to American governance was taking us. "Any Republicans who stray from the party line can expect the full weight of Dobson to come down on them. Beneath the placid demeanor I sensed an urgency and intensity—a man close to the boiling point at what he sees as the iniquities of political leadership. Are members of Congress unruly children needing discipline from the *Dare to Discipline* author? Maybe so, but we don't know how they will respond to Daddy Dobson. And we don't know how Dobson himself will react if they defy him. He's kept his cool so far, but that would be the ultimate test."[18]

There was a time when I thought that Dr. Dobson would burn himself out trying to run the government and Focus on the Family at the same time. Then I discovered that even while he was rushing about enforcing fundamentalist policy, Dobson was also creating Family Policy and Family Action Councils across the country that would "enforce" the fundamentalist doctrines in their states long after Dobson had passed from the scene.

I have to admit that with all the monitoring we do at Soulforce, the presence and power of Dobson's Focus Action almost escaped us before his active councils (many with offices and full-time staff) had been established in almost forty states. There is a kind of hidden-in-plain-view quality to Dobson's operation. Unlike the Moral Majority or the Christian Coalition, names that capture the imagination of the media and the general public alike, Dobson's councils have names that don't grab you and are easy to forget. I wonder if this is part of Dobson's plan, to establish Family Policy Councils (501c3s) and Family Action Councils (501c4) with almost no one outside his circle of support even able to remember the names, let alone get worked up about the long-range goals of both fundamentalist Christian operations.

To add to the confusion, Family Policy Councils and Family Action Councils affiliated with Dobson in other states have names as varied as the Center for Arizona Policy, Family Institute of Connecticut, Hawaii Family Forum, Cornerstone Institute of Idaho, Christian Civil League (Maine), Mississippi Center for Public Policy, Family First (Nebraska), Citizens for Community Values (Ohio), Stronger Families for Oregon, and Free Market Foundation (Texas).

Focus Action affiliates across the United States are "pro-family" (against granting lesbian and gay couples their civil rights) and "pro-life" (against *Roe v. Wade* and abortion rights). Focus Action is building this new political force by joining powerful statewide organizations already in place with start-up operations guided by Dobson allies. Whatever their origin, these groups are officially independent of Dobson and Focus on the Family, with their own 501c3 and 501c4 organizations.

In Virginia, Dobson's affiliate is The Family Foundation, founded in 1985, almost twenty years before Dobson launched Focus Action in 2004. And yet on their home page you'll find these words: "The Family Foundation is proud to be associated with James Dobson's Focus on the Family and its network of nearly forty independent state policy councils." When Virginia's Family Foundation joined with Dobson, he added to his power base a well-established Virginia organization with a full-time professional staff in the state capital networking "tens of thousands of pro-family citizen activists throughout Virginia."[19]

Dobson's Family Action Councils are the 501c4 political arm of his Focus on the Family 501c3 empire. As Dobson explained on its public launch in 2004, "The primary difference between the two ministries is that FOF can provide a tax deduction for its contributors but is extremely limited in its ability to lobby for its core principles. By contrast, Focus Action can devote every dollar contributed to defend what we believed…All the funds contributed to it go straight to the battle for righteousness."[20]

When Dobson launched Focus Action in 2004, less than six months before the presidential election, the *New York Times* reported that prominent liberals had already acknowledged that "Dr. Dobson's efforts could hurt their cause." "There is no question," stated Ralph Neas, president of People for the American Way, "that James Dobson is the most powerful and most influential voice on the religious right."[21]

Creating fear and loathing of gay and lesbian Americans has proven, year after year, to be the most effective way for Dobson and the other fundamentalist Christian leaders to raise millions of dollars and recruit millions of volunteers to support their long-range campaign to "take back America." In the first six months, Focus Action raised nearly $9 million to support Dobson's political goals. "Nonprofit experts say raising that much money so quickly—the equivalent of $50,000 per day—is astounding," reported the *Denver Post*, "more evidence of the goodwill the child psychologist has built among supporters over a quarter-century of preaching conservative values."[22]

Dobson promised those 25 million Americans who hear him weekly that Focus Action and Policy Councils at work in every state would help them build a more effective force "…in fighting for the Marriage Protection Amendment and against judicial tyranny…Too many Christians have been no-shows," he explained, "but by working together we can change that. We can tackle head-on the most troubling problems facing our great nation and begin changing its direction before it is too late."[23]

After the reelection of George W. Bush, Dobson praised his not-yet one-year-old coalition for its influence "in state capitals, in the media, and in grassroots lobbying among the citizenry." He noted that his new pro-family network was "… especially effective in the battle to protect traditional marriage in all thirteen states that passed constitutional amendments defending marriage as being exclusively between a man and a woman." Then he promised his Family Policy Councils would be "vital in securing support for amendments in additional states and in their ratification."[24]

What Dobson promises, Dobson usually delivers. And in the process of delivering enough votes to elect his allies or defeat his enemies, this unsmiling, round-faced, pink-cheeked, rather harmless-looking family psychologist has, as *Slate* reports, become "America's most influential evangelical leader, with a following reportedly greater than that of either Falwell or Robertson at his peak."[25]

During my time in the entourages of Jerry Falwell and Pat

Robertson, I never saw either of them attack and punish those who disagree, as Dobson does on a regular basis. It may not be official and certainly not on public display, but I believe there is an unwritten blacklist, and anyone who offends him in any way never appears again on his radio broadcast. And because an author is almost guaranteed that his or her book will sell out in bookstores across America after appearing with Dobson on *Focus on the Family*, that kind of punishment leads to serious financial loss.

I don't doubt that in his 1994 letter condemning me, Dr. Dobson was sincere when he said, "I've never tried to hurt you or anyone else." But he is sincerely wrong if he believes that his antihomosexual rhetoric is not hurtful. In fact, there is a sufficiency of evidence even in his letter that I was not exaggerating when I claimed his antigay rhetoric leads to intolerance, suffering, and death. We had an example of the consequences of Dr. Dobson's rhetoric just one day after his letter was read to the public by a Rush Limbaugh—like talk-show host on a Colorado Springs radio station.

Gary and I, with friends and supporters, were holding a seven-day "Fast for Understanding" during the week of July 10 to 17, 1994, in front of Dobson's massive headquarters. Immediately after hearing Dobson's "Response to Mel White Letter" read on the air, listeners began to flood the station with calls condemning me. "Someone ought to go up there and take him out," one caller exclaimed, and in the hour of calls that followed, no one challenged his remarks. By early evening, there had been enough death threats that the police suggested we move from our trailer near Focus on the Family to a nearby hotel for the night.

In his letter Dobson claims that "on all occasions" when he spoke or wrote publicly about homosexuality and homosexuals "the comments made were respectful, caring, and compassionate." However, in that same letter Dobson went on to support my accusations against him by caricaturing and condemning lesbian and gay people as he had repeatedly on his daily broadcasts across the United States, in his books, pamphlets, videotapes, films, and especially in his fund-raising letters. Here are just a few examples from his full-page letter to me:

- "...gay activists utilize public schools to undermine heterosexual marriage and the institution of the family..."
- "...programs like Project 10 [a voluntary program in the Los Angeles School System designed to assist gay and lesbian youth who have suffered mental and physical abuse] have been used for homosexual recruitment."
- "...we oppose the attempt by gay activists to capture the hearts and minds of children."

And that's just the beginning. Dobson spent approximately one-fourth of his letter quoting from an article written to condemn the Rainbow Curriculum in New York City, an attempt by Joseph Fernandez, superintendent of the New York City public school system, to help stop the abuse of gay students and to help all students understand the nature of homosexual orientation. Fundamentalist Christians in New York and across the country opposed the Rainbow Curriculum with such ferocity that the curriculum was dropped and the superintendent was fired from his job.[26] In his letter to me, Dobson quoted extensively from the article retelling that sad story.

...In the guise of presenting health information...used the occasion to engage in raw homosexual propaganda aimed at teen-agers...pictures of a woman with her legs spread to an approaching clenched fist (swathed in latex) to illustrate

lesbian "fisting."...instructions for trying "golden showers" (a sexual activity with urine), enemas, scalpels and razors... instructions to clean your canes, crops and whips...Clorox and soap, condoms and dental dams, fists and knives, whips and chains, this is the stuff the New York City Board of Education presents to 12 year-olds.

For the record, the article Dobson used to "illustrate" the "gay agenda" was in fact out-of-context information from a "safe-sex manual" prepared by the Gay Men's Health Crisis Center in New York. The explicit warnings in that brochure were given to sexually active men and women who were most vulnerable to the HIV/STD epidemic. The brochure was never given to twelve-year-olds, let alone distributed through the Rainbow Curriculum to junior-high and senior-high students in the New York City School System.

In his letter, Dobson also claims that of his four thousand programs during his seventeen years on the air "...only a handful have been devoted to the subject of homosexuality." It wasn't true then. It isn't true now. Even as I write these words, the lead story on Dobson's Web site is a press release ending the long-term banking relationship Focus had with Wells Fargo because of "the bank's ongoing efforts to advance the radical homosexual agenda."[27] Today alone on Dobson's home page, there are fifteen thousand—plus words warning of the "gay agenda," and advertisements for sixteen books, booklets, and DVDs caricaturing "the homosexual lifestyle" and offering ways "to over come your homosexuality." And when I searched for titles on Dr. Dobson's Web site under the category "Fighting the Homosexual Agenda," there were 11,299 references to old Dobson broadcasts, guest interviews, and articles on Citizen Links, a Focus on the Family Web site presenting "Issues in Policy and Culture."

The description of the *Focus on the Family* program scheduled for the day I happened to be writing these words makes it clear that once again Dobson is using his half-hour broadcast heard by millions of Americans to launch another attack on homosexuality and homosexuals: "What Companies Embrace Pro-Gay Policies: Dr. James Dobson examines the increasing number of U.S. corporations embracing pro-homosexual policies." At the heart of that December 1, 2005, broadcast, "Corporate America's Attack on the Family,"[28] was Dr. Dobson's advice for Americans to "Buy Christian" this Christmas and boycott products from corporations that offer domestic partnership or any other benefits to their lesbian or gay employees. It's a familiar call to arms. During the months leading up to the reelection of George W. Bush, it was "Vote Christian" and defeat any candidate (local, state, or national) who favors granting any rights or protections to gay and lesbian Americans.

All it takes is a quick look at the Focus on the Family Web site and its archives to put to rest Dobson's claim that "only a handful" of his broadcasts are attacks on homosexuality and homosexuals. And his fund-raising letters consistently echo those attacks. In his 1994 full-page open letter to me, Dobson goes on to say that I have "never documented" any of my assertions about his "supposed extremism or bigotry." "I'm asking you now in this letter," Dr. Dobson added, "which will also be released to the press, to come forward with the evidence. I invite you to quote chapter and verse. Cite the dates. Provide the basis for your incendiary charges against me and Focus on the Family...Check the record. You'll find not a word that dehumanizes any individual or classification of people."[29]

Dobson was correct when he criticized us for not including the original sources of the thirteen pages of evidence against his inflammatory rhetoric that we presented to his staff in 1994. We have tapes of the broadcasts and copies of the books, magazines, and fund-raising letters from which we quoted his words against us. But we didn't footnote each quote with its source. In 2005, Soulforce released a thirty-two-page booklet and a twenty-nine-minute DVD[31] confronting Dobson's false charges with even more up-to-date scientific, psychological, historical, and even biblical evidence, and every Dobson quote is documented, as he says, "chapter and verse."

In his open letter to me, Dobson also claims that every time he did speak of homosexuality, "there was not a word of disrespect aimed at individuals who are homosexual or lesbian." And yet in the thirteen pages of evidence we presented in "Our Case against the Anti-Gay Words and Actions of James Dobson & His Focus on the Family Ministries," even the title of the book quoted most by James Dobson is offensive: *The Homosexual Agenda: Exposing the Principal Threat to Religious Freedom Today*. On the back cover, amid all the endorsements of the book by fundamentalist Christian leaders, you read this disgusting untruth: "The homosexual agenda has as its primary aim to 'trump' the rights of all other groups, especially those of people of faith."[32]

Inside you will read, "Homosexuals are attempting to force their lifestyles and its consequences upon society…They want special rights…social acceptance and privilege…They desire to teach homosexuality as an 'alternative lifestyle' in public schools, and want their immoral relationships both recognized and subsidized with government funding by means of 'domestic partnerships' laws that redefine the nature of the family."

The book's opening words call Christians to "…promote morality in society, rather than immorality…calling homosexuals to repentance…Homosexual rights legislation not only promotes immorality in society, but spreads the many diseases that result from the practice of homosexuals. Promiscuity and sodomy have been blamed for the worst epidemic in the twentieth century: AIDS."

Could it be that Dobson honestly believes that when he attacks homosexuality and homosexuals that there is "not a word of disrespect aimed at individuals who are homosexual or lesbian"? Has he convinced himself that this kind of rhetoric is harmless, that it is neither extreme nor bigoted, that it doesn't have tragic consequences in the lives of lesbian and gay Americans, their friends and families? You would think that James Dobson, a practicing psychologist with millions of dads and moms listening to his antihomosexual broadcasts and reading his antihomosexual books, pamphlets, and fund-raising letters, would feel responsible to examine the empirical evidence collected over the past century that homosexuality is neither a sickness nor a sin. Does he take time off even occasionally to take one small step out of the Dark Ages into the twenty-first century by reading an occasional psychological journal, or by talking to professional colleagues who specialize in sexual-orientation issues, or even by doing research on his own? Instead, James Dobson bases his understanding of the cause and treatment of homosexuality on a few isolated verses from the writings of Paul and Moses, who knew a lot about God and nothing about sexual orientation.

Dobson surrounds himself with people who are loving and sincere but who know even less than Dobson about sexual orientation and gender identity. He staffs Focus on the Family and his Love Won Out Conferences with sincere celebrity parents like Nancy Heche, mother of Anne Heche, the actress who had a rather notorious relationship with Ellen DeGeneres; with pseudoscientists like Joseph Nicolosi, an outdated Freudian who is a founder and current president of NARTH, the National Association of Research and Therapy of Homosexuality; and with a collection of attractive and articulate gay men and lesbians who have "left the lifestyle" to get married, have families of their own, and work full-time in ex-gay programs.

As far as I can tell, there isn't one real social scientist on Dobson's payroll. His current ex-gay director of the Homosexuality and Gender department is working on a master's degree through a correspondence course offered by Jerry Falwell's Liberty University. Worse by far are the consequences in the lives of many of these ex-gay leaders who finally admit that the "reparative" or "transformational" therapies haven't worked in their lives. When that happens—and it happens over and over again—they feel trapped between two worlds, alienated from their fundamentalist Christian friends and from the gay community as well.

Like Dobson, the leaders of these ex-gay organizations are sincere. I do not question their motives, but they are ignorant and in their ignorance they are making victims of my gay sisters and brothers. Here is a sample of that ignorance in the words of Joseph Nicolosi, Dobson's in-house expert on the origins of homosexuality:

- "There is no such thing as a homosexual...We are all heterosexual, but some heterosexuals have a homosexual problem."[33]
- "I've never met a homosexual man that had a loving respectful relationship with his father."[34]
- "The mother is over-emotionally involved, a dominant, strong personality...the father is quiet, withdrawn, non-expressive, and/or hostile."[35]
- "I've never seen a male with a homosexual problem think fondly of his older brother...I've never heard that...never do hear it."[36]
- "We advise parents to use clear and consistent messages: 'We do not accept your effeminacy. You are a

boy. God made you a boy. Being a boy is special.' When parents do this, especially fathers, they can turn their boys around."[37]

James Dobson shows equal ignorance in his basic understanding of homosexual orientation. His view of Scripture blocks any new insights that might come from scientific or psychological research. So he passes on that ignorance to millions of fundamentalist Christians (and others) who hear his claims that homosexuality is a sin that must be forgiven and a sickness that can be healed. In his own words:

DOBSON: "What do we know about this disorder? Well first, it is a disorder, despite the denials of the American Psychiatric Association."[38] (And I might add the American Psychological Association, American Academy of Pediatrics, American Association of School Administrators, American Federation of Teachers, American School Health Association, National Association of School Psychologists, National Association of Social Workers, and the National Education Association.)[39]

DOBSON: "When you're living outside of God's will for your life—whether by experimenting with homosexuality or willfully embracing any other sin—you will feel the effects one way or another. And probably the biggest result of living a sinful life is not having peace with God"[40]

My response to Dobson's biblical confusion: "What the Bible Says and Doesn't Say About Homosexuality,"[41] and a long list of other publications by America's preeminent Bible scholars, demonstrate clearly that the biblical authors knew nothing and therefore say nothing about homosexuality in either the Hebrew or Greek testaments. The Bible literally is silent about homosexual orientation as we understand it today.

James Dobson's teaching that homosexuality is a sin or a sickness has tragic consequences in the lives of parents, usually Christian parents with lesbian or gay children. When they discover the sexual orientation of their son or daughter, they suffer terrible, sometimes lifelong guilt. It took several years to convince my own father and mother that they hadn't failed, that my homosexual orientation was a gift from God, not due to any mistake they might have made.

Other parents feel they haven't failed. Those who make it clear to their children that homosexuality is a sin may reject or even discard sons or daughters who "continue in their sinfulness" or force them into ex-gay programs that promise to "transform" or "repair them." This "tough love," as they call it, suggests that living in "a state of rebellion against God" must not be tolerated or supported in any way.

It is not difficult to relate to the suffering of gay and lesbian youth and young adults who have been rejected or discarded by their parents. But it is important, as well, to imagine the suffering of those parents who think they are doing right by rejecting their children or forcing them into endless sessions with Christian counselors (like Dobson or Nicolosi) or into "reparative" therapy programs associated with Exodus or other ex-gay ministries. Teaching that homosexuality is a sickness and a sin leads directly to broken homes, ruined relationships, and tragic endings.

Fundamentalist Protestants like James Dobson and fundamentalist Catholics like Joseph Nicolosi truly believe that all we know about sexual orientation can be found in Leviticus and Romans. They are a threat to the families they focus on and should wear labels that read "The Surgeon General warns that taking Dobson and Nicolosi seriously can be dangerous to your mental and spiritual health and to the health of those you love."

Unfortunately, James Dobson is not satisfied to mislead millions of his listeners about the origins of homosexuality. Dobson goes on to demean, dehumanize, and demonize homosexuals, as well.

I am also tired of Dobson's attacks on "homosexual activists" who supposedly have a "master plan" that has as its centerpiece "the utter destruction of the family."[42] I am proud to say that I am a "homosexual activist." Every gay and lesbian person who comes out is also an activist, and Dobson is absolutely wrong when he accuses activists of working to destroy the family. We have families of our own and our struggle for the rights and protections of marriage are no more and no less than a struggle to protect those families.

Dobson claims that "discrediting of Scriptures"[43] is one of my end goals as a homosexual activist. Don't accuse me of "discrediting Scriptures" when I spent ten years of my life in seminary getting two graduate degrees and learning Greek and Hebrew just to understand them better. I love the Scriptures and have spent my life reading, memorizing, teaching, and preaching them, and when I ask groups of my fellow activists what caused them to care about doing justice, it is almost always the same. Most of them were shaped in Sunday or Sabbath schools by the Hebrew prophets' call to do justice and/or by the words of Jesus, who said to the fundamentalists in his day, "You know the law by heart but you've forgotten the heart of the law: justice, mercy and truth."

Dobson accuses me and my fellow activists of "muzzling the clergy,"[44] when in fact I am clergy in good standing with the Metropolitan Community Church and I would defend the rights of other clergy, Catholic and Protestant alike, to disagree with me publicly in their writings, their sermons, or through Christian media without even a threat of censorship and certainly without being muzzled either by the law or by lawlessness.

Dobson says that I am demanding "special privileges and rights in the law."[45] In fact, Gary Nixon and I have had a loving, committed, faithful relationship for twenty-five years yet we are denied more than a thousand rights and protections that go automatically with marriage. We don't want "special rights." We just want to share the civil rights guaranteed all Americans. And in his efforts to soil the U.S. Constitution with his so-called Marriage Protection Amendment (and in the process superimpose his fundamentalist Christian values on our nation), Dobson is using the highest law of the land not just to deny millions of Americans our basic civil rights but to make all gay Americans outcasts in our own land.

Dobson accuses me of "trying to overturn laws prohibiting pedophilia."[46] That dangerous and "baseless claim" comes from his distorting the truth once again. In several countries, gay activists have lobbied to have the age of consensual sex for homosexual adults lowered to match the age of consensual sex for heterosexual adults. It has been quite common for governments to use age-of-consent laws to punish gays for loving, consensual acts long after loving, consensual acts between heterosexuals are legal. Instead of explaining the real reasons behind the effort to equalize the age of consent, Dobson misuses the issue to falsely support his claim that gay men want to exploit children. In fact, we have children of our own, and as responsible, committed parents we are as determined to protect our children from pedophiles as Dobson is.

Dobson accuses me of "indoctrinating children and future generations through public education."[47] He makes "indoctrinating" sound like we use our educational programs for brainwashing, misleading, and even recruiting children. In fact, the word is defined by *Webster's* as teach, instruct, or train.

These are our real goals for the curricula activists have designed to help children and youth understand sexual orientation. Gay youth are victims of those who have been "indoctrinated" by James Dobson and his troops. We are simply trying to help end that cycle of victimization that flows out of ignorance and fear.

Dobson accuses me and my fellow activists of attempting to secure "all the legal benefits of marriage for any two or more people who claim to have homosexual tendencies "[48] Look at the prejudice just beneath the surface of that misleading phrase. When he says "for any two or more people," he is summoning up pictures of polygamy, promiscuity, partner sharing, and group sex. And when he says "homosexual tendencies," he is implying once again that homosexual orientation is a choice and a sick and sinful choice at that. Dobson is right that we are seeking all the legal benefits of marriage for same-sex couples in loving, committed relationships, but once again he twists the truth to create fear and loathing of gay and lesbian people.

I would like to remind Dobson and his fundamentalist Christian friends of these words of Jesus: "I say unto you, that every word that men shall speak, they shall give account of thereof in the day of judgment; for by your words you shall be justified, and by your words you shall be condemned" (Matthew 12:36-37).

I've spent much of this chapter on James Dobson's antihomosexual rhetoric. Dobson really believes that homosexuals are a threat to the family and to the nation. Don't doubt that. To suggest that he is not a true believer or to say he's only doing it for the money is to underestimate Dobson's determination to deny us our rights, drive us back into our closets, or worse. But his attacks on gay Americans, though sincere, have proven to be the means to help achieve a much greater end than to "stop same-sex marriage" or "keep gays out of the military."

In that full-page "open letter" ad that Dobson took out to condemn me on Sunday, July 17, 2004, I got my first experience of his penchant to punish. His condemnation included: "sinking degree of dishonesty," "distorting the truth," "misrepresenting the facts," "constructing a fraudulent basis," "your propagandistic motives," "your manipulations of the press," "your elaborate publicity campaign wrapped in the cloak of human rights." He ends his letter with these words: "Despite the candor of my reply to your charges, Mel, I extend my best regards to you. While we disagree on some very critical issues, I do not intend any ill will or malice to you."

I believe Dr. Dobson is sincere when he does not "intend any ill will or malice" in his full-page ads, but we didn't spend seven days fasting in Colorado Springs because we "disagree on some very critical issues." This is not a philosophical, psychological, or biblical debate. This is a matter of life and death. James Dobson uses his massive media empire, over and over again, to dehumanize our lives, demean our relationships, and demonize our struggle for justice, and his words and powerful political actions lead to intolerance, discrimination, spiritual violence, suffering, and even death. And I can't even imagine what might happen to us if he manages to place his version of the Bible at the center of American life or even elect his judges to the Supreme Court.

D. JAMES KENNEDY (THE EXTREMIST)

Of all the fundamentalist Christians who exploit the fear and hatred of homosexuals, D. James Kennedy embodies the most extreme. If James Dobson represents a clear and present danger, Kennedy's words and actions give us some idea of what the future might hold for gay and lesbian Americans living in a nation dominated by fundamentalist Christians.

I first met Kennedy in the mid-1960s while working on my doctorate at Fuller Theological Seminary. Billy Zeoli, president of Gospel Films, called me with an urgent request to fly to Fort Lauderdale, where his production team was making *Like a Mighty Army*, a ninety-minute film that would introduce Kennedy's "Evangelism Explosion" to the nation. "Cast and crew are in place," he explained, "but no one likes the script. Will you fly to Florida tonight and rewrite it for us?"

Billed as a lay-witnessing training program that "leads to explosive congregational growth," Kennedy credited "Evangelism Explosion" for increasing his church membership from seven to 2,500 in just nine years. According to Kennedy's bio, EE was conceived in 1953 when he was startled awake by the question a preacher was asking on his radio alarm: "Suppose you were to die today and stand before God and He were to ask you, 'What right do you have to enter into my heaven.'"—what would you say?" Apparently that question led to Kennedy's conversion and, in 1962, to Kennedy's "Evangelism Explosion," a program that teaches people to base their own person-to-person witness on that question and help grow their church in the process.

In the four hours of research I had before taking a TWA red-eye to Fort Lauderdale, I learned that Kennedy's church was located in the heart of Broward County, South Florida. Even without Google the demographics were clear. Broward County promised sunshine and security for middle-class to wealthy conservative Protestant Americans who could afford to move into this predominantly white enclave with its gated communities and high-rise security systems. Kennedy's Coral Ridge Presbyterian Church was growing not because masses of non-Christians were being converted through Kennedy's "Evangelism Explosion" but because masses of tired, fearful, older Christians were moving to Broward County (and to Coral Ridge Presbyterian Church) because it was a comfortable, conservative oasis for people fleeing the problems of the city.

And their pastor, D. James Kennedy, was the perfect shepherd to guide his flock away from the real problems of justice, mercy, and truth every Sunday with a fundamentalist Christian mix of patriotism, cheap grace, pseudopsychology, and scary apocalyptic warnings of what might happen to America if...If the evil Soviet empire triumphs...If homosexuals have their way with our children...If feminists destroy the family... If pro-abortionists continue killing a million unborn babies yearly...If criminals, teenage gangsters, drug peddlers continue to roam our streets...If pornographers...If the Internet...If Hollywood...If activist judges...If Hillary Clinton...

In our first meeting in his office at Coral Ridge Presbyterian, Dr. Kennedy was most gracious until I raised the possibility that at least a part of the reason for his congregation's amazing growth was "white flight." After that our relationship spiraled downward into grim silence and occasional head nods when needed. I may have been wrong, but it seemed rather apparent that his congregation was not growing simply because new converts were filling the pews but primarily because long-term Christians were shifting from one section of the country (usually the cold North) to another (the sunny climes of Broward County) and from small churches (with large demands on their time and money) to a mega-church (where they could "just get fed"). If true, it didn't seem honest to promise that his Evangelism Explosion would result in similar growth to struggling little churches in depressed cities or rural, low-density-population areas across the country.

For whatever reasons, Kennedy's church was booming in the mid-sixties and it is booming now According to the Coral Ridge Web site, Kennedy's congregation has nearly ten thousand members, and his Sunday sermons on the *Coral Ridge Hour* are broadcast to forty thousand cities and towns across the United States and on satellite to stations in nearly two hundred nations around the world. The Web site claims that the *Coral Ridge Hour* has "the greatest number of TV station affiliates of any religious program in the U.S."[49] Late at night, in hotel rooms when I just can't sleep because Gary and our dog Bentley aren't with me, invariably I will find Kennedy preaching on some independent TV station sandwiched between old movies and infomercials. Don't underestimate Kennedy's influence just because you've never heard his name.

For fifteen years, Coral Ridge Presbyterian was the fastest-growing Presbyterian church in America. *Decision* magazine named the church one of the "Five Great Churches of North America." Besides his *Coral Ridge Hour*, Kennedy has a film and television production ministry, a daily half-hour radio show *(Truths That Transform)*, and a daily ninety-second radio spot in English ("The Kennedy Commentary") and in Spanish *("Verdades Que Transforman")*.

Kennedy's Coral Ridge campus includes Westminster Academy, a fully accredited school for children in kindergarten to senior-high teens. Kennedy's Knox Theological Seminary provides lay and clergy leaders from around the world "an education grounded in the historic Reformed faith and shaped by commitments to the sovereignty of God, the inerrancy of the Bible, and obedience to the Great Commission and the Cultural Mandate."

Beware of preachers who use high-sounding expressions like "cultural mandate." Be on guard when Kennedy and other fundamentalist Christian preachers, political candidates, or televangelists speak obsessively of "reforming culture" or "redeeming society" or "reclaiming America for Christ." Those catchy phrases may sound comparatively benign when Kennedy and the others preach them in their Sunday sermons or proclaim them in books and magazines, on television and radio. They are not benign. They are malignant ideas eating away at democracy under the pretense of saving it. Kennedy may look like a patriot and a prophet on the *Coral Ridge Hour*, but we get a better look at his long-range goals when we understand the extremist company he keeps, fundamentalist Christians who define themselves with such words as "reconstructionist," "dominionist" or "theophonist."

On July 4, 1986, D. James Kennedy and 459 other Christian fundamentalists who identify in varying degrees with the theological labels cited above gathered "in solemn assembly" on the steps of the Lincoln Memorial in Washington, D.C., to sign *A Manifesto for the Christian Church*. Kennedy, one of the signers, served on the original steering committee of the Council on Revival, the organization that brought these fundamentalist Christian leaders together. And though Dr. Jay Grimstead, editor of the *Manifesto*, acknowledges that some signers have since "...retracted their support for COR, its vision and its goals," the original list includes a veritable *Who's Who* of America's fundamentalist Christian leaders and their powerful organizations."[50]

If you want to understand the ultimate goals that fundamentalist Christians have for our country (and even for the world), read this frightening document. In short, the mission of the fundamentalist Christians among us is to help the church rebuild (reconstruct) society so that God's will may be done on earth as it is in heaven (dominion), guided not by man's law but by the laws of God (theophony) as found in the inerrant Bible.

In the *Manifesto's* "Statement of Essential Truths" (subtitled "The Church Must Learn What Is Reality"), the first truth listed is, you guessed it, the inerrancy of the Bible. "Human authors." the *Manifesto* states, "wrote the exact words and sentences God inspired in them to write without error and without misrepresenting God, history or the created world in any way."[51]

The *Manifesto* signers are determined to make their inerrant Bible the test for all truth, including philosophies, books, values, actions, and plans, and the final measurement of all God wants mankind to know about law, government, economics, business, education, arts and communication, medicine, psychology, and science.

The *Manifesto* states that the person or nation who obeys biblical law will be blessed, and a person or a nation who disobeys God's law will be "cursed and destroyed." Therefore, the goal of those fundamentalist Christians who signed the *Manifesto* is to bring a nation's judicial and legal systems into "as close an approximation to the laws and commandments of the Bible as its citizens will allow," and they are building a coalition of Americans to see that the systems are reconstructed to that end.

According to the *Manifesto*, the Christian church must be "the world's teacher." and they warn that there is no way for nations of the world to know "how to live" without "the Church's biblical influence on its theories, laws, actions, and institutions." When this nation obeys God's law, the nation will be blessed. But when the nation disobeys God's law, the nation will be cursed.

The *Manifesto* concludes the "Call to Action" demanding "full obedience to the Bible" with a list of twelve social evils to oppose. Abortion on demand and homosexuality (included with "other forms of sexual perversion") are numbers one and two on the *Manifesto's* list. You get a clear idea of a fundamentalist's "moral values" when opposing abortion and homosexuality are more important than opposing the unjust treatment of the poor (#5) or racial discrimination (#8).

Early in July 1993, I asked one of our volunteers to write a letter to R. J. Rushdoony, founder of the Chalcedon Foundation, the father of Re-constructionist theology, and a primary force behind the *Manifesto*, to see if the Bible must be taken literally in "opposing" homosexuality. We have his handwritten response dated July 8, 1993: "God in His law requires the death penalty for homosexuals as restated in Romans 1:32." Before this father of Reconstructionist theology died, he made it clear that this death sentence should be applied to homosexuals if God were to bless this nation once again.

Rushdoony used that verse in the book of Romans to prove that the Laws of Moses, written roughly thirteen centuries before Christ, still apply to twenty-first-century Christians. In Leviticus, the author makes it clear that men who sleep with other men are an abomination and should be executed (Leviticus 20:13). I have met fundamentalist Christians, clergy, and laity alike who take the whole verse seriously and warn me in letters and on radio talk shows that it is God's will that I be executed for accepting my homosexuality as God's gift.

Fortunately, most fundamentalists don't go that far—at least not yet. Most literalists are really selective literalists. In reading the biblical text they pick and choose what verse (or parts of a verse) they want to take literally and then ignore the rest. For that reason, most fundamentalists are satisfied to call me an "abomination." But hard-core literalists like Rushdoony—and a yet to be determined number of fundamentalists—would go much further. It would be catastrophic if one day these fundamentalist Christians gain enough political power to enforce their literal understanding of Mosaic Law, not just for lesbian and gay Americans, but for all Americans.

For example, in Leviticus, the third book of the Jewish Testament or Torah, the death penalty is decreed not only "… for a man who lies with mankind as he lies down with a woman"

(Leviticus 20:13), but also "Everyone who curses his father or mother shall be put to death" (Leviticus 20:9), and "Any man that commits adultery with another man's wife, the adulterer and the adulteress shall be put to death" (Leviticus 20:10).

Rushdoony and his fundamentalist friends are "dominionists" who believe that Christians should have dominion over all the earth because God has given it to them. They are "reconstructionists" because they believe that they have a biblical mandate to reconstruct our nation to reflect the kingdom of God here on earth. And they are "theophonists" who believe that God's Word should govern conduct in this new kingdom. To these extremists, democracy is a heresy. The U.S. Constitution should be replaced by biblical law. The law should be administered by a committee of church elders with capital crimes punishable by stoning. Rushdoony boils down biblical law to eighteen capital crimes: homosexuality (of course), murder, striking or cursing a parent, adultery, incest, bestiality, rape, witchcraft, blasphemy, the desecration of the Sabbath, and refusing to obey a court order—all from the list of capital crimes described in Leviticus, the third book of the Jewish Torah.

In *Stranger at the Gate*, I recalled my experience in a fifty-thousand-watt Seattle radio station where I had gone to debate a Reconstructionist Presbyterian pastor on a popular call-in talk show. When I asked him how he interpreted that passage in Leviticus that calls for the death of a man who sleeps with another man, he replied without hesitation, "It means you should be killed." After swallowing hard, I asked him, "Who should do the killing? You church folk?" He answered without a pause: "No, that's the civil authority's job. That's why we have to get more good men of God elected into government." In the silence that followed, he added, "I know that must be hard for you to hear, Dr. White, but God said it and it's our job to obey."

This wasn't the first time I had met a fundamentalist

Christian who reads the Bible literally, but it was the first time I had met a fundamentalist who would enforce its Old Testament Laws in the same way. It was unreal to be seated in a radio control room sharing a mike with one of my fellow Americans who was polite and soft-spoken but who believed with all his heart that God wanted me dead. When I asked the independent Presbyterian pastor if he would apply the death penalty to men and women who commit adultery (Leviticus 20:13) and to children who curse their parents (Leviticus 20:9), he answered, "Absolutely." Today, my stomach churns and my mouth goes dry when I hear any fundamentalist Christian declare that the Bible must be taken literally, who really means it.

For the past thirty to forty years, fundamentalist Christians have been working to superimpose God's law over the laws of this country in ways both symbolic and real. On July 31, 2001, in the middle of the night, Judge Roy Moore, chief justice of the Alabama Supreme Court and a fundamentalist Christian, installed a 5,300-pound granite monument to the Ten Commandments in the central rotunda of the state judicial building. On Thursday, November 13, 2003, Judge Moore and the granite monument were both removed from the Alabama Court. In just eight words, Presiding Judge William Thompson explained the reasoning behind the court's verdict: "The chief justice placed himself above the law." Judge Moore is a hero to Christian fundamentalists because placing Mosaic Law over the laws of this land is exactly what they plan to do. In 1997, Judge Moore received the "Christian Statesman of the Year" Award from none other than D. James Kennedy.

Sneaking that 5,300-pound granite monument into the courthouse at midnight was a symbolic act. But the Federal Marriage Amendment proposed by D. James Kennedy and his fundamentalist Christian colleagues is no symbol. It is a very real attempt to superimpose (what they think is) God's law on the rest of us even if it means using the highest law in the land to make second-class citizens of lesbian and gay Americans and rob millions of us the rights and protections promised us in the U.S. Constitution and its Bill of Rights. And if somehow they manage to amend the U.S. Constitution with a watered-down version of that Leviticus passage that condemns us to death, what would happen next? What long-range plans do the fundamentalist Christians have, not just for lesbian and gay Americans but for all Americans who do not take the Bible literally?

So many people ask, "Why are they [fundamentalist Christians] so hung up on homosexuality?" The *Manifesto for the Christian Church* shows us why. Because their inerrant Bible says homosexuals are condemned by God, homosexuals must be condemned by this nation, as well. If this country honors sinful lesbian and gay Americans (through legal recognition of their relationships), it disobeys God, causing Him in turn "to remove his hand of blessing from the nation."

It seems to me that Jerry Falwell, Pat Robertson, and their fundamentalist Christian colleagues are serious when they say homosexuals are a threat to the nation, responsible in part for the 9/11 attack on the World Trade Center and the hurricanes that ravaged the South. In their view, the more rights and protections lesbian and gay Americans gain in city, state, or nation, the angrier God gets. These calamities, whether caused by terrorists or by nature, are seen by fundamentalists as precursors of what God might do to our nation if we continue to ignore God's laws as found in their inerrant Bible.

This morning, as I write, our local Lynchburg paper has a front-page photo of Pat over the caption: "Pat Robertson apologizes for remarks."[52] The story explains that a day after Ariel Sharon suffered a massive stroke, Robertson suggested that the Israeli prime minister was being punished by God for pulling Israel out of the Gaza Strip. His comment drew widespread criticism and enough political pressure that Robertson apologized for his remarks in an open letter to Sharon's son, Omri.

Reading the letter, you can see that Pat was not apologizing for (let alone retracting) his suggestion that God was punishing Sharon. He was apologizing for its timing. "My concern for the future safety of your nation led me to make remarks which I can now view in retrospect as inappropriate and insensitive in light of a national grief experienced because of your father's illness." Robertson is a pre-millennialist fundamentalist Christian who believes sincerely that Jesus cannot return until Israel has occupied all the original territory once ruled by King David. Anything that hinders God's plan endangers the guilty man and nation.

Fundamentalist Christians see themselves as prophets warning the nation of the consequences of this kind of disobedience and in turn calling the nation to repent and follow God's way once again. To this end, in 1996, D. James Kennedy founded the Center for Reclaiming America "for the purpose of mobilizing America's Christians at the grass roots level." Kennedy claims that he already has a nationwide e-mail network of more than five hundred thousand "concerned Christians" being trained "to positively affect the culture and renew the vision of our Founding Fathers."

More recently, Kennedy launched his Center for Christian Statesmanship with a director and staff in Washington, D.C. He describes the center as "a spiritually based outreach to men and women in positions of authority in our nation's capital," equipping national leaders "to make our nation truly Christian once again." His D.C. center offers regular Bible studies to elected officials and their staffers, "Politics and Principles" luncheons, training in Evangelism Explosion, and an annual "Distinguished Christian Statesman" reception. A primary goal of Kennedy's center is "to inform the American public and motivate people of faith to defend and implement the biblical principles on which our country was founded." What appears to be an innocent source of spiritual growth for politicians in the nation's capital is in fact another very successful lobby with the executive, legislative, and judicial branches of government on behalf of Kennedy's long-range goal, reclaiming America for Christ.

Kennedy breaks down this overriding goal into "five key fronts in the modern day culture war": (1) religious liberties (which means no separation of church and state); (2) the sanctity of life (which means no abortion on demand); (3) the Homosexual Agenda (which means deny lesbian and gay Americans their rights, deprive them of any influence, drive them back into their closets, or worse); (4) pornography (which means fundamentalist Christian censorship and control of print and electronic media including the Internet); and (5) promoting creationism (which means eliminate the teaching of evolution from the classroom).

Every year Kennedy hosts a nationwide Reclaiming America for Christ Conference. In 2005, keynote topics included: "The surprising history of church and state in America"; "The war on Christianity within our borders"; "How to take on the ACLU and win"; "What happens when a trial attorney takes on Darwin"; "What a leading scholar says about Jefferson's 'wall of separation'"; and "What a former gay rights activist has to say about the homosexual agenda!'

In 1999, I registered to attend Kennedy's Reclaiming America for Christ Conference. When I arrived at the Fort Lauderdale Convention Center with my friend the Reverend Dr. Nancy Lee Jose, now rector of St. Thomas Episcopal Church in Washington, D.C., we were immediately surrounded by security personnel and not allowed to enter. Eventually one of Jim Kennedy's staff took us aside, made us promise to "be on our best behavior," and only after we promised did they allow us to enter as observers. The convention center was packed with delegates listening intently to Kennedy's welcome and the plans for that day. The atmosphere was far more political convention than religious event. The massive meeting room was decorated in red, white, and blue. The delegates wore patriotic ribbons and badges. Flags from all fifty states hung above the platform, and three stadium-sized screens broadcast the proceedings to those of us a football field distance from the platform.

Off and on for at least twelve months before Nancy Lee and I walked into the lion's den, I had been writing Kennedy requesting time together to consider the truth about gay and lesbian Americans. Kennedy had refused to see me, let alone to negotiate an end to the false and inflammatory antigay rhetoric that spiced up his sermons on radio and television and in the flood of toxic misinformation that flowed out of his Coral Ridge Ministry office in his antigay media specials, antigay audio and videotapes, antigay books and pamphlets, and especially his antigay fund-raising letters.

In a letter just before arriving in Fort Lauderdale, I told Kennedy that I would attend his Reclaiming Conference and that I would appreciate meeting him just long enough to hand him the fifty page case we had produced to demonstrate the half-truth, hyperbole, and lies he was telling about homosexuals and, I hoped, time to respond to the lies with a summary of the latest scientific, psychological, historic, pastoral, and biblical evidence that homosexuality is neither sickness nor sin but another of God's mysterious gifts.

Kennedy had responded with a personal letter politely refusing my request, saying that he could not possibly spend time with me during the conference. During that rather awkward confrontation with security guards upon our arrival, one of Kennedy's associates reminded us again that there was no chance for a meeting with Kennedy.

The keynote speaker that first day was Ralph Reed, then executive director of Pat Robertson's Christian Coalition. Like every fundamentalist on the program, Ralph spiced up his speech with apocalyptic warnings about abortion and homosexuality. When the standing ovation ended and the delegates headed for lunch, Nancy and I slipped into Ralph's entourage and walked with them into the pressroom, where camera crews and print reporters waited to interview this powerful and persuasive young man.

Toward the close of the press conference, I stood quietly at the front of the room hoping for a chance to confront Ralph's misinformation about gay and lesbian Americans. But before I could speak, Ralph's handlers led him and his entourage out the door. I joined the camera crews as they headed into the lobby, hoping for one more chance to confront Ralph Reed's fundamentalist Christian views. At that moment, in the crowded lobby of the Fort Lauderdale Convention Center, with the press corps looking on, Ralph walked up to me, his hand outstretched, a genuine smile lighting up his boyish face.

"Mel," he said, "I've been hoping to meet you since you were arrested at CBN trying to see Pat."

Surprised that he had even noticed me, I mumbled some pleasantry in return.

"I wanted to visit you during your twenty-one days in jail," he said, still shaking my hand, "but the time just got away from me. I'm sorry."

I thanked him for his concern and stood dumbfounded as Ralph's handlers led him away. At that very moment, the same Kennedy staffer who had reminded me that there would be no meeting with Reverend Kennedy during the conference approached at double time, a group of security personnel in his wake.

"Dr. Kennedy will see you now," he said quietly, and surrounded by convention security we were ushered into a room just off the lobby and left alone to share our surprise.

After a few moments of silence, the door literally flew open as Kennedy rushed in, followed by his aides. He walked up to where I was still seated, put his finger in my face, and said angrily, "What you need, Mel White, is to repent your sin and get right with God."

"Hello, Jim," I said, standing to shake his hand. "I'm glad we can meet again at last."

Before I could finish that thought, Kennedy shouted once again, "You need to repent. There's nothing else to talk about."

"But, Jim," I replied, "I have repented my sins but my homosexuality is not a sin, but one of God's mysterious—"

"Repent, Mel White," he interrupted.

"Jim, couldn't we spend a few minutes talking about our diff—"

"Repent," he said again. "You need to repent and then we can talk."

"I have repented, Jim," I answered, holding up the materials we came to present him. He refused to accept our case against his rhetoric. "Will you just read this—"

"Repent," he said, and that one-word command was getting under my skin.

"I have repented," I responded one more time, trying not to give way to my growing anger and frustration.

"Repent," he said again, and I thought maybe he had lost his mind.

"Repent," he said for the sixth or seventh time, unwilling to enter into civil conversation. I am committed to nonviolence of the heart, tongue, and fist as described by Martin Luther King, Jr. But I admit my commitment was wearing thin.

"Repent," Kennedy repeated over and over again.

"I have repented," I replied, and back and forth it went until my friend Nancy Lee took me by the hand, saying, "Nothing can be accomplished here, Mel. Let's go."

I can still see Kennedy staring down at me with fire in his eyes. I can still hear his one-word command: "Repent!" I've not seen or heard from D. James Kennedy since that strange meeting in the Fort Lauderdale Convention Center. It's a memory I don't cherish. Looking back, I feel embarrassed for both of us.

In the meantime, if anyone needs to repent it is D. James Kennedy, who continues to use every possible venue to caricature and condemn my sisters and brothers in his televised sermons; his full-page "Love Won Out" newspaper ads featuring "former homosexuals" and promising "deliverance" in newspapers across the United States; in his special campaigns against corporations, like Disney, that celebrate "Pride Days" and offer domestic partnership benefits; in special antigay bulletins, reports, and White Papers from Coral Ridge; in his "Homosexual and State of the Union Surveys" featuring questions like "Would you want your child to be taught by a homosexual teacher?"; with particularly heinous books, pamphlets, and videotapes; his so-called petitions to national leaders; his year-end campaigns to end government/taxpayer support of the "homosexual agenda"; in his television specials; and especially in his incendiary fund-raising letters.

In 1993, when we began to monitor D. James Kennedy and the other fundamentalist Christian leaders, we collected hundreds of examples of the false, misleading, and inflammatory rhetoric Kennedy used to help stop President Clinton from ending the ban on gays and lesbians in the military. One mailing he sent to grandparents read: "Would you want your grandson in a foxhole facing the enemy in front afraid that he would also be attacked from behind?" In 2005, Kennedy joined with other fundamentalist Christians to use every possible medium to deny lesbian and gay couples the civil rights basic to heterosexual marriage and to support their so-called Marriage Protection Amendment. Whether in 1993 or 2005, the underlying half-truth, hyperbole, and lies Kennedy uses to caricature and condemn us remain the same.

Why is D. James Kennedy so terrified of granting gay and lesbian Americans the rights and protections that go with marriage, or ending the ban on gays in the military, or including us in hate-crime legislation or recognizing us as a legitimate (let alone a protected) class in any way? Is he just raising the alarm to recruit more volunteers and raise more funds? No. Absolutely not. Kennedy is truly convinced that homosexuality is a sin, that practicing homosexuals are sinners, and that once a nation accepts sin and sinners without a call to repentance, that nation is doomed.

Kennedy bases his fears on a literal reading of the story of Sodom. He claims unequivocally that "the evil of Sodom was homosexuality." Then he reminds his listeners of the consequences of that evil. "Then the Lord rained brimstone and fire on Sodom and Gomorrah from the Lord out of the heavens. So He overthrew those cities," Kennedy warns, "all the plain, all the inhabitants of the cities and what grew on the ground." "In the Law code in Leviticus," Kennedy continues, "homosexuality is referred to as an abomination, and anyone guilty of a homosexual act was to be punished by death" (Lev.20:13).

Kennedy seems obsessed with condemning homosexuality and homosexuals but his condemnation always has a greater context. Will God punish our nation as God punished Sodom? Over and over again Kennedy sounds the warning: "The path our nation is taking invites God's judgment." "…No civilization has ever made such an arrogant break with God's law and survived." "...We are pushing the nation perilously close to crossing a cultural Rubicon from which we may not return." "... God will not honor the nation that descends into sinfulness." "... The nation that will not obey God will perish." "...The wicked return to the grave and all the nations that forget God." "...It will destroy our nation's foundations." "...God will abandon our nation."

During the Iran/Contra hearings in 1988, Senator George Mitchell listened carefully as Colonel Oliver North sounded like the fundamentalist Christian he is when he defended his illegal actions, inferring that he had acted on behalf of God and country. At an appropriate moment, Senator Mitchell leaned into his microphone and shared his own personal convictions. "Please remember," he advised North, "that it is possible for an American to disagree with you on aid to the Contras and still love God, and still love this country, just as much as you do. Although He is regularly asked to do so, God does not take sides in American politics."[53]

D. James Kennedy would disagree. Kennedy and his fundamentalist sisters and brothers believe that God has chosen America to redeem the world and that anyone or anything that gets in God's way has two options: "Repent or suffer the consequences." The logo on the Kennedy Web site reads (ever so humbly): "Glorifying God. Proclaiming Truth. Reclaiming America."[54] He promises to "reclaim America" weekly on the "greatest number of TV station affiliates of any religious program in the U.S." And yet most progressive Americans have never heard his name. I don't know exactly what Kennedy means by "reclaiming America," but I know he is determined to do it, and I suspect that doing it could have tragic consequences not just for me and my gay sisters and brothers but for all Americans.

Part Two

HOW FUNDAMENTALISTS FIGHT AND WIN THEIR WARS

FOUR

THE SECRET MEETING AT GLEN EYRIE: DECLARING WAR ON HOMOSEXUALS

*I*n May 1994, just eight weeks before James Dobson took out his full-page ad to say "...there is no such [antihomosexual] campaign in progress," fifty-five fundamentalist Christian leaders who were organizers and activists in their own communities assembled secretly behind locked gates in a castle at the Glen Eyrie conference center just six miles from Colorado Springs, Colorado. According to transcripts of those meetings, these fundamentalist activists had just one purpose: to plan their "short-term" solution for the problem of lesbian and gay Americans.

The forty-three men and twelve women from seventeen states and the nation's capital gathered in a second-floor conference room to share their mutual fears about the consequences of the "militant homosexual agenda," to determine how they could "take back the ground" that homosexual rights organizations had gained, and to prevent homosexuals from ever being recognized as a "protected class."[1]

There was no press release announcing that fateful May 1994 event. In fact, there was a complete media blackout... with one exception. Before the meeting was called to order, the story was leaked conveniently to Valerie Richardson, a reporter with the *Washington Times*. Owned by Sun Myung Moon's Unification Church, the *Washington Times* was especially kind to fundamentalist Christian organizations. Reporter Valerie Richardson described the Glen Eyrie event in a brief article that went generally unnoticed:

> Leaders of anti-homosexual-rights groups across the nation wrapped up two days of top-secret meetings here yesterday aimed at strengthening their movement before the critical November elections. In the first national meeting of its kind, representatives from about 40 state organizations gathered at the birthplace of Amendment 2, the only statewide anti-homosexual-rights measure to be approved by voters, to discuss strategies for repeating its success?[2]

Sue Hyde, then coordinator of the National Gay and Lesbian Task Force (NGLTF)'s[3] Fight the Right Project, did notice the "tantalizing but sketchy" *Washington Times* story. Immediately she began to look for background materials on the May 16-18, invitation-only, closed-to-the-media national conference. In the process, she discovered that Skipp Porteous, founder of the Institute for First Amendment Studies, had managed to acquire a complete set of documents and seven audiotapes of the speeches and Q&A sessions from the conference.[4]

Those tapes, describing in detail the events at Glen Eyrie, were rediscovered recently in the Tufts University Library

Archives by Kaylynn LaGamma and Barbara Henson, a lesbian couple living in Colorado Springs. It is very painful to listen to the fundamentalist activists at Glen Eyrie plotting to deny us our rights, end our influence, drive us back into the closet, or worse. But it is even more painful to realize how much momentum their campaign to "end homosexuality in America" has gained in just twelve short years.

To miss (or to ignore) the warning signs posted at Glen Eyrie—not just for sexual and gender minorities, but for all Americans—would have been a serious mistake. That secret meeting in a castle in Colorado was a turning point in the war that fundamentalist Christian leaders were waging against gay and lesbian Americans, but it was also a turning point in the fundamentalist Christian attempt to exercise absolute power over our nation—church and state alike—the ultimate sign of religion gone bad.

The secret meeting was called to order by Will Perkins, the used-car salesman and committed fundamentalist Christian who led the successful drive in 1992 to pass Colorado's Amendment 2. To understand his goals for gay Americans is to understand the ballot measure he convinced Colorado voters to support on the basis of "No Special Rights." In fact, Amendment 2 had nothing to do with "special rights." The amendment repealed existing antidiscrimination ordinances in Aspen, Boulder, and Denver and prohibited the passage of any such future antidiscrimination ordinances that included sexual orientation in any Colorado city or town.[5] These representatives of grassroots fundamentalist organizations from across the country had come to Glen Eyrie not just to celebrate the fundamentalist Christian victory in Colorado but also to learn how to duplicate in their states what Will Perkins's Colorado for Family Values had accomplished through the political process in the Mountain State.

"There is not a more important meeting being held anyplace

in these United States," Perkins began. "If we lose this battle [against homosexuality and homosexuals], there are no moral absolutes left for this nation." After a round of applause, Perkins added, "I'd like to lead us in a word of prayer to seek God's direction like Benjamin Franklin suggested in 1776, that God does put his hand on us today and tomorrow."

Actually, Ben Franklin's motion (to open with prayer the remaining sessions of a hopelessly deadlocked Constitutional Convention) was made and defeated in 1787.[6] But Perkins's use of Franklin to support his call for prayer at the Glen Eyrie conference sent a dangerous signal. From the opening moments of their Glen Eyrie conference, these fundamentalist Christians were evoking God's guidance on their plan to deprive lesbian and gay Americans of all the civil rights and protections guaranteed them by the U.S. Constitution. It was obvious that they believed that the war they were waging against us was a holy war and that their efforts to "end homosexuality in America" were done in God's name and with God's blessing.

At the top of the Glen Eyrie pile of materials we had received was a list including the name, address, and organization of every person present. Carefully, we sorted through them. There wasn't a fundamentalist Christian celebrity among them. It didn't take much to realize that this conference was officially opening a new front in the war they were waging against us. Originally the war was fought from the top down by fundamentalist superstars like Jerry Falwell, Pat Robertson, James Dobson, and D. James Kennedy, who used their media muscle to caricature and condemn us. At Glen Eyrie, the big guys nationally were recruiting and equipping the little guys locally to fight the war more effectively at the grassroots level in towns and cities across America. Superstars like Dobson supported the meeting but did not attend. The keynote speakers explained why.

John Eldredge, representing Dobson's Focus on the Family,

set the pace. "I thought it was interesting to read last week in the *Wall Street Journal*," he said, "that in Virginia Beach, which is obviously Pat Robertson's home turf, five candidates that were running for the school board there, all endorsed by Pat Robertson, all lost. And they lost...because it was perceived to be something of a takeover. It wasn't perceived to be a genuine expression of the community."

"I don't mean anything derogatory about the person," Robert Skolrood added in his keynote address, "but they're determined to say that if Jerry Falwell will support us, then the whole issue revolves around Jerry Falwell...instead of sticking with the merits of the case." Eldredge even named his boss, James Dobson, and Dobson's massive Focus on the Family organization, as a possible liability if they "weighed in" on local issues"...because we are out of state and perceived to be something of the eight-hundred-pound gorilla. People don't like that, even people who are with us...People resent the top-down approach," he added. "We're able to win on commonsense values as long as it's perceived as a genuine grassroots movement..."

During those two fateful days at Glen Eyrie, Eldredge and seven other powerful strategists of the fundamentalist Christian revolution took pains to explain carefully to a roomful of lay activists that the fundamentalist superstars would continue waging war against homosexuality and homosexuals nationally but that in the long haul that war would be won through their local, grassroots efforts.

It is interesting to note that it wasn't just the fundamentalist gurus who were missing from the Glen Eyrie conference. There were no pastors, priests, bishops, moderators, or superintendents present at Glen Eyrie even from the largest evangelical denominations or the independent mega-churches. And no clergy were there to represent the mainstream Protestant let alone Roman Catholic congregations.

Edward John Carnell, an esteemed evangelical theologian himself, describes one of the first steps Christians take on the road to idolatry: "[There is] a curious tendency," he says, "to separate from the life of the church...And those fundamentalists who remain in the church demonstrate, in Dr. Carnell's words, "the perils of ideological thinking." They are, he explains, "...rigid, intolerant, and doctrinaire..." And, he adds, they exhibit "a highly censorious spirit" that is "hypercritical, stern, disapproving." The speakers at Glen Eyrie brought Carnell's words to life.

From the very first keynote address, these activists at Glen Eyrie exhibited "a highly censorious spirit" as one by one they expressed their low esteem for the church, especially for the Christian clergy who until that time had been "worse than useless" in achieving the fundamentalist Christian's revolutionary goals. At Glen Eyrie, all clergy took a pounding. Will Perkins, founding chairman of Colorado for Family Values, warned, "The message from the church is not a solid message... We need to hold accountable those pastors, churches, and denominations who are promoting homosexual behavior, who are condoning homosexual behavior by making them realize that by doing so, they are also condoning adultery, fornication, bestiality, and polygamy."

Colonel Ronald Ray, who served in the Department of Defense under President Reagan, declared without qualification that "the problem is the church." Dobson's man, John Eldredge, called the average church member "a sheep without a shepherd who knows that homosexuality is wrong but doesn't know why and doesn't know how to make a compelling argument against it." And Robert Skolrood, then president of the National Legal Foundation, warned the delegates to "be careful of clergy. Our pastors don't know anything, and most of them are wimps. You've got to get out there and we've got to get these issues before the people." Eldredge summarized this new phase in the fundamentalist campaign against lesbian and gay Americans.

> There is tremendous confusion within the church on the basis of moral issues. The critical thing to understand is that most pastors are terrified that this issue in particular will split their church. We need to be sympathetic and understanding of their concerns and help them help us without drawing them personally into controversies they don't want to be a part of...I think there are ways to do that. I think this is a lay movement, for example. I don't think it's a clergy movement because of the other current reality. We need to draw the laity out of the churches into more or less community coalitions. That's why we need independent groups like Colorado for Family Values that are not denominationally oriented, that are not necessarily even church based, can draw the committed laity together and provide them a vehicle for involvement without sacrificing the priest or pastor or the board of elders.

The local fundamentalist Christian leaders summoned to this meeting in the Rocky Mountains were local Christian activists who were drawn, in Eldredge's words, from the laity "out of the churches into more or less community coalitions." It is important to note early on that these community coalitions—organized around the fundamentalist Christian agenda—have become de facto churches for their members. The Glen Eyrie delegates represented local congregations in the new "denominations" being organized and presided over by fundamentalist Christian celebrities with strong national voices. There were delegates from Beverly LaHaye's Concerned Women for America, Pat Robertson's Christian Coalition, Gary

Bauer's Family Research Council, Lou Sheldon's Traditional Values Coalition, Don Wildmon's American Family Association, Howard Phillips's Conservative Caucus, James Dobson's Focus on the Family, Peter LaBarbera's Accuracy in Media, Paul Cameron's Family Research Institute and Exodus, the umbrella organization representing local ex-gay ministries springing up across the country.

Other delegates represented a fascinating diversity of fundamentalist Christian organizations all working in their various ways to "make this a Christian nation once again" (and especially to fight the "homosexual agenda"). For example, New Mexico's Warriors Not Wimps for Jesus was there alongside Texas-based Truth before Consequences and Mothers Against Bad Government. The Kansas State Education Watch was even accompanied by a state representative, Darlene Cornfield.

There is a moment in Sir Richard Attenborough's *Gandhi* that haunts me when I think of Christian leaders holding secret meetings to disenfranchise lesbian and gay Americans (or to do anything else, for that matter). Gandhi stands before a crowd of angry South Africans who have been humiliated by another oppressive law. There are four white policemen sitting in the front row, obviously there to learn how Gandhi plans to resist their injustice. "I welcome you," Gandhi says to the crowd, "all of you." With that he looks down at the policemen and adds, "We have no secrets."

Glen Eyrie was a secret session of fundamentalist Christian laymen and women representing local congregations of this new fundamentalist Christian church. The primary goal of their meeting was to end the political rights of lesbian and gay Americans, but these same fundamentalist activists were hard at work turning their traditional churches against us, as well.

Long before 1994, the fundamentalist activists who maintained their membership in local congregations of the mainline denominations had begun their efforts to take control of those denominations, to elect fundamentalists like themselves into every important leadership position in those denominations, and thus to guarantee that those denominations would turn against us, as well.

For example, in 1993, just one year before Glen Eyrie, Diane Knippers became president of the Institute for Religion and Democracy. Their mission statement describes the IRD as "...an ecumenical alliance of U.S. Christians working to reform their churches' social witness, in accord with biblical and historic Christian teaching." In fact, this turned out to be just one more veiled call to action by fundamentalist Christian leaders against the "rising power of homosexuals within our churches."

The IRD mission statement says it this way: "They [the mainline Christian denominations] have turned toward political agendas mandated neither by Scripture nor by Christian tradition. They have thrown themselves into multiple, often leftist crusades—radical forms of feminism, environmentalism, pacifism, multi-culturalism, revolutionary socialism, sexual liberation and so forth." The IRD promises its members to be "...a watchdog on behalf of church members. On their behalf, we monitor the statements of church leaders and the programs of church agencies."

In fact, during the next dozen years, the IRD did far more than monitor. Mrs. Knipper and her colleagues on the religious right raised and spent tens of millions of dollars to stop the United Methodist, the Presbyterian, and the Episcopal churches from granting gays and lesbians the rights of ordination and marriage and to prevent any vote that would recognize us in any way as legitimate members of the Christian church.

In every denomination, similar fundamentalist-based organizations were organized and generously funded. With names like Presbyterians for Renewal and the United Methodist

Confessing Movement, these organizations used every available medium—films, videotapes, DVDs, books, magazines, brochures, colorful Web sites, and direct letter appeals especially to convention delegates where important votes would take place—to turn the minds and hearts of their fellow Protestants and Catholics against gay and lesbian Americans.

Organizing these antigay political and religious forces was carefully orchestrated from the top by leaders of these new fundamentalist "denominations"—you might call them bishops of the new fundamentalist churches. For at least a dozen years before Glen Eyrie, these powerful fundamentalist leaders had also been holding secret meetings (in something like a fundamentalist council of churches) to coordinate their efforts to "purify" (exert their will over) church and state alike.

This rare convergence of powerful fundamentalists to coordinate the religious war they were waging against secular culture began in 1981 with the creation of a Council on National Policy. The CNP, still powerfully active, is concerned about creating and implementing the overall fundamentalist strategy for "reclaiming the nation for Christ." The Arlington Group, founded in June 2003 in a condo in Arlington, Virginia, now represents at least seventy national fundamentalist Christian organizations and their allies who meet regularly in Washington, D.C., primarily (at least at this moment) to defeat the "homosexual agenda" and to superimpose their antigay agenda on the U.S. Constitution through their bogus "Save Marriage Amendment."

It must have dawned quickly on the fifty-five delegates gathered at Glen Eyrie that they were being recognized as equal partners in the war their gurus were waging against homosexuality and homosexuals. No longer would this war be primarily in the hands of Dobson broadcasting daily his antigay rhetoric to tens of millions of Americans, or Robertson and

Falwell spreading antigay propaganda through their satellite and cable television networks. The national superstars were admitting that they couldn't succeed at defeating the "gay agenda" and superimposing their absolute moral values on the nation without organizing a grassroots movement that would include every city, town, and village in America.

"THE GAY AGENDA"

John Eldredge, then director of seminars and research in the Public Policy Division of James Dobson's Focus on the Family, was the first speaker at the Glen Eyrie Conference. He expressed the ultimate short-term goal for their meeting. "Obviously," he began, "over the short term we are trying to roll back the militant gay agenda wherever and however it manifests itself."

When I first heard the term "gay agenda" or "militant gay agenda," I laughed it off as another invention by fundamentalist Christians. It was fairly obvious from my first days as an activist that a roomful of gay men and women could hardly agree on three toppings for a deep-dish pizza, let alone lay out an agenda to "destroy the nation's values." Then I discovered that our adversaries were basing their fears on an actual "Homosexual Agenda" written in 1987 by Michael Swift, a gifted gay writer with a flair for satire.

In reality, Swift's angry (but very clever) article was a caricature, a lampoon, a satire of the ridiculous accusations being made against us by leaders on the religious and political right. To demonstrate the absurdity of those charges, and to call gays to take positive actions against them, Swift wrote a satirical essay portraying what a homosexual agenda would look like if homosexuals actually did all the disgusting things they say we do. In 1987, Swift's send-up of the fundamentalists' antigay rhetoric appeared in the *Gay Community News*, a popular gay paper that loves to push the limits of political satire. Unfortunately, leaders on the religious right didn't understand satire (or consciously misused this satiric essay in their campaign against us).

In February 1987, Swift's "Homosexual Agenda" was read into the *Congressional Record* by "a shocked, a very, very shocked" legislator: "We shall sodomize your sons…" the satire begins. "We shall seduce them in your schools…If you cry faggot, fairy, queer at us we will stab you in your cowardly hearts and defile your dead, puny bodies." Unfortunately, the *Congressional Record* omits the first twenty-five words of Swift's article. "This essay," he began, "is an outré, madness, a tragic, cruel fantasy, an eruption of inner rage on how the oppressed desperately dream of being the oppressor."[7]

From the day Swift's "Homosexual Agenda" was read into the *Congressional Record* (without its opening sentence or any explanation of its satiric nature), televangelists and radio preachers, conservative Protestant and Catholic clergy and laity, even presidents, legislators, governors, mayors, and school officials, misused this unfortunate satire to demonize homosexuals and to support the crazy idea that there is a "militant homosexual agenda." Swift's "Homosexual Agenda" is still being misused to create fear and loathing of lesbian and gay Americans.

There is no doubt that the men and women who created the Glen Eyrie Protocol were sincere. Taking on homosexuality and homosexuals was not just a way to raise funds and mobilize volunteers. Those Christian fundamentalists really believed that eliminating homosexuality was a battle between light and darkness, good and evil.

Not knowing or not caring that his words were being recorded, one plenary speaker began his description of the "gay threat" with these words. "I think the gay agenda—and

I would not say this as frankly as I will now in other cultural contexts...I think the gay agenda has all the elements of that which is truly deceptive at every turn...It deceives those who are drawn into it. It presents an extraordinarily deceptive face to the public at large, one of the primary marks of something that is truly evil. And while it is offering all the pleasures and liberties of happiness, autonomy, and personal fulfillment, it is destroying the souls and the lives of those who embrace it... And," he added, "homosexuality has a corrosive effect on the society that endorses it explicitly or even implicitly."

Ronald Ray, a Reagan Defense Department appointee and another keynote speaker at Glen Eyrie, went even further. "We have domestic enemies," Ray said, referring directly to homosexual Americans. To enthusiastic applause, Ray illustrated the danger of this "homosexual threat to the nation" with Lincoln's words spoken in Springfield, Illinois, in January 1837:

At what point then is the approach of danger to be expected? I answer if it ever reaches, it must spring up from among us. It cannot come from abroad. If destruction be our lot, we ourselves must be its author and finisher. As a nation of free men, we must live through all time or die of suicide.*

Ray praised George Washington for his strict enforcement of the prohibitions against sodomy inherited from laws enacted by colonists in Virginia and Massachusetts. He explained that George Washington "...approved the termination, the radical termination of a Lieutenant in the Continental Army who attempted sodomy with an enlisted man and lied about it. In the military we call it drumming out." he added, "which is a public

*Abraham Lincoln (age twenty-eight), in Lyceum Address, January 27, 1838, before the Young Men's Lyceum of Springfield, Illinois.

military display of abhorrence with the entire company turning their backs on the guilty party who has been stripped of all rank, badge and identity as an American soldier."

Glen Eyrie conferees agreed that seeing the sodomy laws returned and enforced in all fifty states was one of the first steps necessary for this "radical termination" of homosexual rights (if not the "radical termination" of homosexuals). Those sodomy laws that traveled with the Pilgrims and the Puritans from England were based on the "buggery law" passed by the English Parliament in 1533 during the reign of Henry VIII. The Parliament defined "buggery" as "the Detestable and Abominable Sin of Buggery with Mankind, or Beast, which is contrary to the very light of Nature..." But this religion-based violence against homosexuals didn't begin with our Protestant forefathers.

Gay historian David Bianco reminds us that historically, up until 1533 "the Roman Catholic Church had been responsible for judging and meting out punishment for sodomy, which was considered a mortal sin."[8] When Henry VIII took power over the Church of England he secularized the sodomy laws but continued citing biblical passages to make the sin of sodomy also a crime punishable in the courts by hanging.

In 1656, a book of suggested *Lawes for Government in New England* was published in London quoting the same biblical passages that the Vatican and later the "Reformation Parliament" of King Henry VIII used to criminalize sexual acts between men and between women:

> If any man lyeth with mankinde, as a man lyeth with a woman, both of them have Committed abomination, they both shall surely be put to death. Levit. 20. 13. And if any woman change the naturall use, into that which is against nature, as Rom. 1. 26. she shall be liable to that same Sentence...

Three hundred and thirty-eight years later, Glen Eyrie delegates were still quoting those ancient texts to support the war they were waging against us...only this time they were quoting from the King James "authorized" version of the Bible.

> If a man also lie with mankind, as he lieth with a woman, both of them have committed an abomination: they shall surely be put to death, (Lev. 20:13)." And if "... their women did change the natural use into that which is against nature, (Romans 1:26)" she will be liable to that same sentence.

It is ironic that today's fundamentalist Christians use the King James Version to build their case against us when historians have no doubt that King James himself was a rather flaming homosexual. In 1603 when he was crowned King of England, elite and educated members of the royal court were mocking James with this Latin play on words: *"Rex fuit Elizabeth: nunc est regina Jacobus."* (Elizabeth was King: Now James is Queen.)[9]

As a teenager, King James's love for the young Earl of Lennox caused the Royal Court to force Lennox to flee England under the threat of death. King James I went on to appoint his page boy, Robert Carr, the Earl of Somerset, and his royal cupbearer, George Villiers, the Duke of Buckingham. In one of his many love letters to Buckingham, King James wrote, "I desire only to live in the world for your sake, and I had rather live banished in any part of the world with you, than live a sorrowful widow-life without you. And so God bless you, my sweet child and wife, and grant that ye may ever be a comfort to your dear dad and husband." King James explained his relationship to Buckingham in eight short words: "Jesus had his John. I have my George."[10]

Buckingham was removed from power upon the death of

King James I in 1625 and was given command of a military unit fighting the French. He failed miserably, and during a 1628 visit to Portsmouth to help calm his angry troops, Buckingham was murdered by John Felton, a soldier under Buckingham's command who saw King James's lover as "the antichrist." (Sound familiar?) Buckingham, once the King's lover, is buried in the Henry VII Chapel of Westminster Abby, until then reserved for the remains of royalty alone. He lies near the body of his beloved James I. On a tablet facing Buckingham's tomb is a Latin inscription describing James's lifelong lover as "THE Enigma of the World."[11]

Not until four years after the Glen Eyrie Conference did King James's sexual orientation become controversial among fundamentalist Christians. In 1998, fundamentalist organizations including the Family Research Council, the Christian Coalition, and Americans for Truth about Homosexuality asked their supporters to quit using the King James Bible because historical research made it clear that James I of England was "indisputably gay." At a press conference that year, Gary Bauer, a presidential candidate and the founding executive director of the Family Research Council, explained, "I feel uncomfortable that good Christians all over America, and indeed the world, are using a document commissioned by a homosexual. Anything that has been commissioned by a homosexual has obviously been tainted in some way."[12]

Whatever version of the Bible you prefer (if any), we still can't blame the King James Bible or the Protestants who used it. The Roman Catholic Church, the largest of all Christian denominations with approximately one billion adherents worldwide, is without doubt the original source of suffering for gay and lesbian people. The election of Pope Benedict XVI will only make things worse. Claude Summers, professor emeritus in the humanities and English at the University of Michigan—

Dearborn, summarizes the case against Roman Catholicism for its role in turning "the Western world" against us.

> Through its interpretation of biblical passages and its embrace of a "natural law" theology, that heavily influenced the secular laws of most of the Western world, the Church is deeply implicated in and has sometimes actively promoted the brutal persecution of sexually variant people throughout the Christian era. These persecutions range from the torture and execution of "sodomites" during the Middle Ages and the early modern period to the imprisonment of thousands of homosexuals on charges of "crimes against nature" in the nineteenth and twentieth centuries, to say nothing of the guilt, alienation, and despair (sometimes leading to suicide) that millions of glbtq [gay, lesbian, bisexual, transgender, and queer] people have felt as the result of the Church's pronouncements.[13]

In other words, the religious teachings that made same-sex intimacy a "sin" originated in the Vatican in the Middle Ages, became a crime in England in 1533 under Henry VIII, and migrated to the "new world" with the religious settlers who founded the first American colonies. However, in this "new world," there were no recorded executions for sodomy until 1624.

The first gay person to be executed in the Americas was Richard Cornish, a ship's captain accused of sexually assaulting his indentured servant, William Cowse. The charge, as chronicled in the minutes of the Virginia court, sounds today like a case of sexual harassment—Cornish wanted to have sex with Cowse, who refused and then was given extra work by Captain Cornish. On the basis of the testimony of another crew member who overheard Cornish proposition Cowse, Cornish was tried and hanged. Two men who publicly objected to the execution as unjust were pilloried and had their ears cut off for questioning the religious authorities. I wonder if today's fundamentalist Christians remember this shameful history when they call for a return to our Puritan roots.[14]

Gay historians have found approximately twenty recorded cases of sodomy charges being brought against individual male colonists from 1624 to 1740 and just four resulted in the death penalty. We can take some comfort from this small number, for it illustrates conclusively that our founding fathers were not preoccupied with sodomites or with arresting and prosecuting those who participated in same-sex intimacy.[15]

Our forefathers were even less eager to punish women for same-sex acts. In a case of "lewd behavior...upon a bed" between two women in Plymouth, Massachusetts, both women were merely given a warning. Using the Bible as their authority, the New Haven colony was the only colony to threaten the death penalty for "filthiness" between women, but there are no court records that this sentence was ever carried out.

And so that my transgender friends don't feel left out, in 1629, when Thomas Hall (also known as Thomasine Hall) was arrested at Jamestown for dressing as a woman to have sex with men, the Virginia courts punished Hall by requiring she wear both men's and women's clothing, not much of a penalty for one who preferred cross-dressing in the first place.[16]

In 1777, Thomas Jefferson proposed a new law code for the people of Virginia that replaced the death penalty for homosexual acts with the castration of the male offender. Modern males might find no consolation in Jefferson's proposition any more than modern females will find relief in Jefferson's suggestion that women who committed same-sex acts have a telltale hole bored in their nose. However horrible this new option seems, we can find consolation that even by suggesting the Bible-based penalty of death be replaced, he was standing firmly against centuries of Roman Catholic, Anglican, and Protestant tradition.[17]

After the American Revolution, separation of church and state became one of the founding principles of the new republic. The death punishment for sodomy based on biblical law was gradually reduced to jail time and loss of property. Until 1961, all fifty states had laws making sodomy an illegal act. In 1994, when those fundamentalist Christians gathered in their Glen Eyrie castle, thirteen states still had sodomy laws in place and the U.S. Supreme Court's 1986 *Bowers v. Hardwick* still upheld the constitutionality of those laws. And the fifty-six fundamentalist activists were determined to outlaw sodomy in every state. Happily, they failed (at least for now).

Seventeen years later, June 26, 2003, in *Lawrence v. Texas*, the Supreme Court reversed itself. By giving homosexual and heterosexual adults "the right to engage in private consensual sexual activities, even if society generally disapproves of the behavior," the court effectively struck down the sodomy laws. As though he were speaking directly to the fundamentalist Christians waging war against us, Justice Kennedy, writing for the majority, apologized for the court's error in its 1986 decision to uphold the sodomy laws. He stated that Bowers's "continuance as precedent demeans the lives of homosexual persons…[That decision] was not correct when it was decided, and it is not correct today. It ought not to remain binding precedent. *Bowers v. Hardwick* should be and now is overruled."[18]

And though we celebrated the demise of those ancient sodomy laws, it is important to remember that just one wrong appointment of a fundamentalist Christian jurist to the Supreme Court could cause the court to reverse itself again. A very slight shift of the court's makeup could lead to the recriminalization of homosexual behavior in private between consenting adults. The court might even then apologize to the American people for ruling that homosexuals have equal rights.[19] And the delegates to Glen Eyrie and the millions of Americans they represent have gained enough political power to see that happen. As I write this, George W. Bush has presented to the Senate for confirmation a candidate to fill the seat of Justice Sandra Day O'Connor after first getting approval from fundamentalist Christian leaders who sponsored that 1994 secret meeting in Glen Eyrie.

Those fifty-five fundamentalist leaders met secretly in Glen Eyrie to create a strategy for eliminating the threat that lesbian and gay Americans present to society's very foundation. The transcripts of that conference—especially the first keynote address by Dobson's representative, John Eldredge—reveal much about their plan to deny us our rights, end our influence, drive us back into the closet, or worse. And a dozen years later, it is becoming more and more apparent that with all the advances we have made, step-by-step their goals are being reached.

FIVE

THE GLEN EYRIE PROTOCOL:
HOW THE WAR WILL BE WAGED

*J*ohn Eldredge, the keynote strategist from Focus on the Family, explained to the local activists assembled in the castle at Glen Eyrie that the American people must be convinced of three basic truths before this war against homosexuality and homosexuals could be won:

First, they had to show "why heterosexuality is best for individuals and society" (inferring that homosexuality was destructive to the individual and to the state).

Second, they had to prove that homosexuality is NOT "immutable" (inferring that homosexuality is a choice and that homosexuals can be changed).

Third, they had to demonstrate "why society needs to make certain demands on people sexually" (inferring that the government might be influenced to use its power to enforce fundamentalist Christian morality on homosexual Americans).

GOAL 1:
PROVE TO THE AMERICAN PEOPLE THAT
"...HETEROSEXUALITY IS BEST FOR INDIVIDUALS
AND SOCIETY"

Mr. Eldredge made it very clear that to prove his first truth—that heterosexuality is best for individuals and society—they must support their case "...by what Americans consider to be gospel truth that is empirical science." He called scientists "the new priests of modern culture" and advised the Glen Eyrie conferees to use scientific not biblical data to persuade the American people that homosexuality was a destructive force in the lives of individuals and the nation.

It is particularly interesting that John Eldredge and the other keynote speakers seldom referred to the Bible in building their antihomosexual case. Quite to the contrary, they advised against using it. Eldredge referred instead to "the now infamous statement of Coach Bill McCartney that 'homosexuality is an abomination before God.'" During the debate over Colorado's Prop 2, McCartney, the former University of Colorado football coach who founded Promise Keepers, supported his case against gay rights by quoting that famous passage from Leviticus 20. "If Colorado for Family Values had made that the theme of their [Prop 2] campaign," Eldredge warned, "I doubt that they would have succeeded..." He then advised that while quoting the Bible "...may resonate with a religious sector of the American public, it flies against the rest of these cultural presuppositions, which a number of religious people also hold to be true."[1]

It is also interesting to note that Eldredge promised to make a positive presentation— "why heterosexuality is best" —and then he and the other speakers focused entirely on the negative— "why homosexuality destroys lives and ruins nations." They never speak of the joys of heterosexuality. They just blast homosexuals over and over again. Eldredge leads the way. To support his first point that heterosexuality is "best for individuals and society," Eldredge reads from what he describes as "a letter from a young man, raised in a solid home, writing to his family to explain why he is homosexual and dying of AIDS."

"Solid family" very likely means fundamentalist Christian family. The young gay man is reaching out to his parents. If he is "dying of AIDS," why aren't they with him? And why does he have to explain to his mom and dad who he is and why he's ill? We can only guess, but if his parents are fundamentalist Christians who shared their son's letter with Focus on the Family, then they are victims of Dobson's misinformation about homosexuality and homosexuals.

In all probability they loved their son but have condemned his "lifestyle" and now feel that God must be punishing him for his sinfulness and them for their failure to "raise him right." Rather than accepting their son and loving him without qualification, these poor parents had to love their son with conditions. Imagine the wall that raises between them. Most gay people don't have to imagine it. We have stood on the other side of that wall shouting for somebody to hear us, but the ignorance drowns us out. James Dobson and his crew should feel shame and guilt for raising that wall between parents and their children all across America. Here's the first excerpt from the letter that Eldredge read at Glen Eyrie:

> *Dad and Mom, the truth is science is just now on the threshold to discover a fact that millions of us already know: that the sexual orientation of an individual is determined biologically. It is not a choice I made. Perhaps that which will be all the more painful to you, Mom and Dad, is I can offer no apology for being gay. It was not a choice. It was how I was created.*

After reading those words, Eldredge comments: "Science is not even in the front yard of providing near absolute proof, let alone on the threshold. But most people don't know that."

First of all, Eldredge, Dobson, and his entire Focus on the Family crew are ignorant about sexual orientation and have never seriously considered the mass of evidence to prove the young man's point. Instead, they are using this poor kid's death to pass on that ignorance one last time to his parents and the world.

Second, who cares where science is? I'm afraid that if they ever find the gay gene, they'll do something to abort it. Like the young man says, "millions of us already know" that our sexual orientation is NOT a choice. Why do those parents trust Dobson and refuse to trust their own son? Why do fundamentalist Christians continue this "there is no homosexual gene" routine? How many creative, courageous, committed gay people do they have to meet before truth will dawn in their brains? How can parents be so brainwashed by untruth that they can ignore the truth and condemn and reject their own children? How soon will the Christian community help people to embrace their gay child and say: "You are not sick or sinful. You are one of God's children. We love you and accept you without qualification!"

Third, it appears that the young man's parents are asking for their son to apologize for who he is and how he contracted HIV. I will never forget a conversation I had with a ghostwriting client appointed by President Reagan to be on his first AIDS Commission. I asked my friend, one of the kindest men I know, why with all his millions he hadn't contributed anything to HIV/AIDS research or services.

"I've met hundreds of men with AIDS," he answered, "and not one of them has apologized for what he did to contract this disease. Why should I contribute when they aren't even sorry?"

I couldn't believe it. The man who had just survived bypass

surgery to clean up the gunk in his coronary arteries had not apologized for his "lifestyle" or the contribution he had made to his illness, but he wanted the men with AIDS to apologize before he would help them in any way. Since when was it necessary to apologize for an illness? Answer: Since Dobson and the others started calling homosexual "practice" a sin. In fact, if they would recognize homosexual intimacy as another of God's loving gifts, they would be well on their way to stopping this plague, at least among gay men. When we are ashamed of our sexuality and have to "get it" on the side, we take terrible, desperate risks. Celebrate our relationships. Grant us the rights and protections of marriage. Honor our families. And until you do, accept your part in the blame for the consequences of dangerous sexual behaviors.

Eldredge read one other paragraph from the young man's letter: "One final thought, Mom and Dad. In spite of everything in this letter, please know that my life has not been difficult. It's been very rewarding, and I could not imagine myself happier."

Eldredge can't believe that a homosexual "dying from AIDS" can see life as rewarding, let alone be happy.

Apparently, that young man has managed to overcome the torrent of misinformation about homosexuality. Apparently he has accepted himself and even forgiven the Christian church and American society for the lies they told him. He may not have gotten unconditional love from his parents, but because he said earlier that he had been "created," I am guessing that somehow he knows that his Creator loves him unconditionally and that makes all the difference. I hope that young man is alive and well somewhere, that he conquered the virus or is at peace while living with it. I want to throw my arms around him and tell him how special he is. I just hope that his parents learned that in time.

So Eldredge begins his demonstration of "empirical data"

to prove heterosexuality is best with this letter from a young man dying with AIDS. He offers no other examples. Instead, he encourages them not to be overtaken by evil, but to overcome evil with good. He has no "empirical data" that heterosexuality is best for the individual and society, so he skips to his second point.

Unfortunately, conference planners had invited Paul Cameron, the worst possible source of "empirical data," to show "scientifically" why heterosexuality is "best." Cameron has spent his lifetime creating false and misleading data about homosexuality and homosexuals that to this day are the primary "empirical data" being used against us.[2]

Apparently not one of the Glen Eyrie delegates noticed (or perhaps no one cared) that more than ten years previously, on December 2, 1983, Paul Cameron was officially dropped from membership in the American Psychological Association, at that time representing sixty thousand professional psychologists in the United States and Canada, for violating the "Preamble to the Ethical Principles of Psychologists."[3] On October 19, 1984, the Nebraska Psychological Association formally disassociated itself "from the representations and interpretations of scientific literature" offered by Dr. Paul Cameron "in his writings and public statements on sexuality."[4] And in August 1986, the American Sociological Association "officially and publicly states that Paul Cameron is not a sociologist and condemns his consistent misrepresentation of sociological research."[5]

Twice, Paul Cameron is mentioned in the autobiography of Dr. C. Everett Koop, President Reagan's Surgeon General and a committed evangelical Christian. Koop describes Cameron as "one of the country's most outspoken anti-homosexuals" who "perpetuated a number of myths about AIDS transmission and called for unnecessary quarantine and testing." Koop also recalls being surrounded by picketers "led by anti-homosexual

Paul Cameron, who were shouting obscenities as they milled around carrying placards: 'Quarantine Manhattan Island,' 'Burn Koop,' and other encouraging messages."[6]

"The Gay Agenda," a videotape that misled millions of Americans in the late 1980s, used Paul Cameron's discredited research to demean, dehumanize, and demonize gay Americans. Produced by televangelists Ty and Jeannette Beeson's Antelope Valley Springs of Life Ministries, copies of the video were given to each Glen Eyrie delegate. During the year before, an estimated ten thousand copies of the video, featuring Paul Cameron's outlandish antigay diatribes, had been distributed to voters in Colorado and Oregon in time to influence voting on antigay initiatives that were on the ballots in those states. According to Bill Horn, video producer for the Antelope Valley Springs of Life Ministries, exit polls in Oregon showed that 70 percent of "yes" voters said they were influenced by the video featuring Cameron's distorted data.[7]

According to Horn, in December 1993, Marine Commandant General Carl E. Mundy received a copy of "The Gay Agenda." "After viewing it," the general wrote in a letter to Representative Pat Schroeder, "I reproduced copies for each of my fellow service chiefs, the chairman and the vice chairman of the Joint Chiefs of Staff. It appears to be extreme, but its message is vivid and, I believe, warrants a factual assessment."[8]

All of Paul Cameron's data are extreme (to say the very least), but the marine commandment didn't take the time to see if they were true before widely circulating "The Gay Agenda" through his chain of command. Like General Mundy, millions of fundamentalist Christians still believe Cameron's data when they hear it parroted by their clergy or their favorite media guru even though the scientific community has clearly labeled Cameron's data false, contrived, inadequately supported, and tragically misleading.

For example, in his booklet *The Medical Consequences* of *What Homosexuals Do*, Cameron claims *quite falsely* that gays average somewhere between 106 and 1,105 different partners a year, that 80 percent of those interviewed admit to ingesting a medically significant amount of feces, and more than 25 percent admit to drinking or being splashed with urine.[9]

In his booklet *Child Molestation and Homosexuality*, Cameron claims *quite falsely* that homosexuals are responsible for one-third of all child molestations, and a fifth to a third of surveyed gays admitted to child molestation.[10]

In Cameron's *What Causes Homosexual Desire and Can It Be Changed?*, he describes *quite falsely* the causes of homosexuality as: "a dominant, possessive, or rejecting mother; an absent, distant, or rejecting father;...the lack of a religious home environment;...divorce...parents who model unconventional sex roles; and...condoning homosexuality as a legitimate lifestyle—welcoming homosexuals (e.g., co-workers, friends) into the family circle"[11]

And in Cameron's most recent booklet, *Same Sex Marriage: Til Death Do Us Part?*, the author claims again *quite falsely* that "homosexual coupling undermines its participants' health, has the highest rate of domestic violence, shortens life, and is a poor environment in which to raise children."[12]

When professional mental and physical health organizations representing more than 1.5 million psychologists, psychiatrists, family counselors, scientists, and professors at prestigious academic and research institutions refute this kind of antihomosexual propaganda, why are my Christian sisters and brothers so easily deceived? I discovered at least one answer while researching a film/book documentary on Jim Jones and the Jonestown tragedy in Guyana. I spent six months with the survivors of that tragedy whose family and friends came home in body bags. The almost one thousand people who drank

Kool-Aid laced with cyanide and died in the jungles of South America were people just like you and me. Unfortunately, they trusted their pastor too much. Even when our religious leaders are totally trustworthy, our worship practices make us all the more vulnerable to deception, especially during stressful times.

Congregants sit in rows facing forward with no opportunity to respond to the authority figures who lead them. Pastors speak almost ex cathedra with hardly any fear of being questioned, let alone contradicted. Is it blind trust or just not caring that makes the annual congregational meeting (when budgets are discussed and goals are decided) the lowest-attended meeting of the year? How many of the millions who send in donations ever check to see if televangelists like Falwell, D. James Kennedy, and Charles Stanley or fundamentalist radio gurus like James Dobson, Chuck Colson, and Bob Enyart are telling the truth, let alone spending our donations wisely?

John Eldredge, Dobson's man at Glen Eyrie, advised the delegates to use empirical data (scientific evidence) to prove to America that heterosexuality was good and homosexuality was bad. And those delegates turned to Dr. Paul Cameron without questioning his credibility, let alone testing his so-called empirical data that still flows like toxic waste from Cameron's Family Research Institute polluting the national discourse and poisoning hearts and minds against us.

GOAL II
PROVE TO THE AMERICAN PEOPLE THAT "...HOMOSEXUALITY IS NOT IMMUTABLE"

It isn't enough to prove that heterosexuality is good and homosexuality bad. Eldredge explained that it is equally important to convince Americans that homosexuality is NOT "immutable" (consequently that homosexuality is a choice and that homosexuals can be changed). In his keynote, Robert Skolrood places the issue of immutability at the top of the list. "The first problem we have to deal with legally," he warned them, "is that most homosexuals and their heterosexual supporters argue that homosexuality is an inborn condition and furthermore it is no less valid than heterosexuality. As a result they maintain that to discriminate against a person because of sexual orientation is the moral equivalent of discrimination on the basis of color or religion. They call that just plain bigotry."

Both men blamed the media for leading a majority of the American people to believe that homosexuals are "born gay." These reporters, Eldredge said, "who have latched on to a couple of those [recent scientific] stories have spun them in favor of the immutability of homosexual orientation." During the years leading up to the Glen Eyrie Conference, scientists were announcing all kinds of exciting but partial answers to the question "What happens differently in the development of a homosexual person from the development of a heterosexual person that causes that person to be gay?"

At the time of Glen Eyrie, the nature-versus-nurture debate had grown intense. Theories of biological and nonbiological causation were tested. The influence of hormonal mechanisms and brain mechanisms were studied as was the possibility that stress experienced by the fetus during pregnancy was the causative agent. Scientists compared the sexual orientation of siblings, especially twins, trying to determine if there was a genetic influence on sexual orientation. Hearing acuity, fingerprints, the sense of smell, left-handedness, even gay rams all got into the act.

The media were having a field day as the scientific community edged closer and closer to solving the mystery of sexual orientation, and the fundamentalist Christians at Glen Eyrie were instructed to counter each new discovery with their own "empirical data" declaring homosexuality a sickness that could and should be cured. The primary source of data, then and now, proving that gays can become ex-gays, is the National Association of Research and Therapy of Homosexuality.

Less than two years before Glen Eyrie, three Christian psychologists, Charles Socarides, Benjamin Kaufman, and Joseph Nicolosi, founded NARTH, dedicated "to the research, therapy, and *prevention* of homosexuality." At the time of Glen Eyrie there were only a handful of well-meaning people involved in NARTH, but in 2005 the organization claimed to have more than one thousand members, including "psychoanalysts, psychoanalytically-informed psychologists, certified social workers, and other behavioral scientists, as well as laymen in fields such as law, religion, and education."

Like Cameron, the men and women of NARTH begin their research, their therapy, and their efforts to "prevent" homosexuality with the assumption that homosexuality is a pathology to be changed or at least controlled through "reparative" therapies of one kind or another. At this moment, Joseph Nicolosi serves as president of NARTH. The current vice president is Dr. Jerry Harris, director of LDS (Mormon) Family Services and an adjunct professor at Brigham Young University. All it takes is a quick glance at the Suicide Memorial in the Book of Remembrance on the Affirmation Web page to realize that the antigay teachings of the Mormon Church and especially the treatment of gay students at BYU may be responsible directly and indirectly for the death by suicide of more gay men than any other religious institution in the country.[13]

NARTH's official response to more than a century of research into the causes of sexual orientation can be summarized by the statement on their Web site: "the disorder is characterized by a constellation of symptoms, including excessive clinging to the mother during early childhood, a sense that one's masculinity is defective and powerful feelings of guilt, shame and inferiority beginning in adolescence."[14]

NARTH offers a large number of articles contradicting the "born that way" theory, reviewing and rebutting the latest scientific research on sexual orientation (that threatens in any way their conviction that homosexuality is a pathology), offering information and assistance to parents, pastors, school board officials, mayors, governors, and state and national legislators, attacking statements against reparative therapy by the major emotional health organizations, telling the stories of men and women who have been "delivered" from their "homosexual lifestyle," and linking to the growing number of local and national ex-gay organizations springing up across the country that offer "deliverance from homosexuality" promised by the people of NARTH.

Courage is the Roman Catholic's ex-gay organization ministering to those with same-sex attractions. "By developing an interior life of chastity, which is the universal call to all Christians, one can move beyond the confines of the homosexual identity to a more complete one in Christ."

The Mormons have Evergreen International, "the most complete resource for Latter-Day Saints who experience same-sex attraction...who want to diminish their attractions and overcome homosexual behavior..."

The Orthodox Jews have JONAH, "a non-profit international organization dedicated to educating the world-wide Jewish community about the prevention, intervention, and healing of the underlying issues causing same-sex attractions...."

Our transgender sisters and brothers are victims of misinformation distributed by Gender Benders (nonreligious) and Reality Resources (religious), exposing "...the many discrepancies and outright blatant lies/fantasies promoted by the transgender population...Transsexuality," they insist, "is not the result of a genetic or hormonal flaw, but an emotional disorder, which can be corrected with proper treatment and education."[15]

Exodus (primarily an Evangelical/Fundamentalist ministry) "...promotes the message of 'Freedom from homosexuality through the power of Jesus Christ.'" Since 1976, Exodus has grown to include more than 120 local ministries in the USA and Canada...linked with other Exodus world regions outside of North America, totaling over 150 ex-gay ministries in 17 countries.

PFOX (Parents and Friends of Ex Gays and Gays), "supporting the right of homosexuals to choose change," is the fundamentalist Christian alternative to PFLAG (Parents, Family and Friends of Lesbians and Gays).[16] PFLAG, founded in 1973, has two hundred thousand members and supporters in more than five hundred affiliates in the United States who "celebrate diversity and envision a society that embraces everyone including those of diverse sexual orientations and gender identities."

PFOX, founded by fundamentalist Christians just four years after Glen Eyrie, now claims approximately forty-six chapters or supportive individuals in nineteen states and the District of Columbia providing "outreach, education, and public awareness in support of the ex-gay community and families touched by homosexuality." One line in the PFOX mission statement tells it all: "As responsible parents, we must seek the facts and love our children unconditionally without having to affirm their homosexual behavior."

PATH (Positive Alternatives to Homosexuality) is the nonprofit coalition uniting "all these organizations promising hope for homosexuals...helping people with unwanted same-sex attractions to realize their personal goals for change."

Although fundamentalists continue to use data from

Cameron's Family Research Institute and NARTH to reach their second goal, the rapidly growing ex-gay movement is the most powerful tool fundamentalist Christians have to convince Americans that homosexuality is NOT immutable. It is almost impossible to go a day without hearing another moving testimonial from an ex-gay who has been "delivered from the homosexual lifestyle."

On a regular basis, religious broadcasters feature ex-gay testimonials on their television and radio programs. Ex-gay speakers share their stories in churches, large and small, and in chapel services on Christian high-school and college campuses. Christian books, magazines, even full-page ads in newspapers across the United States feature pictures of former lesbians and gays who are celebrating "their new freedom in Christ." Now James Dobson's Love Won Out weekend conference program is taking the ex-gay message on the road to cities across America. Currently there is a PFOX campaign to fill billboards nationwide with the faces of beautiful young people and the words: "Ex Gays Prove That Change Is Possible." Even as I write this in late 2005, the Vatican has released a document approving for the priesthood ex gays who have been "free of homosexual tendencies for the past three years."[17]

If you recall, there were no clergy at the secret meeting in Glen Eyrie. In fact, keynote speakers denounced evangelical pastors for their silence on the homosexual issue: "Most of them are wimps" (Robert Skolrood). "The church is the problem" (Colonel Ray). "Pastors are terrified the issue will split their churches" (John Eldredge). "We need to hold them accountable" (Will Perkins). That was 1994. Twelve years later, the nation's clergy have joined the chorus of fundamentalist Christian voices caricaturing and condemning us from their pulpits across America. A 2003 survey by the Pew Forum on Religion and Public Life shows that those clergy voices are supporting the fundamentalist line that homosexuality is a sin, that gays and lesbians can change their orientation, and if they refuse to change and continue in their sin, their rights should be denied:[18]

Two-thirds of evangelical Protestants who attend church services at least once a month say their ministers speak out on homosexual issues, compared with only about half of Catholics (49%) and just a third of main-line Protestants (33%).

Compared with others who attend services where homosexuality is discussed, substantially more evangelicals (86%) say the message they are receiving is that homosexuality should be discouraged, not accepted and (76%) believe it is a sin to engage in homosexual behavior.

Similarly, evangelicals who hear sermons on this issue are much more apt than others to believe that gays and lesbians can change their sexual orientation and to view homosexuality as a threat to the country. Religiosity is clearly a factor in the recent rise in opposition to gay marriage. Overall, nearly six-in-ten Americans (59%) oppose gay marriage, up from 53% in July. But those with a high level of religious commitment now oppose gay marriage by more than six-to-one (80%-12%), a significant shift since July (71%-21%).

People who believe homosexuality is a choice, as opposed to a trait people are born with, are far more opposed to gay marriage, as are people who believe homosexuals can change.

We cannot know where it all will end, but Eldredge's third point suggests it might end badly.

GOAL III
PROVE TO THE AMERICAN PEOPLE THAT "...SOCIETY NEEDS TO MAKE CERTAIN DEMANDS ON PEOPLE SEXUALLY"

It's very difficult not to conclude from his third goal that John Eldredge is suggesting that sexual morality of fundamental Christians needs to be enforced by law. His first gentle example is a reference to the laws that help enforce heterosexual marriage. He points to the fact that marriage requires a license from the state. "We need to address the issue of why society needs to make certain demands on people sexually," he said. "Because our culture views pain as such a great evil, because culture is so pro-victim, and because sexual happiness is considered to be such a fundamental right, we need to answer the question why society will actually cause people sexual pain and by that I mean sexual restraint."[19]

There are two suggestions in this paragraph that raise alarm, because we don't know exactly how Eldredge and his fundamentalist Christian friends will apply them to our lives. What sexual demands would they like to make on homosexual people if they ever gained such power over us? And if we resisted their demands, what kind of "sexual pain" or "sexual restraint" do they have in mind?

Eldredge begins to lay down a legal foundation for condemning us when he attacks the "cultural norm" that "sexual happiness in not merely desirable but it is considered to be our right." He illustrates his point that sexual happiness is NOT a constitutional right by quoting out of context C. S. Lewis in an unnamed essay written forty years ago that "we have no right to happiness" by which he [C. S. Lewis] "...understood most people to define happiness as four bare legs in a bed."[20]

Eldredge also condemns the "American value of radical personal autonomy" and adds with a touch of sarcasm his disapproval of "absolute freedom, right to choose, freedom of choice, all that." Eldredge reviles that kind of thinking—"that we are free to do with our own lives whatever we want—because it leads to suicide, abortion, euthanasia," and he adds "the homosexual movement is milking this for all its worth."

"If feelings are our moral compass," Eldredge warns, "on political questions, on questions of fidelity, marriage, human sexuality, et cetera, then you can see why you add in the ingredients of personal autonomy, sexual fulfillment, the right to happiness, the commitment not to offend anyone, the high value of sensitivity, and thus you have the one last American value, which is tolerance."[21] Apparently "tolerance" is NOT a good thing for Eldredge, because he calls it "the explanation of why the homosexual movement has been able to make the ground it has."

Before Eldredge explained what restraints he has for gay Americans, he presented the Glen Eyrie conferees Fundamentalist Communications 101 in the following rather alarming directive: "We must never appear to be bigoted or mean spirited. To the extent we can control our public image we must never appear to be attempting to rob anyone of their Constitutional rights. We must be shrewd to build a consensus for our position by appealing to shared values and concerns, issues of fairness and justice. We grapple with restoring our country to its moral moorings. The absolute values that were stipulated by God are still absolute, and if we want to pursue life, liberty and happiness, we've got to have those absolute values."

Later in his keynote address, Eldredge shared two basic rules for fundamentalist Christian communicators: "We must avoid the very appearance of bigotry" and stay clear of any "overt appeal to biblical morality in the public square."

In their conference information packet, Glen Eyrie delegates found a single page describing what conference planners hoped would be the four "Foundational Principles," or four basic goals, the conferees would adopt for their local, regional, and statewide organizations. They would work together:

1. "to convince elected officials to take principled stands against pro-homosexual legislation."
2. "to eliminate government dollars/resources as a result of improper behavior brought on by their lifestyle (ex. AIDS)."
3. "to see spiritual revival."
4. "to strengthen the male/father image. The mom and dad family would be restored to such a place of prominence, with legal and cultural support, that homosexuality would be regarded as a sad pathology by implication. Most present sex education would be eliminated from schools, replaced by a marriage and family course in the higher grades which emphasizes abstinence as the only acceptable alternative to sex within marriage."[22]

It's only natural to wonder why the two-word phrase "spiritual revival" is included (#3) in a list calling elected officials to deny us our legal rights (#1), to discontinue desperately needed government funding (#2), and to demean our lives (#4). What could "spiritual revival" mean in such an antigay context?

I grew up attending "spiritual revivals" held by evangelists in week-long meetings at my local church, in tents at youth camp, and at crusades in coliseums. A "spiritual revival" has three parts: First, the preacher warns of sin and its consequence; second, he invites sinners to repent; third, he asks the sinner to walk down the aisle as a sign of genuine repentance. When the service ends and the sinner gets up from the altar or returns from the prayer room, family and friends are waiting. (During every invitation Billy Graham used to say, "Don't worry. If you've come by bus your friends will wait for you.")

It was true in the local church or at camp meetings, as well. The new convert was greeted with smiles, tears, and hugs all around. But if you had never walked that aisle, never knelt to seek God's forgiveness, never "received Christ as your Lord and Savior," you felt like an outcast. No one tried to make you feel that way. Your friends and family didn't reject you overtly, but you knew that you would never really be one of them until you had taken that step. "We'll be praying for you, son" meant "We love you, but we're worried about your soul." "We'll be praying for you, daughter" was a clear sign that until you "got right with God" you wouldn't really be right with your family or friends, either. People in the church knew who was saved and who wasn't saved and every revival became a kind of test that you passed or you failed in the eyes of God and in the eyes of "the people of God."

An e-mail I received from a thirty-three-year-old gay man in Ohio expressed it perfectly. "I have sat through many services," he begins, "under many top evangelists, in many different denominations only to learn again and again that I am evil and hell bound. I was actually at a service where an evangelist invited alcoholics, adulterers, drug addicts, and…LITTLE FAIRIES to come forward. I was horrified that he had spotted me."

I think "spiritual revival" was on that list for two reasons. First, the fundamentalist Christian leaders at Glen Eyrie were genuinely convinced that homosexuality is a sin with devastating consequences for the individual and the nation. The only way out of that sin is to confess it and be forgiven. Therefore, in this antihomosexual context, calling for "spiritual revival" is reminding these antigay activists to provide opportunities for "conversional" or "transformational" ex-gay therapy in their communities. But second, it is also a clear call to give lesbian and gay Americans one more (or is it one last?) chance to confess their sin, "get right with God," reject their homosexual "life style," or face the consequences.

At Glen Eyrie, the "short term" consequences for unrepentant homosexuals were made very clear by keynote speakers, conference leaders, and in lists drawn up by the delegates themselves. They would recruit, train, equip, and mobilize an army of fundamentalist Christian activists...to deny same-sex couples the rights, benefits, and protections of marriage, civil unions, or domestic partnerships;...to end all sex education classes that went beyond abstinence;...to stop government support of safe-sex and condom distribution programs;...to reduce if not eliminate government spending on HIV/AIDS research or services;...to prohibit homosexuals from adopting, co-parenting, or offering foster care to children;...to remove lesbian or gay teachers from public and private schools;...to defrock gays or lesbians in ministry;...to rescind all bills that include sexual orientation in hate-crime legislation or ban discrimination against homosexuals in housing, employment, and interstate commerce;...to support and enforce the ban on gays and lesbians in the military;...to reinstate and /or enforce the sodomy laws and through the sodomy laws to criminalize homosexual behavior;...and to use everything in their power to stop the homosexual's "pursuit of minority status, however that represents itself."[23]

While reading the Glen Eyrie transcripts, I was bothered that several keynote speakers described this rather exhausting list as "short-term goals." Even during their secret sessions at Glen Eyrie, not one person alluded to whatever "long-term goals" they might have for us. There are times I wonder if fundamentalist Christians have thought that far ahead. If these are their "short-term goals," what are their long-term goals for gay Americans? Is it possible that the extremists among them are discussing an ultimate solution behind the scenes? Could it be based on a literal reading of their inerrant Bible? Isn't it inconceivable that they would ever enforce the death penalty on men who sleep with other men that the second book of the Torah demands?

Even though we are certain that our fellow Americans would never go to that extreme, we need to seriously consider the question. Once fundamentalist Christians have successfully dehumanized our lives, demeaned our relationships, denied us our rights, devastated our families, destroyed our influence in church and society, and driven us back into our closets, what comes next?

I get very nervous when fundamentalist Christians speak of resurrecting God's "absolute values" in order to restore the "moral moorings" of our country, especially when they have agreed "to avoid any overt appeal to biblical morality in the public square." Stealth is a primary strategy in the war that fundamentalist Christians are waging against us. They speak in coded language that only they really understand. What do they mean by God's "absolute values"? It was without doubt the phrase most repeated at Glen Eyrie, and reclaiming those "absolute values" continues to be the fundamentalists' coded call to arms. Where is Alan Turing when we need him?[24]

Will Perkins began the Glen Eyrie conference with these words: "If we lose this battle there are no moral absolutes left for this nation." Robert Linden followed with: "The absolute values that were stipulated by God are still absolute." Robert

Eldredge declared that God's absolute values have been replaced by "the last American absolute, which is tolerance."

Robert Skolrood made this loaded accusation: "Homosexuality denies, really, the fundamental values of Christianity. It denies life, it denies God's expressed desire that men and women cohabit, and it denies the root structure that the Bible prescribes for all mankind and the family. What these people are against is absolute values. And Christianity is one of the stumbling blocks in their way."

To a fundamentalist Christian, heterosexuality is one of the primary "absolute values." We need to stop laughing when Robertson, Dobson, or Falwell declares that homosexuality is a threat to the family and the nation. Fundamentalists aren't laughing. In Skolrood's words, homosexuals deny "the root structure that the Bible prescribes for all mankind and the family." God has given each of us a role to play in sustaining life on this planet. A gay man who refuses to do his God-given duty as husband and father helps bring down the entire structure.

From ancient times, same-sex intimacy between men, the wasting of the seed that brought life, was a threat to the future of the tribe and an act of disobedience that angered God and caused him to turn away from his people. So fearing both the practical and the spiritual consequences of that same-sex act, Moses declared in Leviticus that "a man who sleeps with another man is an abomination and should be executed."

Because fundamentalist Christians pride themselves on taking the Bible literally, we gain little comfort from scholars who assure us that the author of Leviticus says nothing about homosexual relationships as we understand them today or that these ancient holiness codes have nothing to do with men and women living in the twentieth-first century. Fundamentalist Christians are no more interested in biblical scholarship than they are in empirical evidence. They see same-sex acts through the eyes of Moses as a sin that has both practical and spiritual consequences.

At Glen Eyrie, fundamentalist Christian leaders created a long list of antihomosexual goals without even referring to the biblical mandate that demands capital punishment for practicing homosexuals. Have the literalists decided that they can ignore this part of the text, or are they simply waiting for that day when they have accumulated enough power to enforce it?

When I ask myself if it is possible that—given the opportunity—fundamentalist Christians would sentence me to death, I recall that encounter I had on the radio in Seattle with the independent Presbyterian pastor who insisted that the Bible condemned me to death and that the "civil authorities" are responsible for carrying out that order. When I wonder about their long-term goals for us, I remember our lesbian friend who was monitoring the writings of R. J. Rushdoony, the fundamentalist Christian leader mentioned earlier in this chapter who insists that biblical law should take precedence over constitutional law. She wrote for advice, pretending to be a heterosexual woman who has just left her husband because he was gay. "You must thank God for delivering you from this homosexual," Rushdoony replied in his handwritten letter of July 28, 1993. "Marriage to evil is itself an evil: it is the worst form of unequal yoking. God in His law requires the death penalty for homosexuals. This is restated in Romans 1:32. Scripture tells us that homosexuality is the burning out of man. Thank God for your deliverance. Tell the pastor what this homosexual is and says. If the pastor does nothing, leave the church as quickly as possible. I have seen some very sickening cases of homosexuals who married, and how they worked to destroy their spouses and their children. The corrupt love to corrupt. By calling his sin OK, this young man shows how far gone his nature is."

When I doubt for a moment that fundamentalists would ever

throw the first stone, I recall the many letters I received from clergy across Oregon and Colorado responding to my letter trying to explain the tragic consequences of antihomosexual Propositions 9 and 2 in the lives of my sisters and brothers in those states. Most of the letters I received were on church stationery, signed by pastors or other church leaders. "Your letter is written by the devil and has come straight out of hell," one man wrote. "Please God—don't delay punishment. I fear too many will believe these lies and so many are lost already."

Another ends his letter, "Your sin is perverse, detestable, destructive and deadly (AIDS is killing our population). Seek forgiveness and repent for your sins before it is too late, if it isn't already!" A third man wrote, "Homosexuality is the one sin that God says is worthy of death. You may deceive the people, but there is no deceiving God. I just hate it so that you will take the lives of our children to hell with you."

Over the years, I've received hundreds of similar letters from my fundamentalist Christian sisters and brothers describing my sexual orientation as "a curse," "a terrible sin," "wicked," "vile," "unseemly," "the results of a reprobate mind," "disgusting," "perverse," "perverted," "an unnatural, degrading passion worthy of death," "an illness that God could heal if you had more faith," and "the one sin worthy of death."

After too many talk shows, radio interviews, public forums, and debates where these names and worse were flung in my direction, I'm beginning to think that maybe, just maybe, if the time comes when they have the power to enforce the death penalty prescribed by the Laws of Moses, there are a growing number of fundamentalist Christians who would volunteer to pull down the handle that drops me through the trapdoor or squeeze the trigger that fires a bullet in my direction.

At a 1985 Conservative Political Action Conference, Paul Cameron, founder of the Family Research Institute, announced to the attendees, "Unless we get medically lucky, in three or four years, one of the options discussed will be the extermination of homosexuals." Indeed, according to an interview with former Surgeon General C. Everett Koop, Cameron was recommending the extermination option as early as 1983.[25]

And journalist Mark E. Pietrzyk writes in the *New Republic:* "At least twice Cameron has advocated the tattooing of AIDS patients on the face, so that people would know when they were meeting with an infected person. The penalty for trying to hide the tattoo would be banishment to the Hawaiian island of Molokai, a former leper colony. In the event that a vaccine were developed to prevent AIDS, Cameron has proposed that homosexuals be castrated to prevent them from 'cheating' on nature."[26]

Cameron has called for gay bars to be closed and gays to be registered with the government. In spite of the fact that the Southern Poverty Law Center calls Cameron "one of the most thoroughly discredited researchers in America," this was the man who delivered a keynote address at the Glen Eyrie meeting, where fundamentalist Christians gathered to plan our fate, and who continues to be their primary source of information on homosexuality and homosexuals.

Here are a few more samples of the conclusions Cameron draws from his research that are used by fundamentalist Christians to support their campaign against lesbian and gay Americans. It seems fairly obvious that over the long haul this kind of misinformation leads to the fear and loathing of homosexuals that could have disastrous long-term results.

Cameron's paper "Violence and Homosexuality" begins with these words: "Keeping in mind that only about 2%-3% of adults are homosexual or bisexual, let's examine varieties of violence."[27]

"The top six serial killers in the U.S. were all gay."

"The modern world record for serial killing is held by a homosexual."

"A lesbian holds the female serial killer record."

"Two gays compete for the spot of "world's worst murderer."

"Homosexuals are more apt to harm their sexual partners deliberately."

"15% to 40% of statutory rape (child molestation) involves homosexuality."

"Violence goes hand-in-hand with the 'gay' lifestyle."

"Most violence involving gays is self-induced."

"A fifth to a third of surveyed gays admitted to child molestation."[28]

"Homosexuals account for between 1/5 and 1/3 of all child molestation."[29]

"Homosexual teachers are disproportionately apt to become sexually involved with children."[30]

"The risk of a homosexual molesting a child is 10 to 20 times greater than a heterosexual."[31]

Cameron joined with the other Glen Eyrie speakers in condemning "tolerance" and even called "satanic" the "new religion of equality." In his own strange, convoluted keynote, Cameron didn't quote one of his phony statistics. He just rambled on about this being "a conflict between good and evil." He declared that Christians and Jews both believe that we are "brought here to be productive." Then he adds, "When it comes to sexual productivity, more and more people are abdicating their responsibility."

Cameron says that the Christian word is "responsibility" while the egalitarian word is "rights." "And the key of course from the homosexual corridor." he explains, is "I have the right to at least approach your children to see which of them would be interested in what I have to offer!'

After describing egalitarianism as a religion opposed to Christianity, Cameron says, "I think these two faiths are duking it out, and so far the egalitarian faith is slowly but surely pummeling ours." He warns that "we are below replacement levels in terms of number of children provided just to the system, and falling..." and he adds, "We cannot go very much further down this road of giving people what they want without working for it."

Cameron never makes quite clear what he has in mind when he says, "We cannot go very much further down this road of giving people what they want..." but it's difficult not to think the worst. Cameron used his time at Glen Eyrie to leave the ultimate solution hanging in the air without ever stating it. And no one raised a question.

Each speaker tried to outdo the previous with his or her prophetic warnings. The fearmongering hyperbole of Judith Reisman, who called herself a pornography researcher with the Institute for Media Education, outdid them all: "If the homosexual population is now 1 percent," she began, "hold your breath, people, because the recruitment is loud, it is clear, it is everywhere, and you'll be seeing 2 percent, 5 percent, 10 percent, 20 percent, probably 30 percent or even more than that of the young population will be moving into homosexual activism."

In that conference room overlooking the lush green forests and snowcapped peaks of the Rocky Mountains, the Glen Eyrie delegates were taught by seasoned experts better ways to achieve their ends through the legal and judicial processes; through local, state, and federal elections; through antigay initiatives and constitutional amendments; through recall and protest campaigns.

Look back on the twelve years since Glen Eyrie. How many legal battles have we fought? How many of their candidates have beaten our friends and supporters in local, state, and federal elections? How much time and money have we spent working to defeat their antigay initiatives and constitutional amendments? What will it cost us to defeat fundamentalist efforts to superimpose their antihomosexual doctrines on the U.S. Constitution with a "Marriage Protection Amendment," not just in money but in once again having to hear our lives and our relationships endlessly demeaned in print, and on radio and television?

In the castle at Glen Eyrie, experts also taught the fundamentalists how to use guerrilla marketing in television and radio markets, books, pamphlets, tracts, and fund-raising letters; through the Internet's Web pages, chat rooms, membership lists, and "bulletin boards"; through massive fax, telephone, e-mail, and letter-writing campaigns. Glen Eyrie delegates adopted ways to collect and share information rapidly and efficiently, and they vowed to put aside their differences and to work together in this unprecedented assault on homosexuality and homosexuals.

Although the fundamentalist Christian revolution to "return America to its Christian roots" began in the early 1970s, it is important to remember what happened in the second-floor conference room of a castle in Colorado Springs, Colorado, May 16-18, 1994. Those secret meetings signaled a commitment by fundamentalist Christian leaders to focus on the "homosexual threat" as the nation's worst enemy, and to use that threat as their primary tool for raising hundreds of millions of dollars and for recruiting millions of new volunteers to "reclaim America for Christ." Those forty-three men and twelve women from seventeen states and the nation's capital went down from the mountain with a Glen Eyrie Protocol in their hands that revealed their "short-term" solution for lesbian and gay Americans, and look what they've accomplished since that day. They also left us wondering what their long-term solutions might be.

Part Three

THE GREAT
FUNDAMENTALIST
HERESIES

SIX

IDOLATRY:
THE RELIGION OF FUNDAMENTALISM

*T*he gathering at Glen Eyrie illustrates a much larger issue than the fundamentalist Christian attack on homosexuality and homosexuals. In that Rocky Mountain castle, fundamentalist Christians were demonstrating how badly their Christian faith had veered off course. It brings to mind another mountain, Sinai, and another people of God who had gone astray. The Glen Eyrie speakers quoted Moses (who spent time on the mountain listening to the voice of God); but in fact they stood in the tradition of Aaron (whose actions were determined by the noisy voices of the crowd). And like the people of Israel who created a golden calf to represent God while Moses was away, fundamentalist Christians have built their own idols to represent God until Jesus returns. The religion of fundamentalism is idolatry, and to understand their obsession with the annihilation of homosexuality and homosexuals is to first understand the idols that they worship and exactly why they worship them.

GOD AS IDOL

Who is this god they call upon to bless their war against us? The god of Will Perkins and his colleagues at Glen Eyrie is not the God of the Jewish patriarchs or the prophets, let alone the God we see in the life and teachings of Jesus. The god that Will Perkins calls to bless his antigay campaign is an idol that he and his fellow fundamentalists have created from a string of unrelated biblical verses read literally to sanction their prejudice and consolidate their power.

We've seen this demigod before. The Roman Catholic Church called upon him to bless their bloody inquisitions and crusades. Fiery frontier preachers called upon him to bless their war against Native Americans. White Southern Christians called upon him to bless their efforts to preserve slavery and segregation. White Northern Christians called upon him to bless their efforts to prevent women's suffrage and obstruct child labor laws. At Glen Eyrie, Will Perkins and his friends called upon him to bless their war against gay and lesbian Americans.

These same fundamentalists who persecute my sisters and brothers wear bracelets that read "What Would Jesus Do?" If only they would take that question seriously. More than two thousand years ago, a Pharisee who was a lawyer tried to trap Jesus by asking him which is the great commandment in the law. In all probability, this young lawyer had memorized all 613 commandments in the Torah, 248 positive and 365 negative, including thirty-nine acts that were prohibited on the Sabbath day.

I picture Will Perkins standing there with the Pharisee waiting for Jesus to answer the question "Which commandment is the greatest?" In his pocket, Will has his own prioritized list of commands, and the words of Moses from the second book of the Jewish Torah head the list: "If a man also lie with mankind, as he lies with a woman, both of them have committed an abomination: they shall surely be put to death; their blood shall be upon them" (Leviticus 20:13).

Of course, the words of Paul in his letter to the Romans would be second on Perkins's list: "For this reason God gave them up unto vile affections: for even their women did change the natural use into that which is against nature: And likewise also the men, leaving the natural use of the woman, burned in their lust one toward another; men with men working that which is unseemly" (Romans 1:26-27).

With his literal understanding of the Bible, Perkins believes sincerely that Moses and Paul were condemning homosexual orientation as we understand it today (which they weren't), and that Moses called for the death penalty for homosexuals and that Paul echoed that demand (which they didn't). Will and his Glen Eyrie friends were ready to enforce that command until Jesus speaks. Surely his words confused them, at least for a moment or two: "Love God with all your heart, soul, mind and strength and love your neighbor as you love yourself. On these two commandments hang all the law and the prophets."

Will Perkins, his friends at Glen Eyrie, and the other Pharisees present must have been shocked and surprised by Jesus' words. Wasn't it plain to them that this ancient holiness passage from Leviticus that they were using as a law to support their prejudice was trumped, invalidated, annulled, quashed, overthrown by the two great commandments? Had they learned nothing about how God views the "untouchables" from the example of Jesus, who embraced the "untouchable" leper; who praised the "untouchable" bleeding woman; who drank from the bucket of the "untouchable" Samaritan whore; who dined with the "untouchable" Jews who collected taxes for Rome; who let the "untouchable" prostitute pour expensive perfume on his feet and dry them with her hair; and who healed the "untouchable" homosexual companion of the "untouchable" Roman centurion?

They must have been shocked into silence after hearing Jesus explain that all "laws" were not equal; that it was time for them to discern between what was important in God's eyes and what was not; that they should do away with cultural customs and practices that did not measure up to the two "Great Commandments." I'll bet the Pharisee quietly slipped away knowing that if people took Jesus seriously they would be set free from the legal restraints religious leaders use to keep them in their place.

I wonder if Will Perkins crumpled up and tossed his list to the ground at the feet of this radical young rabbi just as the Pharisees who condemned the "untouchable" woman caught in the act of adultery dropped their stones at Jesus' feet. Or is it possible that Will and his Glen Eyrie cohorts missed the significance of Jesus' words altogether and instead of being saved by them, marched off to campaign for a Federal Marriage Amendment and in the process of persecuting rather than loving the "untouchables" lost their own souls?

A Christian understands who God is by looking closely at Jesus. Both testaments, all sixty-six books, more than a million words, point directly to him. And there is no way Will Perkins, Pat Robertson, Jerry Falwell, James Dobson, or D. James Kennedy can miss the fact that God is defined by Jesus, who said to his disciples just before his arrest and crucifixion: "This one command I give thee, Love one another. By this will they know that you are my disciples, if you have love one to another" (John 13:34-35). In James Finley's words, "The Scriptures are one long love letter from God."[1] Any lesser god is an idol, and anyone who worships that lesser god is an idolater in God's eyes. There is no way that these men and their colleagues can ask God to bless their campaign against gay people without breaking God's heart and risking God's eternal judgment for their idolatry. Nevertheless, they gathered at Glen Eyrie determined to take that risk.

THE BIBLE AS IDOL

At Glen Eyrie—as in recent elections—fundamentalist Christians were obsessed by their vision of "absolute moral values," and the Bible, the "family," and the nation top their values list. These are the idols worshipped by fundamentalist Christians. These are the new gods that have replaced the God of Jewish and Christian tradition, and it is almost impossible for the brightest, bravest, brashest iconoclast to topple those idols from the altars on which they stand.

If you want to understand why reasoning about "the values" with a fundamentalist Christian doesn't change his or her mind, you have to understand how a fundamentalist reads the Bible. Know this up front: I love the Bible. I have read from it, learned from it, preached from it for half a century. I believe it is God's word and that God continues to speak to us through it. But I do not believe—as my fundamentalist sisters and brothers believe—that every verse in the Bible is directed to us in the twenty-first century as a law to be read literally and obeyed without question.

Evangelicals have often called the Bible inerrant in the attempt to protect it from those who ignore or even ridicule God's word. It's also been a kind of code word used to recognize another evangelical who also loves and respects the Scriptures. That's why when I don't use "inerrant" to describe the Bible, people assume, quite incorrectly, that I've lost my original faith in and commitment to the Book of books.

I believe that the Holy Spirit has carefully superintended, watched over, and guided the writing and translating of those sixty-six books to guarantee that over the centuries they remain the Christian's trustworthy guide to faith and practice. But I do not believe that God ever intended that the Bible be a trustworthy guide to biology, geology, or astronomy. Fundamentalists do believe it and in the process refuse to be inspired and informed by what humanity has learned over past millennia about the mystery and wonder of God's creation. When they call the Bible inerrant, they mean it contains the whole truth about everything and in doing that they refuse to hear the Spirit of Truth, God's Spirit, the Spirit Jesus promised would come to comfort us and to "teach you all things" (John 14:26).

Fundamentalists refuse to hear the Spirit of Truth speaking to us, not just through those sixty-six books, but through Copernicus, Galileo, Michelangelo, da Vinci, Bach, Handel, Newton, Darwin, Kepler, Jefferson, Lincoln, Pasteur, Einstein, George Washington Carver, Rachel Carson, and the other women and men through the centuries who were open to new insights and discoveries about creation. When fundamentalists cut themselves off from what the Holy Spirit would teach us now about those things the biblical writers had no way of knowing, they sin against the Holy Spirit and they turn the Bible into a cold, stone idol.

Nevertheless, an inerrant Bible as they define it is the frame through which fundamentalists view the world. That frame can bounce off every idea you throw at it if your understanding of a biblical verse doesn't agree with theirs. They aren't interested in the meaning you find in a biblical passage. They aren't even interested in the truths scholars, historians, and linguists find there. For fundamentalists, the canon is closed. No more inspiration is needed. The Holy Spirit is as unnecessary for understanding holy writ as is the knowledge of Greek or

Hebrew. Fundamentalists know exactly what every verse means and woe be unto those who disagree.

In his *Case for Orthodoxy Theology*, Edward John Carnell explains the difference between the evangelical view of Scripture and the fundamentalist view: "When [evangelical] orthodoxy says that the Bible is the only rule of faith and practice, the fundamentalist promptly concludes that everything worth knowing is in the Bible. The result is a withdrawal from the dialogue of man as man. Nothing can be learned from general wisdom, says the fundamentalist, for the natural man is wrong in starting point, method, and conclusion...Classical [evangelical] orthodoxy says that God is revealed in general as well as in special revelation. The Bible completes the witness of God in nature; it does not negate it."[2]

Because of their excessive commitment to a literal Bible, fundamentalist Christians have fallen into the trap of bibliolatry, which *Merriam-Webster's* online dictionary defines as "having excessive reverence for the letter of the Bible." There is no real concern for the Bible's overall intent, no sense of the God of grace at work in the world, no appreciation for redemptive history or for our new understanding of the God of Moses in the life of Christ. To the fundamentalist, every word, every line, every phrase has equal worth. The Good News in Christ has no more weight than the Ten Commandments. Even when they are in stark contrast, the words of Jesus do not trump the words of Moses. The fundamentalist reads a line in Leviticus and says to himself, "God said it. I believe it. That settles No questions. No discussions. No possible change of mind or heart."

The way the gods were used by the Egyptian Pharaohs and their priests illustrates the way fundamentalist Christians are using their false gods in our times. There were roughly 1,500 different ancient Egyptian gods, from Aken (ferryman of the underworld) to Yah (the second moon god). They didn't live on a mountain like Sinai or dwell in a distant heaven somewhere among the stars. They looked and acted exactly like human beings but lived their capricious lives invisibly in the mortal world.[3] Most of the gods were represented by idols on altars in temples and in hieroglyphic symbols on scrolls of parchment. The role of the Egyptian priest was to appease and manipulate the gods through magical formulas, secret oracles, and sacred words. Consequently, by appearing to have power over the gods, the priests also had power over the people.

For example, the idol for Aken, the boatman who delivered the dead to the underworld, was a miniature papyrus boat with a carving of a boatman at the helm. Here's the catch. A priest was required to awaken the boatman on behalf of a departed friend or relative. So, your mother dies. You bring an offering to the priest. He mumbles the magic words to the meta-divine, that mysterious power over and above the gods. If the magic works, the meta-divine awakens the boatman, who ferries your mother safely into the land of the dead.

Idolatry is defined by that cycle of Egyptian priests using magic to manipulate the gods and collect offerings from the people in return. And the one true God had chosen the Jews, this little tribe of former slaves, to end that cycle of idolatry forever. For the first time, humankind learned that there was only one God who was not simply a human fantasy invented to explain the natural world and all its terrors. This God was Creator, Redeemer, and Sustainer of the natural world. Yahweh didn't look or act like a person (that would come later). This God was a mysterious presence in and above and beyond the world. No priest could use holy words or magical formulas to control this mysterious God at work redeeming the world.

Fundamentalist Christians use Bible verses just as Egyptian priests used oracles. Because Pat Robertson's CBN is available to 1.6 billion viewers in two hundred countries in seventy languages, I'll use him as my primary example of idolatry (or bibliolatry) at work in the fundamentalist Christian community.[4]

You want to be wealthy? Why not! Pat's "law of reciprocity" is based on one verse from the Gospel of Luke: "Give and it shall be given to you; good measure, pressed down, shaken together, and running over (Luke 6:38)." In describing his law of reciprocity, Pat declares that "If you give to God, He gives back thirty-, sixty-, and one hundredfold. Regarding tithes," Robertson continues, "He [God] said in the Old Testament, 'Prove Me now in this' and see 'if I will not open for you the windows of heaven and pour out for you such blessing that there will not be room enough to receive it.'"

What bothers me with Pat's law of reciprocity is not what he says but what he implies when saying it. Like the priests of Egypt who for an offering would provide a magic formula that would manipulate the gods into doing man's will, Pat has turned Luke's description of a loving, generous creator into a law that God must obey. The dictionary defines reciprocity as the exchange of obligations, licenses, or privileges between individuals or nations. Pat promises his television viewers that if "they do this," then God "will do that." He doesn't promise wealth, but that promise is implied, especially when he's asking for a large donation to *The 700 Club*.[5]

You want to be healthy? Why not! Pat's "law of miracles" is based on a short paragraph from the Gospel of Mark: "Have faith in God. For assuredly I say to you, whoever says to this mountain, 'Be removed and be cast into the sea,' and does not doubt in his heart, but believes that those things he says will come to pass, he will have whatever he says. Therefore I say to you, whatever things you ask when you pray, believe that you receive them, and you will have them." (Mark 11:22-24). Explaining the meaning of this verse, Pat exhorts his listeners (in two hundred countries), "Do not ask the storm to stop. Tell it to stop!! Do not ask cancer to leave a sick body. Command it to leave."[6] I've seen this second heresy at work undermining the self-esteem of a member of my own family who believed that healing came automatically with spiritual rebirth and when he wasn't healed blamed himself for not having enough faith.

You want to be successful? Why not! Pat retells Jesus' parable of the rich man who went on a journey after giving three servants five talents, two talents, and one talent to invest. Upon his return, he rewarded the five- and two-talent servants who had doubled their money by investing it but took away the one talent from the servant who had buried his master's money to keep it safe. Calling this the "law of use," Pat explains, "Whatever is given you, however small it is, use it…diligently on an ever-increasing scale…Before long, the amount of your achievement or the opportunity available to you will become absolutely awesome. This is the secret of the kingdom which guarantees success to any Christian who applies it."[7] This third heresy makes me angry. When he "guarantees success," Pat Robertson joins snake oil salesmen through the ages.

You want to be saved? Why not! This question—"What must I do to be saved?"—has troubled humankind for millennia. In the sixteenth century, Johann Tetzel sold indulgences that would buy your way out of hell. In the twenty-first century, fundamentalists offer an even simpler (and much cheaper) formula from Paul's letter to the Romans: "If you confess with your mouth the Lord Jesus and believe in your heart that God has raised him from the dead, you will be saved" (Romans 10:9).

I knelt at an altar as a child and confessed Jesus as Lord and Savior of my life. At sixty-six, I still believe the verse I learned when I was five: "For God so loved the world that He gave His only begotten Son, that whosoever believes in him shall not perish but have everlasting life." But when I became a man, I saw the danger of reducing the life, death, and resurrection of Jesus to a kind of "Get Out of Jail" card that I could use to escape the fires of hell. Getting saved is not like joining a very special club where.membership guarantees you health, wealth, and happiness. Getting saved isn't graduation but the first day of class. Getting saved happens all at once and yet it happens on a daily basis, as well, as we follow Jesus' example. Paul describes Jesus as the Son of God who had equal status with the Creator and yet he gave up that privileged status to become a servant of humankind (Philippians 2:5-8). Getting saved is a gift of God's grace through faith, and the beginning of that journey into faith (Ephesians 2:8-9) requires that we don't cling to some mistaken privileged status but become servants of humankind as Jesus did (Phil. 2:7).

Jesus compared the final judgment to a time when those who feed the hungry, clothe the naked, and care for the outcast are separated from those who live greedy, self-centered lives. Jesus died to save the world, but he was arrested, tortured, and killed because he offended the religious and political leaders with his demands for justice, mercy, and truth. When I hear Pat Robertson and other fundamentalist preachers say that "getting saved" is all it takes to please God and to escape eternal death, I have to respond, it takes much more than that to follow Jesus. Anything else, in the words of Deitrich Bonhoeffer, is cheap grace.

During their current campaign to get the Ten Commandments posted in every possible public place, fundamentalist Christians would be wise to stop long enough to read and heed those first three commands.

(I) *Thou shalt have no other gods before me.* Unlike the one-true-God, Pat's god offers health, wealth, success, and an easy way to escape damnation. Like an Egyptian priest reciting an oracle, Pat mumbles the sacred words from holy writ and demands his god to perform the desired miracle. (Then suggests the viewer send an offering to support his ministries.)

(II) *Thou shalt not make any graven image...nor bow down to them...nor serve them.* Pat uses his massive television network to present the world an image of a god he can command, a kind of errand boy for the believing Christian. That god is an idol, and on every *700 Club* Robertson bows down before that idol and calls it God. (Then suggests the viewer send an offering to support his ministries.)

(III) *Thou shall not take the name of the Lord thy God in vain.* Pat Robertson doesn't swear, but he takes the Lord's name in vain for one example when he quotes god to condemn Jewish rabbis or Christian clergy who recognize same-sex marriage. "God says, 'I don't recognize it,'" Pat declares. How arrogant of Pat to speak for God. "And I'm for sticking with God."[8] (How arrogant for Pat to assume that he is on God's side and that God is on his side, as well, and then suggest that viewers send an offering to help support his ministries.)

The Bible is not a book of magic. It is a book of mystery. You can't just quote verses that support your prejudices or guarantee your health, wealth, and happiness and demand that God "follow through" as promised. God is not limited to the words of Scripture. God is still speaking to us through them. If we don't maintain an open mind and an open heart while reading the Bible, we may not hear what God is saying to us in our time. Reading the Bible demands a certain dependence on the Spirit of Truth, who helps us get past all the preconceptions we have picked up over the years and hear for ourselves what God needs for us to hear. Reading the Bible demands humility and a willingness to let other sacred writings, spiritual traditions, scientific findings, our friends, and even our enemies help us understand what God is saying to us through the inspired writings found in these sixty-six books, letters, poems, short stories, hymns, and biographies.

In the late twelfth century, a monk we know only as Guigo advised that reading the Bible requires "concentrating all one's powers on it." Then he makes this comparison: "I hear the words read: 'Blessed are the pure of heart, for they shall see God.' This is a short text of Scripture, but it is of great sweetness, like a grape that is put in the mouth filled with many senses to feed the soul...So wishing to have a fuller understanding of this, the soul begins to bite and chew upon this grape as though putting it in a wine press to ask what this precious purity may be and how it might be had."[9]

In the late fourteenth century, Thomas Hamerken or Haemmerlein, known as Thomas "à Kempis," wrote these words: "If you fancy that you know many things, and fairly understand them; remember that the things you do not know are many more than those you do know."[10] The Bible becomes a dead idol when we call the words between its covers inerrant, infallible, to be taken literally. This is not a dead book. It is alive. Open it carefully because the new truth that might come leaping out at you could change your life forever.

THE FAMILY AS IDOL

Fundamentalist Christians are genuinely concerned (actually in a full-out panic) about the "corrosive effect" homosexuality and homosexuals have on the nuclear family. Fairly obvious proof of their concern are the names of the organizations represented at Glen Eyrie: Focus on the Family (Dobson), American Family Association (Wildmon), Family Research Council (Bauer), Family Research Institute (Cameron).

And the other organizations there that didn't include the word "family" in their title usually have the American family as their number one concern. For example, the Web site for

Beverly LaHaye's Concerned Women for America features a *Culture and Family* Institute, a *Family Voice* magazine, and places "the definition of family" at the top of its list of core issues. The headline on Pat Robertson's CBN Web site lobbying viewers to support the Federal Marriage Amendment is: "Pray that God will protect His divine plan for marriage and the family." In his latest book, *As the Family Goes*, D. James Kennedy claims that "...the family is the heart of our culture and if America is going to survive and thrive, it will require a renaissance of the American family."[11] And Jerry Falwell joins the chorus with "The ultimate goal for the homosexual and lesbian couples is to attack the foundation of our society, the biblically based family. They have set out on a course to destroy the meaning of family in America."[12]

The word "family" has become a kind of buzzword for fundamentalist Christians, a way of identifying other fundamentalist individuals and organizations, a password, a litmus test. Their so-called "Christian family" is, of course, a myth, a myth we all aspire to for certain, but a myth nevertheless.

Check out the latest stats on divorce rates among the general population. After a 1999 study of 3,854 adults from the forty-eight contiguous states, the Barna Research Group reported that conservative Christian couples are even more likely to divorce than couples from other faith groups, atheists, or agnostics. George Barna, Barna's president and founder, commented: "While it may be alarming to discover that born-again Christians are more likely than others to experience a divorce, that pattern has been in place for quite some time. Even more disturbing, perhaps, is that when those individuals experience a divorce many of them feel their community of faith provides rejection rather than support and healing."[13]

Looking back on her role as the perfect mom on *Leave It to Beaver*, Barbara Billingsley remembers fans saying, "Nobody lives like that." She agreed. "I didn't live like that, either." Apparently, for the six-year run of that very popular family program, Barbara Billingsley left her own children with a housekeeper at 6 A.M., drove to the studios, and didn't return until evening. In her interview, she said that the Cleaver family was created for entertainment purposes only and that people shouldn't take that picture of the American family so seriously.

The Christian family idol being held up by Dobson and the rest has also been created to entertain, and no one should take it seriously, either. The family model fundamentalists glorify is an idol as far removed from the average American family as the statue of Venus de Milo is removed from a real American woman or Michelangelo's David is removed from a real American man.

However, I do share the fundamentalist Christian's concern for the current state of the American family. I grew up in a Christian home and I wouldn't trade that experience for anything. I love the old family into which I was born, and I love the new family that God has given me. But the fundamentalists' version of the family is an idol that James Dobson and the others have created, a false and misleading standard by which they measure our families and find them wanting.

In Robert Skolrood's keynote address at Glen Eyrie, there are several important clues for understanding the fundamentalists' concern about "preserving" their model of the family. "It's impossible for Christianity to make peace with homosexuality," he declares, "because homosexuality denies, really, the fundamental values of Christianity. It denies life, it denies God's expressed desire that men and women cohabit, and it denies the root structure that the Bible prescribes for all mankind and the family. What these people [homosexuals] are against is absolute values." [14]

Let's break down that amazingly instructive paragraph into its five parts:

1. "IMPOSSIBLE FOR CHRISTIANITY TO MAKE PEACE WITH HOMOSEXUALITY."

This is very important information for those of us who are determined to help change the minds and hearts of our fundamentalist sisters and brothers. On October 20, 2005, Soulforce received a letter from Ron Reno, special assistant to James Dobson, responding to another Soulforce request for a serious meeting with Dobson and his ex-gay staff. "To be candid," he begins, "we question the sincerity of your repeated invitations [to meet] considering Mel White's refusal to participate in a community dialogue we held during Soulforce's last visit to Colorado Springs. The event, which allowed for a frank discussion on the subject of homosexuality, revealed the success that is to be achieved through an amenable exchange of ideas."

Once you realize that fundamentalists have decided that it is "impossible to make peace with homosexuality," these endless invitations to "an amenable exchange of ideas" can be seen for what they are: pretense, sham, deception, a way of silencing criticism and at the same time appear to be open to new truth when in fact they are not.

For the past ten years, I've agreed to endless public and private meetings with fundamentalists to respond to their misinformation campaign against us. I've prepared diligently for those meetings and have presented the latest scientific, psychological, historical, pastoral, and even biblical evidence. Unfortunately, I discovered a long time ago that fundamentalist Christians will sit and smile and look attentive but ignore the evidence. They even seem unable to hear, let alone be moved by, the tragic stories of the gay people who have been wounded by their antigay words and actions.

That's why I've decided that at least for me the debate is over. The verdict is in. Homosexuality is not a sickness, not a sin. No longer do I accept the fundamentalist invitation to participate in their charades. I will dialogue, discuss, debate the issue with anyone who is seriously open to the truth, but fundamentalist Christians are not open and thus we must resist their untruth in other ways.

2. "HOMOSEXUALITY DENIES...THE FUNDAMENTAL VALUES OF CHRISTIANITY"

This is a troublesome confession that illustrates the confusion fundamentalist Christians have about "absolute values." For the Jewish prophets and for Jesus, the fundamental values of Christianity are justice, mercy, truth, and, above all, love. Jesus even promised in his dramatic personal story of the last judgment that the fate of our eternal souls doesn't rest just on getting saved but equally on how well we care for the world's needy and forgotten peoples (Matthew 25:31-46). He said to the Pharisees, "You know the law by heart but you have forgotten the heart of the law: justice, mercy and faith" (Matthew 23:23).

Do fundamentalist Christians agree with the "absolute values" of the Jewish prophets and Jesus? Who better to ask than the Reverend Rick Warren, a man inspired by W A. Criswell to enter the ministry, whose book, *The Purpose Driven Life*, has sold more than 20 million copies, and whose Saddleback Church in Lake Forest, California, has a reported eighty thousand people on its rolls. The *Today* show has called Rick Warren our nation's "most influential pastor," and *Time* magazine suggests he is the man most likely to succeed Billy Graham. Rick Warren is an evangelical to the core, and a man deeply concerned about the poor and oppressed, but he sounded very much like a spokesman for fundamentalist Christianity when he summarized his version of Christian values just before the reelection of George W. Bush.

Warren suggests we ask each candidate what he or she believes "about abortion and protecting the lives of unborn children? About using unborn babies for stem cell harvesting? About homosexual 'marriage?' About human cloning? About euthanasia—the killing of the elderly and the invalid?" Warren said these five issues are "non-negotiable...to me they are not even debatable because God's Word is clear on these issues."[15]

One quick read of the Gospels is enough to make it clear that Jesus would ask the candidates a whole different set of questions. He would ask what they plan to do "about children who are hungry or thirsty? About the poor and homeless who need food, clothing and a roof over their heads? About widows who live lonely fearful lives behind double locked doors? About prisoners who never see a visitor let alone a decent lawyer? About the person who is an outcast because of race, religion, physical disability or sexual orientation?" "Doing justice, loving mercy, seeking truth..." These are the issues God's Word is clear on.

I find it hard to understand why people who claim that the Bible is inerrant and should be read literally are focused on those five absolute fundamentalist Christian values. I also find it hard to understand why their fear that "homosexuality will destroy the family" often heads the list. Skolrood tries to explain in his next point.

3. "...BECAUSE [HOMOSEXUALITY] DENIES...LIFE"

What is he saying? The lesbian and gay people I know celebrate life and live life to the fullest. Or is he reverting to the ancient notion, held by our Jewish ancestors, that the sperm holds all that is needed to make a new life? Does he believe that women are just the garage in which the sperm parks until the baby is born, and that if you "waste that sperm" (as might happen in homosexual intimacy) you actually waste (or deny) a life?

Or is this just another way of saying "homosexuals don't make babies and without babies the nation has no future and civilization will collapse"? Once again ignorance prevails. Loving, committed same-sex couples in long-term relationships have babies, adopt babies, provide foster care for babies, and (by the way) same-sex couples with children make excellent parents.

In a fund-raising letter sent to millions of gullible Americans, James Dobson warned against granting gay and lesbian couples and their children the rights and protections of marriage because "social science confirms that two parents of the same sex, however loving or nurturing they may be, cannot meet the unique needs of children in the same way that a mother and a father can." It is strange that this fundamentalist psychologist heard by an estimated 25 million people a week is so ignorant about "social science" and the family. You would think he would take seriously the research by qualified social scientists instead of making up data to support his prejudice.

"There is no evidence," states the American Academy of Child and Adolescent Psychiatry, "to suggest or support that parents with a gay, lesbian, or bisexual orientation are per se different from or deficient in parenting skills, child-centered concerns, and parent-child attachment."[16] The American Psychiatric Association agrees: "Numerous studies over the last three decades consistently demonstrate that children raised by gay or lesbian parents exhibit the same level of emotional, cognitive, social, and sexual functioning as children raised by heterosexual parents."[17] And research by the American Psychological Association adds: "Studies comparing groups of children raised by homosexual and by heterosexual parents find no development differences between the two groups of children in their intelligence, psychological adjustment, social adjustment, popularity with friends, development of social sex role identity or development of sexual orientation."[18] Maybe Skolrood's next example will make it clear why homosexuals are such a threat to the family.

4. "...BECAUSE HOMOSEXUALITY DENIES...GOD'S EXPRESSED DESIRE THAT MEN AND WOMEN COHABIT"

Okay. We know what this means. It's "Adam and Eve not Adam and Steve," right? Of course God wanted men and women to "cohabit" (although cohabit is most often defined as unmarried couples living together in a sexual relationship or two singles "shacking up"). The Creation story makes it very clear that God is pleased when a man and a woman live and love together. But why do fundamentalists still believe that those proof texts in Leviticus and Romans make it just as clear that God doesn't want same-sex couples to live and love together as well?

This drives us back into the debate about those pesky clobber passages that are used to caricature and condemn us. This I know for certain. For twenty-five years, Gary and I have lived together. We don't "cohabit" as much as we used to, but, hey, that's common for couples after a quarter century. And though our civil rights are denied us by the state and our religious rites are denied us by the church, we are married in God's eyes and in the eyes of our friends and families, and God not only approves of our relationship, God celebrates it. God blesses it. God informs and inspires it.

James Dobson disagrees. His powerful voice condemns same-sex marriage with a kind of growing hysteria: "This is the real deal," he warns. "Most gays and lesbians do not want to marry each other. That would entangle them in all sorts of legal constraints. Who needs a lifetime commitment to one person? The intention here is to destroy marriage altogether...Unless we act quickly the family as it has been known for five thousand years will be gone. With its demise will come chaos such as the world has never seen....Marriage is on the ropes and western civilization itself appears to hang in the balance..."[19] Once again this fundamentalist counselor ignores the evidence, blames gay and lesbian couples for the current breakdown of heterosexual marriage, and creates fear and loathing of homosexuality and homosexuals in the minds and hearts of millions of Americans.

The American Anthropological Association refutes Dobson's charges unequivocally: "The results of more than a century of anthropological research on households, kinship relationships, and families, across cultures and through time, provide no support whatsoever for the view that either civilization or viable social orders depend upon marriage as an exclusively heterosexual institution. Rather, anthropological research supports the conclusion that a vast array of family types, including families built upon same-sex partnerships, can contribute to stable and humane societies...The Executive Board of the American Anthropological Association strongly opposes a constitutional amendment limiting marriage to heterosexual couples."[20]

5. "...BECAUSE HOMOSEXUALITY...DENIES THE ROOT STRUCTURE THAT THE BIBLE PRESCRIBES FOR ALL MANKIND AND THE FAMILY"

This is the problem with homosexuality and homosexuals that most troubles our fundamentalist sisters and brothers. Actually, it's most troubling to our fundamentalist *brothers*, who are certain that God loves them best. They wouldn't say it that way. They would describe their superior relationship to God as Robert Skolrood did at Glen Eyrie in terms such as "root" and "structure." Our fundamentalist brothers know that God loves the sisters equally but that in the chain of command "prescribed for all mankind and the family," God speaks to man and man speaks to a woman on God's behalf. Actually, the fundamentalist chain of command is ordered in their literal Bible: God speaks to Jesus; Jesus speaks to men; men speak to women; women speak to children (and then to men of color, women of color, children of...but that's another story). When I think about the fundamentalist Christians' chain of command, this couplet comes to mind: "Boston, dear Boston, the land of the bean and the cod, where the Cabots speak only to Lodges and the Lodges speak only to God."

While teaching communications at Fuller Theological Seminary, I was invited to keynote a convention sponsored by Mike Yaconelli's Youth Specialties organization. One of Mike's tasks was to edit and publish *The Door*, a *Rolling Stone*—like magazine for the evangelical youth subculture. Mike was a genius at satire. Every month, the magazine would help us evangelicals laugh at our own foibles. He was especially keen on satirizing the rise of fundamentalism and fundamentalists within the evangelical church. Bill Gothard, at the time a rising star in the fundamentalist firmament, often spoke of God's "chain of command." At the Youth Specialties event, about a thousand of us were seated in a hotel ballroom when suddenly Mike burst into the room dressed in a hairy gorilla suit swinging a rusty chain wearing a name tag: Gothard. After a moment of shocked silence, laughter filled the room. Through "Gothard the Gorilla" swinging his chain of command, Mike Yaconelli was attacking the heterosexist, sexist, and homophobic notion held by fundamentalist Christians that God was a male and spoke to males first.

Heterosexism—seeing heterosexuality as superior to homosexuality and bisexuality; *sexism*—seeing men as superior to women and children; and *homophobia*—the fear and loathing of homosexuals—are all three rooted in this chain of command, and the entire family structure or sequence of authority is based upon it.

In the military, the chain of command is everything: president, general, colonel, major, captain, lieutenant, sergeant, corporal, private, and all the subtle ranking in between. If that chain of command breaks down, chaos prevails. On April 11, 1951,

President Harry S. Truman fired General Douglas MacArthur. I was eleven years old, but I still remember the shock waves Truman's act sent through our family and across the nation. MacArthur was the country's hero. Less than one year before, when a massive military force from China almost overran our troops in Korea, it was MacArthur's brilliance as a soldier that managed to push the Chinese almost back to their border; however, when President Truman asked MacArthur to arrange a cease-fire, the general refused, preferring instead to declare war on the Chinese. "General MacArthur was insubordinate," Truman explained, "so I fired him. That's all there is to it."[21]

Insubordinate: "not submissive to authority; disposed to or engaged in defiance of established authority." For fundamentalist Christians, if God's chain of command is broken, chaos will prevail in the family as it does in the military, and homosexuals represent the greatest threat to that chain. So, for centuries, they have denied we exist (they still do), kept us in our closets (where they like us best), and refused to recognize us as Americans in any way, let alone grant us our civil rights.

Then along comes "Steve," the dangerous "homosexual activist" who is definitely not submissive to authority but insists on defying it. He may dress funny, walk funny, talk funny, gesture funny, and run like a girl, but he exists, he's out of his closet, and he's demanding his civil and religious rights. Not only does he want to sleep with another man, he wants to set up housekeeping and adopt and raise children with a man. The "Ich factor" figures in here. (What do they do in bed? Ich!) But for the fundamentalist, this girly man represents far more than "Ich." Rigid gender roles have been established since the beginning of recorded history. Keeping men in charge and women in their place is the way civilization has always worked. Accepting homosexuality not only flies in the face of natural creation (or so they think), but it threatens the overthrow of heterosexism, sexism, and homophobia...all established cultural norms.

Gay men and lesbians look to fundamentalist Christians very much as Douglas MacArthur looked to Harry Truman. Only these queer people are not only defying human authority (church and state alike), they are defying the authority of God HIMself. What might happen, the fundamentalist worries, if women get the idea from homosexuals that they don't have to play the female gender role and the whole house of cards—or, in their words, "family values"—comes tumbling down? Motivated by the terror of being ousted from their male position of power and privilege (sexism) and seeing homosexuality as a threat to heterosexual superiority (heterosexism), the keepers of the cultural norms (men) wage their war against homosexuals and produce in the general public the fear and loathing of gay Americans (homophobia).

In her very important book *Homophobia: A Weapon of Sexism*, Suzanne Pharr shares the answers she has received from asking people across the country: "What will the world be like without homophobia in it—for everyone, female and male, whatever sexual identity?" These are typical responses to Suzanne's informal polling.

- kids won't be called tomboys or sissies; they'll just be who they are, able to do what they wish;
- people will be able to love anyone, no matter what sex; the issue will simply be whether or not she/he is a good human being, compatible, and loving;
- affection will be opened up between women and men, women and women, men and men, and it won't be centered on sex; people won't fear being called names if they show affection to someone who isn't a mate or potential mate;

- if affection is opened up, then isolation will be broken down for all of us, especially for those who generally experience little physical affection, such as unmarried older people;
- women will be able to work whatever jobs we want without being labeled masculine;
- there will be less violence if men do not feel they have to prove and assert their manhood. Their desire to dominate and control will not spill over from the personal to the level of national and international politics and the use of bigger and better weapons to control other countries;
- people will wear whatever clothes they wish, with the priority being comfort rather than the display of femininity or masculinity;
- there will be no gender roles.[22]

The idol fundamentalist Christians have made of the nuclear family is based in no small part on the ignorance and misinformation of James Dobson and his $150-million-a-year Focus on the Family empire. It isn't enough that his psychological insights are so far off the mark. His understanding of biblical history is even worse. For example, in a 2003 fundraising letter Dobson says that if gay and lesbian couples are granted the rights of marriage, "the family as it has been known for 5,000 years will be gone...For millennia, traditional marriage has been celebrated by every culture on earth as the cornerstone of society...the cornerstone of every civilization from the beginning of humanity." Dobson's so-called traditional family (meaning nuclear family with a father, a mother, and 2.5 children) is an idol that he has created out of his own fantasy world that he in turn uses to condemn lesbian and gay relationships. History proves his idol false.

In Genesis (2:24), Adam does leave his parents' home, takes a wife, consummates their marriage, and lives together with Eve in a nuclear family not quite so happily ever after. Perhaps Dr. Dobson is referring to this passage when he describes traditional marriage as the cornerstone of society for thousands of years.

In fact, biblical marriages differed greatly from the traditional marriage Dobson describes. Ancient marriages were not based on love but arranged by the family on the basis of economic advantage. Husbands traded cattle for wives (and often treated their bride no better than they had treated their livestock). Marriage to a non-Jew was prohibited. Children of an interfaith marriage were considered illegitimate. A bride who proved not to be a virgin was stoned to death by the men of her village (Deuteronomy 22:13-21).

The Jewish Testament has many examples of polygamous marriage where a man marries and lives with as many women as he can afford: Esau had three wives; Jacob, two; Ashur, two; Gideon, "many"; Solomon, at least seven hundred who lived together on Zion's Hill; Rehoboam, three; Abijah, fourteen.

The levirate marriage was also common in Jewish history. When a woman was widowed without giving birth to a son, she was required by law to leave her home, marry her brother-in-law, and live in a sexual relationship with him. If love did not grow between them, the woman would have to endure "what was essentially serial rape" by her brother-in-law. A brother-in-law was required to marry not only his brother's widow but any widow to whom he was the next of kin.[23]

The story of Abraham, his wife, Sara, and his concubine, Hagar, illustrates another kind of Jewish family with a man having one or more wives and one or more concubines who were either young Hebrew girls bought from their fathers, slaves taken in war, or young women purchased in a foreign country.

There were families made up of Jewish soldiers and female prisoners of war; female rape victims forced by law to marry their attackers; and male slaves assigned to female slaves by their master. None of these family types was condemned by the Jewish prophets.

Jesus was acquainted with every one of the aforementioned family types: a man and a woman; a man and as many women as he could afford; a widow and her brother-in-law or closest next of kin; a man with one or more wives and as many concubines as he could pay for; a Jewish soldier and a female prisoner of war; female rape victims forced by law to marry their attackers; and male slaves assigned to marry female slaves by their masters. Jesus condemned divorce but did not condemn any of the family types common to his day.

We know that Jesus' best friends—Mary, Martha, and Lazarus—were sisters and brother living together as a family (John 11:1-36); that Peter lived in an extended family including his mother-in-law (Luke 4:38); that Jesus healed the daughter of a single mother (Matthew 15:21-28); that Jesus didn't denounce the Samaritan woman divorced from five different husbands and living with a man who wasn't her husband at the time (John 4:1-30); that Jesus didn't condemn the Roman centurion who lived with his special male servant (Matthew 8:5-13); that when his mother and brothers wanted to speak with Jesus, he turned his back on his birth family and said to those following him, "You are my mother and my brother" (Matthew 12:46-50); that Jesus asked his followers to love him more than they loved their families, "...he who loves son or daughter more than me is not worthy of me" (Matthew 10:37-39); and claimed quite openly that the so-called traditional family was not his concern. In fact, Jesus warned that following him would "...set a man against his father, and the daughter against her mother, and the daughter in law against her mother in law. And a man's foes shall be his own household" (Matthew 10:35-36). Jesus would not condone James Dobson's campaign to save the family. Nor would he join with Dobson, Robertson, Falwell, and Kennedy in holding up that idol for the nation to worship.

Dobson's traditional (nuclear) family has not been around for five thousand years. It is a daydream of the 1950s and '60s with perfect children, perfect fathers, and, most of all, perfect mothers like June Cleaver (*Leave It to Beaver*), Donna Stone (*The Donna Reed Show*), and Carol Brady (*The Brady Bunch*).

With *The Brady Bunch* in perennial television reruns in the United States and, most unfortunately, around the world, it is a rare American who can't sing along with the TV theme song praising the female who is white, lovely, ladylike, perfectly coiffured, and blond: "Here's the story, of a lovely lady..."

The *Leave It to Beaver* Web site describes June Cleaver as "the quintessential TV mom—really, really swell. Being there for her family and keeping her home neat and orderly are June's main concerns...Like any good mother, June often worries about Wally and the Beaver, but she never fails to greet life's daily challenges with the sweet and gentle demeanor that most of us wish our mothers had. A sensible wife, mother and home-maker, her cookie drawer is always full, the coffee is always fresh, and she never has a hair out of place."

For mothers who watch *Leave It to Beaver*, there are nine suggestions as to how they, too, can become a perfect "June Cleaver" wife, from "Put on your prettiest dress every morning" to "Vacuum while the family is gone so the house is ship shape when they get home." Though millions of us were entertained by these programs, all too often our definition of the family was shaped by them.

The creator of our Soulforce archives, Daryl Lach, still remembers his three-year-old sister's response to being spanked: "That's it. I've had it. I'm moving in with Donna Reed." Now, looking back, we can see how those seemingly harmless TV series affected the nation, and the not-so-harmless effects they had on women, people of color, the poor, and any other underprivileged or oppressed minority. The idealized family they held up for the world to see was all white, all pretty or handsome, all healthy and smart, all well dressed and perfectly coiffed, all living in perfectly furnished middle-class homes with sparkling kitchens, spacious well-decorated living rooms, tidy children's bedrooms, and a new car in the garage.

Hollywood has always idealized the family, whether it's *Leave It to Beaver* (the ideal suburban family of the 1960s), the "Waltons" (the ideal rural family of the 1970s), the "Cosbys" (the ideal black family of the 1980s), the "Addams family" (the ideal haunted family of the 1990s), or *Everybody Loves Raymond* (the ideal Italian family of the 2000s). Idealizing the family has its problems. Indeed, one critic describes *Leave It to Beaver* as "the most misleading and shallow presentation of family life ever produced for the airwaves. Not only did its presentation of a conservative, patriarchal lifestyle do injustice to progressive social behaviors, but it also served as a radical fabrication of family life that was to have adverse effects on generations of children to follow."[24]

But there is a difference between what Hollywood does to idealize the family and the family idol that James Dobson uses as a standard of measurement for the rest of us. In *The Way We Never Were: American Families and the Nostalgia Trap*, Stephanie Coontz warns us that the strategies and values of the traditional family "offer no solution to the discontents that underlie the contemporary romanticization of the 'good old days.' The reality of these families was far more painful and complex than situation-comedy reruns or the expurgated memories of the nostalgic would suggest."[25]

The Dobson family idol was created to denounce families

that don't conform to it. We shouldn't take Dobson's portrayal of the "typical Christian family" any more seriously than we take the family of June and Ward Cleaver. It is not based on biblical truth, Old or New Testament. It is totally out of touch with real families over the centuries. It was not created to include but to exclude. And it is totally out of touch with the amazing variety of families that bring life to this planet. How many families have been torn apart because they cannot live up to Dobson's family idol? How many Christian parents have denounced and even discarded their gay child because they believe Dobson's misinformation?

Jesus came into the world to widen the circle of acceptance and bring every family in. Because of their distorted view of the family, Dobson and his fundamentalist allies shrink the circle and leave families out.

THE NATION AS IDOL

Like Jerry Falwell, Pat Robertson, D. James Kennedy, and James Dobson, the activists at Glen Eyrie (and millions like them in cities and towns across America) believe sincerely that if the nationwide trend continues to "accept, legalize and celebrate homosexuality as a virtue," God will "withhold his hand of protection from America and the nation will be destroyed." To fundamentalist leaders who have made an idol of this "Christian nation," the decline and eventual destruction of the United States of America is the ultimate evil posed by gay and lesbian Americans.

On a *700 Club* telecast on October 14, 2003, Robertson declared: "Every society which has embraced homosexuality—normalized it, legitimized it, et cetera, embraced it as part of their culture—every one of those societies has gone down in flames. And if we want to destroy the United States of America, take it down, this is the best way to do it. So the homosexuals will have managed to win what's known as a pyrrhic victory— they may win their temporary battle, but they'll lose the war 'cause they will destroy the society, and that's happening."[26]

"To pass a national gay and lesbian rights act," D. James Kennedy warns, "which would grant minority status—civil rights—to those who are practicing the homosexual lifestyle… to enact into a law those things which are clearly violations of God's Ten Commandments…is to attempt to destroy our nation's foundation. 'It is impossible to govern without God and the Ten Commandments,' said John Adams—and we are now going to attempt to do so."[27]

Unfortunately, fundamentalists—for whatever reasons— genuinely believe that homosexuality and homosexuals are the primary obstacle in the way of restoring the "Glory of God" to this nation or, in Kennedy's favorite phrase, "Reclaiming America for Christ." And though it is still difficult to understand why we are at the top of their enemy list, these words of Pat Robertson help make clear how dangerous we appear to be: "From a biblical standpoint, the rise of homosexuality is a sign that [American] society is in the last stages of decay." The first three keynote speakers at Glen Eyrie elaborated on that theme.

In his opening remarks, the conference moderator, Robert Linden, a retired lieutenant colonel in the air force and a former Hewlett-Packard executive, explained further. "While our founding fathers grappled with the issues of breaking away from their former country and establishing a new form of government, we grapple with restoring our country to its moral moorings. The absolute values that were stipulated by God are still absolute, and if we want to pursue life, liberty and happiness, we've got to have those absolute values."[28] In the second keynote address, Robert Skolrood, president of the

National Legal Foundation, shared his belief that the gradual acceptance of homosexuals by the American people was the primary obstacle to restoring America's greatness.

> Homosexual rights is the issue that's going to affect all of the other issues. Remember in Isaiah 5:20 it says, "Woe to those who call evil good and good evil." And that's what we're doing [by accepting homosexuality and homosexuals]. I mean, we're calling evil good and good evil. We have to stop that sort of thing from progressing any more in America.[29]

With growing fervor, leaders of fundamentalist foundations, think tanks, and a variety of activist organizations have joined with fundamentalist television and radio broadcasters to make the connection between the rise of homosexual acceptance and the various signs that God is removing His hand of protection from America.

I cringe when people laugh at Falwell or Robertson for warning that the World Trade Center tragedy and Hurricane Katrina are signs of God's displeasure (especially with the nation's acceptance of homosexuality and homosexuals). Pat, Jerry, and millions of their friends and fellow fundamentalists truly believe it. As Robert Linden said at Glen Eyrie, "We cannot take this [homosexual threat to the nation] any less seriously than our founding fathers took their adversaries in their time."

One speaker went even further back in our history. "There are no more *Mayflowers* sailing," he said. "That's all there is." The little wooden sailing ship that carried religious separatists to the "new world" is arguably history's most important symbol to fundamentalist Christians. They point back to that moment on November 11, 1620, when the Pilgrims signed the Mayflower Compact, clearly indicating that America began as a Christian nation founded "for the Glory of God, and Advancement of the Christian Faith." Now fundamentalist Christians are asking all Americans to board that little boat, line up behind the Pilgrim Fathers, and sign the Mayflower Compact as a kind of loyalty oath to the Christian nation they envisage.

Fundamentalists like Kennedy often forget that Pilgrims were a minority on the *Mayflower* passenger list. The majority were Englishmen and women coming to the New World to create better lives for themselves with no particular religious convictions. These, too, are our forefathers and foremothers. And Christian or not, they, too, deserve those inimitable rights including life, liberty, and the pursuit of happiness.

It isn't just Will Perkins and the other fundamentalist Christians gathered at Glen Eyrie who looked to the Mayflower Compact as the ultimate sign that this nation was a Christian nation from its birth. Those eleven words from the compact— "for the Glory of God, and Advancement of the Christian Faith"—have become a credo for every fundamentalist Christian committed to returning America "to its Christian roots."

Fortunately, our eighteenth-century forefathers were wise enough to draft a constitution that moved beyond the sectarian goals of our seventeenth-century forefathers to create a democracy that would welcome all, protect all, and guarantee the rights of life, liberty, and the pursuit of happiness for all Americans. Fortunately, too, the Mayflower Compact was placed in a government archive somewhere and the governance of this longest-running experiment in democracy was based on the U.S. Constitution and its First Amendment guarantee that Congress "shall make no law respecting an establishment of religion, or prohibiting the free exercise thereof." Unfortunately, though, our fundamentalist friends also see themselves as our twenty-first-century forefathers, working with grim determination to replace the U.S. Constitution with the Mayflower Compact and complete the Pilgrims' wish to establish a "Christian nation" on these shores.

With his massive television, radio, and print outreach, D. James Kennedy leads the way in calling his fellow fundamentalists to "Reclaim America for Christ." In 2005, Kennedy announced that his Center for Christian Statesmanship was increasing its five-hundred-thousand-strong "e-mail army" to one million and planning to recruit, train, and equip more Christians to run for office. The center has plans for twelve regional offices and activists in all 435 U.S. House districts. A new lobbying arm in Washington will target judicial nominations and the battle over marriage.[30]

Kennedy predicts that by cooperating with dozens of other fundamentalist Christian ministries lobbying for a "Christian nation" in the capital, "We will RECLAIM AMERICA FOR CHRIST...ONE HEART AT A TIME ."[31] The following are a sampling of Kennedy's beliefs that guide his efforts to make this a "Christian nation." Most fundamentalist leaders and millions of their followers share Kennedy's beliefs.

BELIEF: *This nation began as a "Christian nation."*

"Indeed, this is a nation that was founded by men and women who were Christian. Some were not. But even those who were not embraced the Christian world and life view that was almost universally prevalent at the time and according to the dictates of the Word of God."

BELIEF: *The Constitution and the Declaration of Independence support the Christian intent of the Mayflower Compact.*

"I would urge you to recommit yourself to the great principles that our Founding Fathers gave us in the founding documents of this nation; to strive by our prayers, our efforts, by our work, by our evangelization, to make this nation a Christian nation once more."

BELIEF: *This nation will collapse if it doesn't return to its Christian roots.*

"I am afraid that unless this country is taken over by Christians so that we have a Christian consensus, we are going to find that when it really gets tough, the unbelieving world, the Western world, is not going to be willing to stand."

BELIEF: *There should be no "separation of church and state."*

"That doctrine exists only in the minds of liberals....It is not in the Constitution, First Amendment, the Bill of Rights, or anywhere else for that matter. It appears only as a passing comment in a personal letter from Thomas Jefferson that carries no constitutional weight. The wall of repression erected against religious values through the deliberate misrepresentation of Jefferson's words, however, has led to a plague of relativism and moral decay that has eroded civic responsibility and moral decency in this country for the past 100 years."

BELIEF: *Christians understand what's going on in the world; non-Christians don't.*

"It seems that somehow or another only the converted mind (the regenerate mind) is able to understand what is going on in the world; what the Communists are really up to; what Satan's intentions are. Most unbelievers do not even believe in Satan and cannot understand his tactics:"

BELIEF: *To restore our nation's heritage, Christians must run the nation.*

"Though Christianity is growing in this country, it is still far from being the controlling force. I am sure that only a Christian-controlled country is going to be able to stand up to the impending threat and avert the approaching disaster that our nation is facing."

BELIEF: *God has given our Christian leaders the cultural mandate to extend their influence into every phase of society.*

"As the vice-regents of God, we are to bring His truth and His will to bear on every sphere of our world and our society. We are to exercise godly dominion and influence over our neighborhoods, our schools, our government...our entertainment media, our news media, our scientific endeavors—in short, over every aspect and institution of human society."

BELIEF: *The fundamentalist Christian's eventual goal is to rule the world.*

"Man is to subdue the earth and have dominion over all its creatures. This is called 'The Cultural Mandate' because it deals with all culture as we know it. As God's junior partners, we are to rule over the earth in His name."

BELIEF: *Converting people to Christ is a political action.*

"The most significant political action that any Christian can take...is to convert his neighbor."[32] "Our only real hope for reclaiming America is to lead people to a true and personal relationship with the Savior Jesus Christ. America must be reclaimed one heart, one life, one household at a time...That is our mission."[33]

BELIEF: *New converts can be used by fundamentalist Christians to increase their political power.*

"There are forty million people who claim to have been converted. If every one of those would simply win one other person to Christ, we could control this country."[34]

BELIEF: *Until now, fundamentalists have used the political process to accomplish their goals; but they don't see this as a normal political issue about which people of goodwill can* *disagree. Making this a "Christian nation" is a battle between good and evil that must be won at any price.*

"It is important that we understand that this is ultimately a theological battle in which we are engaged, not a battle between mere economic outlooks or various political philosophies. It is a battle between Christ and Antichrist and his [followers]. Therefore, ultimately, it is a battle that will be won, not by bullets, but by beliefs."[35]

BELIEF: *Judges who rule against the "absolute values" of fundamentalist Christians must be impeached and replaced.*

"When judges with anti-Christian views impose their own views on the people, Christians must beware!…We must no longer allow federal judges to impose their private agendas at the expense of our rights and freedoms as American citizens. In America, the people are sovereign, not the judges."[36] "Thousands of Christians Across America Agree: Anti-Prayer Judge Must Be Impeached."[37] "When a federal judge goes this far—when our Christian freedoms are this oppressed—we must take action."[38]

BELIEF: *Art, theater, and film that do not reflect fundamentalist Christian beliefs should not receive government aid.*

"Congress should totally de-fund the callously anti-Christian National Endowment for the Arts…a taxpayer funded agency with a notorious record for subsidizing disgusting, immoral, anti-virtue works of art, theater, and film. No more of our money for blasphemy!"[39] (Commenting on an NEA grant to the Manhattan theater club that was producing *Corpus Christi*, a highly regarded passion play by Terrence McNally that portrayed a gay Jesus.)

BELIEF: *The American Civil Liberties Union stands in the way of the ultimate goal of fundamentalist Christians.*

"For decades the ACLU has worked to undercut the impact and influence of religious faith in American life. Although they declare themselves defenders of tolerance...the ACLU, in fact, actively promotes intolerance when it comes to religion. Stand with us to expose the truth about the ACLU—and its destructive effect on the quality of American life."[40]

BELIEF: *Women belong at home, not in the workforce.*

"Refuse the 'siren song' of feminism and choose the greatest significance and joy in the world—the joy of motherhood."[41]

BELIEF: *There are absolute family values that must be defended at all costs.*

"We are working to achieve the goals of our Family Values Contract...*by opposing* special privileges for homosexuals, taxpayer-funded abortions and pornography, condom distribution in the schools, and the so-called 'separation of church and state'...and *by supporting* moral school curricula, school prayer, respect for the flag, and our Christian heritage."[42]

BELIEF: *Fundamentalist Christians oppose tolerance that "demands the acceptance of another's belief or behavior as equally valid as one's own."*

"[This tolerance that accepts an other's belief or behavior as equally valid as one's own] is well and good unless you happen to believe in God's Word and the absolute standards for right and wrong. If that is the case, watch out. You have just committed the one unpardonable sin—the one belief for which there is no tolerance...We must courageously and boldly stand for what we believe...Unless Christians bring the life-transforming power of Christ to more people, we are going to see an ungodly, unbelieving, power elite go from ridicule, laughter, mockery, and criticism to censure, condemnation, and persecution [of the fundamentalist Christian]. That is exactly what happened in Nazi Germany to the Jews, and it is exactly what is happening in this country today."[43] (Note: This Kennedy "commentary" closed with: "To learn more about the new tolerance and how to neutralize this threat to your faith and family, request *The New Tolerance* offered in the enclosed resources flyer.")

BELIEF: *Kennedy and his fundamentalist Christian colleagues almost invariably place homosexuality at the top of their "enemies of the nation" lists.*

"Homosexuality is called abomination, uncleanness, dishonorable, vile affection, unseemly, an error and a violation of the commandment of God....To enact into law [a reference to any pro-homosexual civil rights legislation] those things which are clearly violations of God's Ten Commandments is to attempt to destroy our nation's foundation...It is a lie to say that no one can leave the homosexual lifestyle. That is a lie. There are more ex-homosexuals in America than there are practicing homosexuals." [44]

WHENEVER I HEAR ANOTHER FIERY FUNDAMENTALIST attack on my gay sisters and brothers, it reassures me to remember that ten days after signing the Mayflower Compact, on November 21, 1620, the Pilgrims landed near today's Provincetown, Massachusetts, perhaps the gayest beach town in America. I'm comforted by this historic fact. Every time Gary and I visit P-Town, I think how important it is for lesbians and gay men to claim our right to share that historic spot. Imagine what the Pilgrims would find if they landed at P-Town today. They would stay in a lesbian-run bed-and-breakfast, eat in a gay-owned restaurant, drink in a transgender-owned pub, be entertained by a bisexual comic, worship in a gay-friendly church, and join that happy crowd—gay and straight alike—ambling down Commercial Street.

But as we amble down Commercial, we need to remember that the old Pilgrims who landed here were determined to create a Christian nation in the New World and that the new Pilgrims gathered secretly at Glen Eyrie 374 years later were (and still are) determined to re-create that "Christian nation" using the Mayflower Compact and the Bible (not the Declaration of Independence or the U.S. Constitution) as their guide.

In a speech he delivered on Ellis Island, September 11, 2002, President George W. Bush joined America's fundamentalist Christians in making an idol of this so-called "Christian nation." He stated:

> This ideal of America as the hope of all mankind…that hope that drew millions to this harbor…that hope still lives. That hope still lights our way and that light shines in the darkness and the darkness will not overcome it.

The original quotation President Bush adapted for his speech to describe America is taken from the Gospel of John describing Jesus as "the light shining in darkness; and the darkness comprehended it not…That was the true Light, which lighteth every man that cometh into the world" (John 1:5, 9). After seeing a replay of Bush's speech, a British commentator pointed out what a lot of people missed. "The president appears to be ranking America alongside Jesus," he said, "as one brought into the world to bring God's plans into fulfillment. To suggest that a sovereign nation state with political priorities and military budgets has somehow a divine status is in my opinion at least as close as you can come to idolatry."[45]

Indeed.

When the Bible, or the family, or the nation are adored,

blindly, excessively, when they are so important that they take the place of God, they become idols. Unfortunately, idols fail. And when the people who believed in those idols with all their heart experience that failure, it leaves their lives in chaos.

Paul Tillich, who watched his own native country idolize Hitler and the Third Reich, recognized the tragic consequences when idols fail. "There is a risk," he says, "if what was considered as a matter of ultimate concern proves to be a matter of preliminary and transitory concern—as, for example, the nation. The risk to faith in one's ultimate concern is indeed the greatest risk man can run. For if it proves to be a failure, the meaning of one's life breaks down; one surrenders oneself, including truth and justice, to something which is not worth it."[46]

SEVEN

FASCISM:
THE POLITICS OF FUNDAMENTALISM

THE WANNSEE PROTOCOL

*F*ifty-two years before Glen Eyrie, on January 20, 1942, fifteen servants of the Third Reich assembled in an elegant guesthouse near Lake Wannsee in a wealthy suburb of Berlin to organize the "Final Solution" for six million European Jews. Over crystal glasses of aged German cognac, they heard keynote speaker Reinhard Heydrick, chief of security police, describe Hitler's solution to the "Jewish threat." In just over an hour, they finished their business, shook hands, and rode into infamy in their chauffer-driven, bulletproof Mercedeses. Only an hysteric would attempt to compare the Wannsee and Glen Eyrie protocols. The holocaust that followed Wannsee will forever stand alone as the ultimate example of man's inhumanity to man. But there are lessons to be learned.

Shortly after the Glen Eyrie meeting, Gary and I learned

one of those lessons. On July 10, 1994, during our seven-day Fast for Understanding in front of James Dobson's Focus on the Family headquarters in Colorado Springs, we heard for the first time of the secret meetings in Glen Eyrie a few weeks earlier. Immediately, we began our search for documents or recordings that would help us understand the fundamentalists' plan for lesbian and gay Americans. During a radio interview, we invited the people of Colorado Springs to bring their children on a visit to our fast site to meet ordinary gay people and see that we were no way like the way Dobson and his friend Paul Cameron described us.

The very next day, a woman and two young children approached us. "I am not a Christian," the stranger began, "and I am not a lesbian. I am a Jew, but I wanted my children to meet you." We poured Gatorade into paper cups and sat down in a circle of plastic chairs to get acquainted. Toward the end of our conversation, our Jewish friend told us exactly why she had come to support our protest. "Because the last time they took you first," she said. "And I will not let that happen again."

Later that evening, in our little house trailer covered with brightly colored "Welcome!" and protest posters and a large sign reading *Fast for Understanding: Day 4*, we discussed her comment "the last time they took you first." In the epilogue to the paperback edition of *Stranger at the Gate*, I compared the war that fundamentalist Christians were waging against homosexuals to those early days of Hitler's Third Reich, when the Nazis tested the average German's tolerance for intolerance on gay Berliners. But this was the first time I had heard the comparison made by a Jewish American.

"Read about Germany in the early thirties," I had written. "On their way to gaining power over that great nation, see what Hitler and his henchmen did to marginalize the Jews and other helpless minorities including homosexuals. The religious right is doing it again, this time straight out of Hitler's book...What could happen next if the shrill, strident, still surging cry of the religious right wins the day? What could happen to us if their leaders take the field?"[1]

You can imagine how most people responded to my words. "You are such a pessimist," a friend complained. "...an alarmist and a pessimist," another chimed in. "What happened in Germany could never happen here!" was the general message of their complaints. Twelve years later, my comparison of Nazi propaganda techniques to the war of words fundamentalist Christians are waging doesn't seem so extreme.

In an interview in the *New York Times*, Dr. Fritz Stern, himself a refugee from Hitler's Germany and a leading scholar of European history, also made the comparison. Reporter Chris Hedges explained Stern's passion for history. "Since escaping Nazi Germany in 1938 at 12 years old, Fritz Stern wanted to grasp how democracies disintegrate, to uncover warning signs that other democracies should heed and to write about the seductiveness of authoritarian movements." At an award ceremony honoring Dr. Stern, a professor emeritus at Columbia University, he startled his audience with a description of the mood in Germany that welcomed Hitler into power with the current mood in America.

"Hitler," Dr. Stern explained, "saw himself as the instrument of providence and fused his racial dogma with a Germanic Christianity...Some people recognized the moral perils of mixing religion and politics, but many more were seduced by it. It was the pseudo-religious transfiguration of politics that largely ensured Hitler's success, notably in Protestant areas... There was a longing in Europe for fascism before the name was ever invented. There was a longing for a new authoritarianism with some kind of religious orientation and above all a greater communal belongingness. There are some similarities in the mood then and the mood now…"[2]

Gary Nixon, my partner of almost twenty-five years and the distant relative of a certain American president, believes there are more than "some similarities." After living with me for all these years and after experiencing the wrath of fundamentalist Christians who seem obsessed with their war against gay Americans, Gary is so certain that a homosexual holocaust could happen here that he has quit using "fundamentalist" to describe the Christians who are waging war against us and calls them "fascists" instead. Don't be too hard on Gary if you disagree. He remembers the painful and frightening experiences we've had with fundamentalist Christians over the years and he finds it very difficult to call them Christian at all.

He remembers one particularly rough encounter I had with a gang of fundamentalist Baptist pastors who invaded a conference room at a university in New Mexico where I had been invited by the campus pastor to speak on being gay and Christian in America. I learned later that when the notice of my visit appeared in a local newspaper, clergymen across the city were enraged. At least twenty-five of these formidable men in black from across the state stood along the walls for roughly thirty minutes before their leader cut in with a loud "It's our turn now!" I tried to continue, but they shouted me down. Students were angry and confused. A young woman was crying. My host finally led me to the door and we left the class in shambles. Recalling that unnerving event and too many others like it, Gary says angrily, "Next time those fascists come to hear you speak you ought to make them leave their guns and their Bibles at the door."

I can't blame Gary for fixing the fascist label on the fundamentalist Christians in our lives. In fact, a good part of the time I think his fascist label is appropriate. During the last twelve years, we've met too many fundamentalist Christian activists who act like fascists in their absolute determination to deny us our rights and drive us back into our closets and even their desire to see us dead, all from reading literally those words of Moses in Leviticus 20:18: "A man who sleeps with another man is an abomination and should be executed."

It may be hard to believe that there are Americans who are committed to carrying out the death sentence on gay men "because God commanded it." It was very difficult for the world to believe that there were Germans determined to eliminate the Jews of Europe. But that, too, happened in my lifetime. Even the not-so-extreme fundamentalist Christians have decided to make gay people second-class citizens or worse, and they are out there right now working hard to gain enough power in government to rob us of our rights and in some extreme cases to string us up legally. Gary and I know the power of runaway fundamentalism because we have spent the last twelve years defending ourselves from their attacks, debating them on talk shows and in public forums, and answering their angry phone calls, letters, and e-mails. After years of studying fundamentalism from the inside out, I am convinced that Christian fundamentalism is a far greater threat to this country than Muslim terrorists could ever be. So we've come full circle. Is there any possibility that fundamentalist Christianity in our times compares in any way to the fascist Third Reich?

On a hilarious episode of Jon Stewart's *The Daily Show*, Stewart pointed out that it was quite in vogue to label your opponent a fascist and that "everyone was doing it." It was a fair warning. Stewart quoted leaders from left, right, and center who were using the fascist label simply to slander their enemy without stepping back from name-calling long enough to see if the name really fits.

So, what is fascism anyway, what are the characteristics of the people called fascists, and do we have any right—or responsibility—to paste the fascist label on the fundamentalist Christians who are waging war against us? We learned in our ninth-grade civics classes that the word *fascist* or *fascismo* comes from the Italian word *fascio*, literally a bundle of sticks, in this case tightly bound around an ax handle with the ax-head (sometimes double-headed) protruding from the top.

The *fascio* symbol currently appears on the American dime, the base of the Lincoln Monument, and behind the speaker's podium in the U.S. House of Representatives. Early Americans used the bundle of sticks to represent the solidarity of our first thirteen colonies. But two thousand years ago, the *fascio* was carried by an attendant before the procession of a Roman emperor to symbolize his absolute power over the people and the people's absolute support for their ruler.

In 1922, Benito Mussolini adopted the ancient *fascio* to symbolize his new army *Fasci di combattimento*, and, just as Hitler's fighters wore the Nazi swastika into combat, Mussolini's troops wore the *fascio* on their black shirts as they swept him into absolute power on a raging tide of nationalism. The ever-present *fascio* symbolized Mussolini's political movement, which held power in Italy for twenty-three years, until April 27, 1945, when Mussolini was shot and killed by Italian partisans while trying to escape to Switzerland. I was only five, but I still remember seeing the picture of his body hanging upside down in Milan's Piazza Loreto, a fitting climax to Mussolini's bloody story. Mussolini, Hitler, and Franco in Spain all headed regimes that can be labeled fascist. But what right do we have to compare Robertson, Dobson, Falwell, and Kennedy to these dictators, or to compare the fundamentalist Christian movement in the United States to the political movements of totalitarian despots of Europe in the first half of the twentieth century?

Actually we have no right to make a direct comparison. It certainly isn't my goal to caricature Robertson with a bristly mustache and his arm in the air or Falwell goose-stepping about Lynchburg. "No critic is saying the United States now mimics the fascism of the 1930s," asserts Canadian professor Henry A. Giroux. "The point is that it happens to be developing a number of characteristics that are endemic to fascist ideology...Fascism is not an ideological apparatus frozen in a particular historical period but a theoretical and political signpost for understanding how democracy can be subverted, if not destroyed."[3]

Umberto Eco, the Italian novelist, describes fascism as "eternal...still around us, sometimes in plain clothes." As a young man, Eco witnessed World War II from a village in the Piedmont Mountains, where his mother moved to keep her son out of the cross fire between fascists and local partisans in their small town just east of Turin. "It would be easier for us [to recognize fascism]," Eco asserts, "if there appeared on the world scene somebody saying, 'I want to reopen Auschwitz, I want the Blackshirts to parade again in the Italian squares.' Life is not that simple. Ur [eternal] fascism can come back under the most innocent of disguises. Our duty is to uncover it and to point our finger at any of its new instances—everyday, in every part of the world."[4]

Almost two years before Jon Stewart scolded us for calling one another fascist so lightly, the reverend Davidson Loehr preached a rather alarming sermon tided "Living Under Fascism." Loehr begins with an acknowledgment that we must be careful to define before we demean. "I don't mean it as name-calling at all," he begins. "I mean to persuade you that the style of governing into which America has slid is most accurately described as fascism, and that the necessary implications of this fact are rightly regarded as terrifying."[5]

Reverend Loehr then suggests to his congregation that if they are genuinely interested in the comparisons of fascism and fundamentalism, they might start by reading an article Mussolini wrote for the *Italian Encyclopedia* in 1932 (with the help of his ghostwriter, Giovanni Gentile). Mussolini's description of fascism makes it all too clear why Loehr sees parallels between fascism and fundamentalist Christianity. It also helps explain why he is terrified by the implications.

"Fascism," Mussolini explains, "now and always, believes in holiness and in heroism...Fascism denies that the majority, by the simple fact that it is a majority, can direct human society... Fascism denies, in democracy, the absurd conventional untruth of political equality...For Fascism, the growth of empire, that is to say the expansion of the nation, is an essential manifestation of vitality, and its opposite a sign of decadence...War alone brings up to its highest tension all human energy and puts the stamp of nobility upon the peoples who have courage to meet it... Empire demands discipline, the coordination of all forces and a deeply felt sense of duty and sacrifice: this fact explains...the necessarily severe measures which must be taken against those who would oppose this spontaneous and inevitable movement... for never before has the nation stood more in need of authority, of direction and order."

After years of monitoring Robertson, Falwell, Dobson, and the others, Mussolini's words sound terribly familiar. The fundamentalist leaders' call to "holiness" and to "heroism" is repeated endlessly, especially in their fund-raising letters. Fundamentalists substitute the word "righteousness" for "holiness" and claim that only the "righteous" are fit to govern the nation, intimating quite frankly that the "unrighteousness" (gays, Muslims, migrants, outcasts, liberals, non-Christians, and pagans of every variety) shouldn't even have the right to vote (let alone have a say in religious or public policy).

In almost every letter he mails to millions of his supporters, Jerry Falwell calls for a return to "holiness." In a year-end letter, Falwell writes: "Sadly, the U.S. has forfeited much of its moral authority in the world...The godly humility that has been our nation's real strength since its founding has been stripped away. Can any of this be restored? Can the God who gave life to America bring it back from the brink of moral suicide...? Of course he can...Join me in proclaiming God's truth by returning your *Morality in America* survey today. And when you do please include a special gift to help us proclaim the truth to America on our weekly *Listen America* broadcasts."[6]

And the call to "heroism" sounds like the closing words of a typical D. James Kennedy fund-raising letter, this time begging for help to support his campaign against the ACLU "for pressuring legislators to give homosexuals 'special rights' under the law—as the fruits of their sexual immorality!" Kennedy warns his people to "take action—effectively—and immediately...I am willing to be called names. I am willing to be the target of hatred. I am willing to stand up and speak the truth, to represent you and your views, to America. *[I am willing to be a hero.]* But I need your prayer support...and I need your financial support today. I am calling on God-fearing Americans everywhere to 'DRAW THE LINE IN '99.' *[Will you be a hero, too?]* "[7]

Mussolini's call for "the growth of empire...the expansion of the nation" is also a common fundamentalist theme. Kennedy says, "As God's junior partners we are to rule over the earth in His name,"[8] and I'm afraid he's not just thinking allegorically. On the one hand, the expansion has to do with Christianizing other countries, regardless of their religious beliefs and traditions, and in the process extending our business and political interests in those lands. But fundamentalist Christians have almost entirely ignored Jesus' appeal to be peacemakers. Like Mussolini's call to use bullets, bombs, and bayonets to expand Italy's sphere of influence "for the nation's sake," fundamentalist Christians give their full support to any bloody conflict that is done "for

God's sake." For example, fundamentalists seem all too eager to support Israel in their war with the Palestinian people.

"Israel is not going to give up Jerusalem," Pat Robertson insists. "Jerusalem is non-negotiable…That is their capital. It was the capital won by King David and they are not about to give it up…Yasser Arafat wants the capital in East Jerusalem…If he insists on it, ultimately, there will be war. But that is what the Bible says—That is going to be the place of ultimate conflict. It's going to be over the status of Jerusalem. I just hope and pray that America comes down on the right side, and the right side is for Israel to continue the land that was given to them by God Almighty."[9] This is foreign policy based on biblical inerrancy. Pat Robertson is pressuring the executive and legislative branches of government to comply with fundamentalist pre-millennial theology.

Of course Roberson has little respect for the State Department. On two different *700 Club* telecasts, Robertson suggests that *we* "nuke" Foggy Bottom, the State Department's location in Washington, D.C. "If I could just get a nuclear device inside Foggy Bottom," Pat exclaimed, "I think that's the answer. We've got to blow that thing up."[10] Whether he's joking (as in "nuking" the State Department) or being very serious (in what follows), Pat Robertson often calls for violence to accomplish what he perceives as God's work in the world.

The media had a field day when he called on U.S. officials to assassinate Venezuelan President Hugo Chávez."[11] Four days later, Robertson thought it was a good idea for someone to murder Jared "the Subway Guy" Fogel.[12] And in 2003, he urged his nationwide audience to pray for God to remove three Supreme Court justices "for their attacks on religious faith.[13] Mussolini described the "necessarily severe measures which must be taken against those who would oppose," and, joking or serious, Pat Robertson recommends on a regular basis rather "severe measures" for individuals and institutions he opposes.

Bill Moyers reminds us that fundamentalist theology began affecting U.S. policy, domestic and foreign, with the Reagan administration. Moyers recalls that "James G. Watt told the U.S. Congress that protecting natural resources was unimportant in light of the imminent return of Jesus Christ." Watt, Reagan's Secretary of the Interior and a fundamentalist Christian, claimed that there is no need to support treaties, protocols, and agreements intended to protect the air, the seas, wildlife, and forest preserves because we don't know how much time we have before Jesus returns." In public testimony he said, "After the last tree is felled, Christ will come back."[14]

Laurence W. Britt is an American businessman (former Xerox executive), a novelist-historian, and a social science sleuth. For decades he has been fascinated with fascism and its effects. The principles of fascism, he says, "are wafting in the air today, surreptitiously masquerading as something else, challenging everything we stand for. The cliché that people and nations learn from history is not only overused, but also overestimated; often we fail to learn from history, or draw the wrong conclusions. Sadly, historical amnesia is the norm."[15]

In 2002, Britt decided to examine the basic principles of fascism as demonstrated by various twentieth-century fascist regimes, including Nazi Germany, Fascist Italy, Franco's Spain, Salazar's Portugal, Papadopoulos's Greece, Pinochet's Chile, and Suharto's Indonesia. "To be sure," he admits, "they constitute a mixed bag of national identities, cultures, developmental levels, and history. But they all followed the fascist or protofascist model in obtaining, expanding, and maintaining power. Further, all these regimes have been overthrown, so a more or less complete picture of their basic characteristics and abuses is possible."

I'm not going to insult you by pointing out how almost every one of Britt's "14 identifying characteristics of fascism" is illustrated by fundamentalist Christians and their political allies. I'm just going to admit that the first time I read this list I was disturbed by the similarities.

1. Powerful and Continuing Nationalism
Fascist regimes tend to make constant use of patriotic mottos, slogans, symbols, songs, and other paraphernalia. Flags are seen everywhere, as are flag symbols on clothing and in public displays.

2. Disdain for the Recognition of Human Rights
Because of fear of enemies and the need for security, the people in fascist regimes are persuaded that human rights can be ignored in certain cases because of "need." The people tend to look the other way or even approve of torture, summary executions, assassinations, long incarcerations of prisoners, etc.

3. Identification of Enemies/Scapegoats as a Unifying Cause
The people are rallied into a unifying patriotic frenzy over the need to eliminate a perceived common threat or foe: racial, ethnic or religious minorities; liberals; communists; socialists, terrorists, etc.

4. Supremacy of the Military
Even when there are widespread domestic problems, the military is given a disproportionate amount of government funding, and the domestic agenda is neglected. Soldiers and military service are glamorized.

5. Rampant Sexism
The governments of fascist nations tend to be almost exclusively male-dominated. Under fascist regimes,

traditional gender roles are made more rigid. Opposition to abortion is high, as is homophobia and antigay legislation and national policy.

6. Controlled Mass Media

Sometimes the media are directly controlled by the government, but in other cases, the media are indirectly controlled by government regulation, or sympathetic media spokespeople and executives. Censorship, especially in wartime, is very common.

7. Obsession with National Security

Fear is used as a motivational tool by the government over the masses.

8. Religion and Government Are Intertwined

Governments in fascist nations tend to use the most common religion in the nation as a tool to manipulate public opinion. Religious rhetoric and terminology is common from government leaders, even when the major tenets of the religion are diametrically opposed to the government's policies or actions.

9. Corporate Power Is Protected

The industrial and business aristocracy of a fascist nation often are the ones who put the government leaders into power, creating a mutually beneficial business/government relationship and power elite.

10. Labor Power Is Suppressed

Because the organizing power of labor is the only real threat to a fascist government, labor unions are either eliminated entirely, or are severely suppressed.

11. Disdain for Intellectuals and the Arts

Fascist nations tend to promote and tolerate open hostility to higher education, and academia. It is not uncommon for professors and other academics to be censored or even arrested. Free expression in the arts is openly attacked, and governments often refuse to fund the arts.

12. Obsession with Crime and Punishment

Under fascist regimes, the police are given almost limitless power to enforce laws. The people are often willing to overlook police abuses and even forgo civil liberties in the name of patriotism. There is often a national police force with virtually unlimited power in fascist nations.

13. Rampant Cronyism and Corruption

Fascist regimes almost always are governed by groups of friends and associates who appoint each other to government positions and use governmental power and authority to protect their friends from accountability. It is not uncommon in fascist regimes for national resources and even treasures to be appropriated or even outright stolen by government leaders.

14. Fraudulent Elections

Sometimes elections in fascist nations are a complete sham. Other times elections are manipulated by smear campaigns against or even assassination of opposition candidates, use of legislation to control voting numbers or political district boundaries, and manipulation of the media. Fascist nations also typically use their judiciaries to manipulate or control elections.[16]

In his sermon "Living Under Fascism," Davidson Loehr warns us that Britt's list describing the fourteen characteristics of fascism "mirrors the social and political agenda of religious fundamentalisms worldwide. It is both accurate and helpful for us to understand fundamentalism as religious fascism, and fascism as political fundamentalism. They both come from very primitive parts of us that have always been the default setting of our species: amity toward our in-group, enmity toward out-groups, hierarchical deference to alpha male figures, a powerful identification with our territory, and so forth. It is that brutal default setting that all civilizations have tried to raise us above, but it is always a fragile thing, civilization, and has to be achieved over and over and over again."[17]

While Britt's research reflects the common characteristics of fascism, the massive study by Theodor Adorno, Nevitt Sanford, Else Frenkel Brunswick, and Daniel J. Levinson describes the personality traits of a fascist. Shortly after World War II, the American Jewish Committee commissioned these four educators to analyze the mind-set of Europeans who allowed six million Jews and uncounted others to be murdered by the Nazis. The one-thousand-page report, *The Authoritarian Personality*, was a joint effort of the Berkeley Public Opinion Study and the Institute of Social Research, also known as the Frankfurt School. It was released by the American Jewish Committee in 1950 and described in detail six personality traits of those who supported Hitler and Mussolini in their war to conquer the world.[18]

The Authoritarian Personality was part of a series called Studies in Prejudice, basic research on the origins of religious and racial prejudice. For the past half century, controversy has swirled around this report, but more than fifty years later it still helps us understand why some people stood by in silent support while their neighbors were dragged away and others risked everything to save them from the holocaust. The personality tendencies of the individual most likely to support fascism were found to include: (1) desire for a strong leader, (2) cultural narrowness, (3) patriotic conformity, (4) stereotyping of the out-groups, (5) anti-introspection, and (6) aggression.

A 356-word "announcement" that Jerry Falwell made to his congregation on Sunday, October 30, 2004, just two days before George W. Bush was reelected president, illustrates rather clearly how fundamentalist Christians share these same six personality traits. I was sitting in the fifth row on the left side of Falwell's Thomas Road Baptist Church, writing furiously to be sure I got every word of this illegal political announcement on the eve of the election.

"This election is clearly light against darkness," Falwell begins. "Vote Christian...and it doesn't take a lick of sense to know what that means. Any dummy knows what it means to vote Christian. Until this year, the Amish haven't voted. This year, they will vote for George Bush. I'm taking my plane immediately after this service and picking up Sean Hannity, Bill Bennett, Ollie North, and Zell Miller. Together, until midnight tonight, we will do Pennsylvania for George Bush. For the past weeks we've done Ohio and Florida. May God bless America one more time.

"Since this church TRBC was founded," Falwell continues, "you've allowed me five out of seven days on the road but always back on Sunday. I've traveled four hundred thousand miles a year rallying this nation to righteousness. As a result of the Moral Majority and the organizations that have flowed out of it—like the Christian Coalition, Concerned Women for America, and the Rutherford Institute, I have...we have rallied one-third of the total number of people who will vote on Tuesday. We, you and I, the people of TRBC, may be God's instrument for saving America. On Monday night, tomorrow [election eve], I've mobilized one hundred thousand pastors to gather their people to pray. We can sow and water, but only God gives the increase [meaning the election of George Bush].

"I will spend the rest of my life mobilizing Christians to be light and salt. It is my goal that before I die, every national, state, local, school board or board of supervisor election will elect and reelect men of God into positions of authority. We must be pro life, pro family, pro strong defense, and pro Israel. Shame on America for killing unborn babies and for recognizing same-sex marriage. America's future will be determined on election day.

"Osama Bin Ladin was used of God (see Psalm 76:10) when he threatened the U.S. and the Bush family on Thursday because it will stir up a few extra million Americans to vote for someone who will not be soft on terrorism, who will hunt down and kill this evil man. If we lose on Tuesday, I will spend the next years raising up another extra million voters to guarantee that Hillary will not get it. We must elect the righteous into office who will see that righteousness prevails."[19]

See if you agree that in this short announcement Jerry Falwell appeals to all six of those personality traits that made Europeans vulnerable to the propaganda efforts of Hitler, Mussolini, and their cronies.

1. Desire for a strong leader resulting in "submissive, uncritical attitude toward idealized moral authorities of the in-group:"[20]

FALWELL: "I have...we have rallied one-third of the total number of people who will vote on Tuesday. We, you and I, the people of TRBC, may be God's instrument for saving America."

2. Cultural narrowness seen in rigid acceptance of the conventional middle-class values of "the culturally 'alike'" and the tendency to reject and punish "the culturally 'unlike'...who violate conventional values."[21]

FALWELL: "We must be pro life, pro family, pro strong defense, and pro Israel. Shame on America for killing unborn babies and for recognizing same-sex marriage. America's future will be determined on election day."

3. Patriotic conformity, rooted in the belief that one's own nation is superior and should rightly dominate and that other nations are inferior and threatening out-groups.[22]

FALWELL: "This election is clearly light against darkness... May God bless America one more time."

4. Negative stereotyped perceptions of the members of "unlike" out-groups.[23]

Rather than seeing them as individuals who also laugh and cry and love and hate, or who, in the words of Joseph Berger, "lived, laughed, cursed, fought, who did the things human beings do."[24]

FALWELL: "...If we lose on Tuesday, I will spend the next years raising up another extra million voters to guarantee that Hillary will not get it. We must elect the righteous into office who will see that righteousness prevail."

5. Anti-introspection, i.e., resistance to self-understanding, to soul-searching, to cause-and-effect analysis of individual and group behavior, unable to tolerate ambiguity, belief in mystical, unexplainable phenomena, disparaging intellectual attempts to perceive life's nuances and complexities.[25]

FALWELL: "Vote Christian...and it doesn't take a lick of sense to know what that means. Any dummy knows what it means to vote Christian."

6. Aggression, involving "the need for an out-group" who represents "the intrinsic evil (aggressiveness, laziness, power-seeking, etc.) of human nature…[that] is unchangeable [and] must be attacked, stamped out, or segregated, wherever it is found, lest it contaminate the good."[26]

FALWELL: "Osama Bin Ladin was used of God (see Psalm 76:10) when he threatened the U.S. and the Bush family on Thursday; because it will stir up a few extra million Americans to vote for someone who will not be soft on terrorism, who will hunt down and kill this evil man."

Analyze Jerry Falwell's preelection campaign speech and you'll find that almost every sentence can be used in one way or another to illustrate the six characteristics of the authoritarian personality. The Adorno study also discovered that there is a definite relationship between individuals with authoritarian personality tendencies and religious practice, especially in the United States: "…belonging to a religious body in America today," the research suggests, "certainly does not mean that one thereby takes over the traditional Christian values of tolerance, brotherhood and equality. On the contrary it appears that these values are more firmly held by people who do not affiliate with any religious group…People who reject organized religion are less prejudiced than those who accept it."[27]

In 1944, Henry A. Wallace, one of three vice presidents who served under Roosevelt, warned that although "fascism is a world-wide disease," the spirit of fascism is also a threat to America. "Its greatest threat to the United States," he writes, "will come after the war" from within the country itself. The editors of the *New York Times* "deplored charges directed by Vice President Wallace against what he called 'American Fascists.'" In fact, the whole country was stunned to hear the vice president claim that fascists in America were a greater threat than the fascists our troops were fighting in Europe. They found it hard to believe that after Hitler and Mussolini were defeated fascism would remain alive and powerful in the hearts of millions of Americans.[28]

The prophetic stand Wallace took against the threat of fascism in the United States (at the exact same time Allied forces were fighting their way up the Italian boot to end Mussolini's fascist reign) might have been the reason why that same year Roosevelt dumped Wallace as his running mate and chose Harry S. Truman to replace him. In his defense, Wallace wrote a compelling editorial for the *New York Times* defining fascism and explaining its powerful hold on millions of Americans.

"The really dangerous American Fascists," Wallace wrote, "are not those who are hooked up directly or indirectly with the Axis. The FBI has its finger on those. The dangerous American Fascist is the man who wants to do in the United States in an American way what Hitler did in Germany in a Prussian way. The American Fascist would prefer not to use violence. His method is to poison the channels of public information. With a Fascist the problem is never how to present the truth to the public but how best to use the news to deceive the public into giving the Fascist and his group more money or more power."[29]

"Always and everywhere," says Wallace, "they [Fascists] can be identified by their appeal to prejudice and by the desire to play upon the fears and vanities of different groups in order to gain power. It is no coincidence that the growth of modern tyrants has in every case been heralded by the growth of prejudice...It may be shocking to some people in this country to realize that, without meaning to do so, they hold views in common with Hitler when they preach discrimination against other religious, racial or economic groups."[30]

A half-century later, Fritz Stern, one of the world's foremost experts in the ways democracies disintegrate, echoed Vice President Wallace's warning of the dangers in an open society of "mass manipulation of public opinion, often mixed with mendacity [dishonesty, deceit, lies, falsehoods] and forms of intimidation [threats, pressure, bullying, fear]." John R. MacArthur, whose *Second Front* examines wartime propaganda in Nazi Germany, was even more explicit. "The comparison between the propagandistic manipulation and uses of Christianity, then and now," he warns, "is hidden in plain sight. No one will talk about it. No one wants to look at it."[31]

So let's talk about it. How can that dark stain on world history help us understand what is happening now? Is it absurd to suggest that the Glen Eyrie and Wansee protocols have something in common? Is there any way to compare the propaganda war that fundamentalist Christians are waging against gay Americans with Hitler's war on Jews during those tragic years in Germany that ended in the Holocaust?

At the heart of fundamentalism is the politics of blame. When times get rough, people need a scapegoat. Richard Plant describes the mood in Germany following the defeat of the Kaiser and the utter collapse of the "Golden Age of German Power." "A tidal wave of shame and resentment...swept the nation. Many people tried to digest the bitter defeat by searching furiously for scapegoats. The belief that internal enemies had brought down the Empire...was widespread"[32]

Plant paints a vivid picture of those days leading up to Hitler's triumph. Germans were afraid of terror from outside the country and equally concerned about racist and nationalist groups that threatened from within. The German mark fell from 192 marks to the American dollar to 4.2 trillion. With the collapse of the economy, the people lost faith in government. Unemployment soared. Hunger and homelessness prevailed. Hope died. Tension grew.

"The Nazi Party," Plant explains, "not only provided food, weapons, and a splendid uniform, it proclaimed a new purpose, a new faith, and a new prophet." That new prophet was a master of the politics of blame. From the beginning of his rise to power, Hitler used fiery speeches to single out his enemies: Jews, Gypsies, homosexuals, union leaders, dissenting politicians, Marxists, scientists, writers, lawyers, but especially the Jews. In *The War That Hitler Won*, Robert Edwin Herzstein describes Hitler's blame game as "the most infamous propaganda campaign in history." Here's where the most obvious comparisons can be made. During his rise to power, Hitler caricatured and condemned the Jews in the exact same way today's fundamentalist Christians are caricaturing and condemning homosexual Americans. We can only hope the similarities end there.[33]

On July 29, 1994, one week after our fast protesting James Dobson's incessant antigay rhetoric, U.S. Senator Paul Wellstone, himself a Jew, made the same comparison. In responding to an antigay comment made by an unidentified "spokesman for the religious right," Wellstone said, "When you say...you [gay Americans] are not a group of people who need special protection. You do well economically. You are an elite. That is precisely the argument that has been made in behalf of the worst kind of discrimination against Jewish people."[34]

In drawing this comparison, I am not in any way suggesting that the suffering of America's sexual and gender minorities is equal to the suffering of European Jewry. However, there is no doubt that propaganda leading to fear and hatred of any people always ends in suffering, one victim at a time. The tragic deaths of Anne Frank, Emmett Till, and Matthew Shepard are a direct result of a very similar sequence of events. Once the blame game begins, the urge to purge follows quickly. The arrest, imprisonment, and murder of six million Jews and the destruction of almost five thousand Jewish communities were an almost predictable consequence of Hitler's propaganda campaign against them.

The blame game is currently being played by fundamentalist Christians against gay and lesbian Americans. The very same techniques that the Nazis used against the Jews during the early stages of their campaign to demean, dehumanize, and demonize them are being used against us today.

Visit the Holocaust Museum in Washington, D.C. Walk through the exhibits describing those early years of Hitler's campaign to demonize Jews. When you see the word "Jew" and substitute just momentarily the word "homosexual," the comparisons become all too obvious.

The quotations I use below to illustrate the variety of ways Nazis caricatured the Jews are from a transcript of *Der ewige Jude (The Eternal Jew)*, arguably the most famous of all Nazi propaganda films. Produced in 1940 by Joseph Goebbels, Hitler's minister of propaganda, this mocumentary uses Polish Jews to stereotype all Jews as "corrupt, filthy, lazy, ugly, and perverse...an alien people which have taken over the world through their control of banking and commerce, yet which still live like animals."[35]

The quotations that I use to illustrate the similarities between anti-Jewish and antihomosexual rhetoric are from the four-star fundamentalist generals I described earlier: Jerry Falwell, Pat Robertson, D. James Kennedy, and James Dobson. And in our archives there are endless quotations from other fundamentalist leaders that are as bad or worse.

"DISEASED"

In a most disgusting sequence at the beginning of *The Eternal Jew*, rats are seen swarming up out of a sewer and into the city streets while the narrator makes this insidious comparison. "In this way, they spread disease, plague, leprosy, typhoid fever, cholera, dysentery, and so on. They are cunning, cowardly, and cruel, and are found mostly in large packs. Among the animals, they represent the rudiment of an insidious and underground destruction—just like the Jews among human beings."

On his *700 Club*, Pat Robertson often dehumanizes gay Americans in the same way. "You know," he said, "one of the great misnomers in our society is the term 'gay'. That somebody who is involved in something that is leading to suicide, where the VD rate is eleven times that of others, which are almost always driven and ashamed and fearful and confused and psychotic and all the others that we read about plaguing this part of our society...They're not gay. They're very, very depressed and miserable."[36]

Using the fraudulent data of Paul Cameron, D. James Kennedy pushes the plague analogy even further. "Some 78% of homosexuals have caught at least one sexually transmitted disease," he writes. "Homosexuals represent 1%-3% of the U.S. population yet they account for 50% of America's syphilis, gonorrhea of the throat and intestinal infections. Their rate of acquiring infectious hepatitis B is 20-50 times greater than that of a heterosexual male...An estimated 50% of all homosexual males are HIV positive; that is, they are carrying the virus responsible for AIDS."[37]

"SEXUALLY PERVERTED"

To illustrate their claim that these "diseased Jews" are also sexually perverted, a man in a tuxedo appears on the screen forcing himself on a scantily clad woman trying desperately to escape. "The Jew is interested instinctively in all that is abnormal and depraved," the narrator explains. "He seeks to disrupt the people's healthy judgment." A book titled *Die Sexuelle Revolution* appears as the narrator says, "For more than a decade Jews wielded their pernicious power here. They meant to turn mankind's healthier instincts down degenerate paths."

In his sermons, on his television broadcasts, and especially in his fundraising letters, Jerry Falwell caricatures the homosexual as a pervert in very similar language. "...the America they [homosexuals] are demanding is...a sewer of moral filth...a place of spiritual anarchy...an environment that's incredibly dangerous to our children...a culture that despises Christian faith and morality."[38]

Pat Robertson describes the homosexual's lifestyle as "at best abominable. Homosexuality is an abomination. The practices of those people is appalling. It is a pathology. It is a sickness, and instead of thinking of giving these people a preferred status and privacy, we should treat AIDS exactly the same way as any other communicable disease."[39]

Knowing that parents and grandparents are his primary audience, James Dobson demonizes gay Americans with an even more specific application of our so-called perverted ways. "This is an issue America has got to wake up to," he warns. "The homosexual agenda is a beast. [It] wants our kids...Moms and Dads, are you listening? This [homosexual] movement is the greatest threat to your children. It is a particular danger to your wide-eyed boys, who have no idea what demoralization is planned for them."[40]

"A THREAT TO CHILDREN"

There is no better way to create fear and loathing of an enemy than to describe him as a threat to children. To make that point about Jews, the popular international film star Peter Lorre, born László Löwenstein, appears on a poster of his 1931 motion picture *M*. Best known for his villainous roles, Lorre stared in Fritz Lange's terror classic as a psychopathic child killer. The narrator says, "The Jew Lorre in the role of a child murderer. Not the murderer but the victim is guilty, according to this film, which presents the criminal sympathetically, to gloss over and excuse the crime." How easy it was for the Nazis to turn fiction into fact, making every Jew a threat to children.

Jerry Falwell has that skill. "Mark my words," he writes in another fund-raising letter. "[The homosexual's] primary target is the nation's public schools and our impressionable children."[41] "For 40 years," adds James Dobson in his Focus on the Family Newsletter, "the homosexual activist community has sought to implement a master plan...overturning laws prohibiting pedophilia, indoctrinating children and future generations through public education."[42] "This agenda must be stopped," echoes D. James Kennedy in his own fund-raising letter, "not because we hate homosexuals, but because of the damage it will do to the precious, innocent children of our land."[43] "It's one thing to say, 'We have rights to be left alone in our little corner of the world to do our thing,'" Pat Robertson warns on *The 700 Club*. "It's an entirely different thing to say, well, 'We're not only going to go into the schools. We're going to take your children and your grandchildren and turn them into homosexuals.' Now that's wrong."[44]

"A THREAT TO THE FAMILY AND FAMILY VALUES"

The Nazi propaganda ministry also uses *The Eternal Jew* to

caricature Jews as a threat to family and the traditional Aryan values. The film begins with pictures of families in the Warsaw Ghetto. "We Germans had an opportunity to look briefly at the Polish ghetto," the narrator explains. Cut to photo inside the propagandist's version of a Jewish home, focused on flies and filth. "Jewish houses are dirty and neglected," the narrator continues while the camera cuts to a woman, assumed to be a wife and mother, outside the home shouting and gesturing wildly as she does business in the marketplace.

"They rush into trade," the narrator says sarcastically, "because it suits their character and natural tendencies." Of course, the last shot in this "family" sequence is the close-up of a young boy alone on the street with blank eyes and a vacuous smile.

"These children," the narrator concludes, "have no idealism like ours have."

Fundamentalist Christians don't waste that kind of time on symbols and subtlety. They rush right to the bottom line. "See how homosexuals target children, attempt to destroy the family and biblical values," claims D. James Kennedy in an ad for his film *Gay Rights: Special Rights*.[45] "This is the climactic moment in the battle to preserve the family and future generations hang in the balance," James Dobson writes in his *Family News*.[46] In a fund-raising letter with the bold headline "SAME SEX MARRIAGE DESTROYING FAMILY," Jerry Falwell exclaims, "They have set out on a course to destroy the meaning of family in America, to re-write the definition of what we hold sacred and dear to include same-sex debauchery."[47] And on a *700 Club* broadcast, Pat Robertson says, "Such people are sinning against God and will lead to the ultimate destruction of the family and our nation."[48]

"A THREAT TO THE NATION"

On March 23, 1933, in its last official act, the German Parliament granted Adolph Hitler dictatorial power over the German people "to save the nation." Hitler, wearing his Nazi uniform, closed down the Parliament with these words: "Treason toward the nation and the people shall in future be stamped out with ruthless barbarity." Less than two weeks later, April 1, 1933, Nazi thugs plastered signs on the front windows of Jewish businesses announcing the official boycott of Jewish merchants.

Hitler was a master at the politics of blame. "Jews the world over are trying to crush the new Germany," he exclaimed. Invariably, the blame game is followed by the urge to purge. By August 29, 1933, Jews, the mentally and physically handicapped, homosexuals, Gypsies, Communists, and other political dissidents, but especially Jews, were being arrested in large numbers and sent to Dachau and other newly constructed concentration camps.

In *The Eternal Jew*, over scenes depicting Jews as parasites and pagans, the narrator explains that the boycotts, arrests, and imprisonment were necessary to stop those who were a threat to race and nation. "The eternal law of nature," the narrator explains, "to keep one's race pure, is the legacy which the National Socialist movement bequeaths to the German people for all time."

In the mind of fundamentalists, homosexuals, not Jews, are the primary threat to the future of this nation and its values. D. James Kennedy: "The anger and shame we feel when the entire nation is held hostage by a few homosexual activists...[49] Jerry Falwell: "They [homosexuals] have a godless, humanistic scheme for our nation...[50] Pat Robertson: "Every society which has embraced homosexuality...as part of their culture has gone down in flames. And if we want to destroy the United States of America this is the best way to do it. So the homosexuals may win their temporary battle, but they'll lose the war because they will destroy society and that's what's happening."[51]

"A THREAT TO CHRISTIANS AND THE CHRISTIAN CHURCH"

The Nazi propaganda film declared that Jews were also a threat to Christians. The narrator reads from the Torah: "Praise to the Lord who has set apart the holy Israelites from other people." Then in solemn tones he reads the fearmongering punch line. "The heathen, who do not keep the law, will be destroyed." The obvious conclusion drawn by Nazis from a literal reading of this biblical text is that Jews are out to destroy Christians.

Fundamentalist Christians see homosexuals as the primary threat to the Christian church, as well. Kennedy: "It's obvious that many in the homosexual community feel intolerance, even contempt for the Christian faith."[52] Dobson: "For more than forty years, the homosexual activist movement has sought to implement a master plan with goals that include muzzling of the clergy and Christian media."[53] Falwell: "Complete elimination of God and Christianity from American society is being designed [by homosexual activists] right now."[54] Robertson: "Just like what Nazi Germany did to the Jews, so liberal America is now doing to the evangelical Christians. It's no different. It is the same thing. It is happening all over again. It is the Democratic Congress, the liberal-based media, and the homosexuals who want to destroy the Christians."[55]

It is interesting to note that after the Nazi narrator calls Jews "diseased carriers of plague, leprosy, typhoid fever, cholera, and dysentery"; and after fundamentalist Christians call homosexuals "ashamed, fearful, confused and psychotic"; both accusers claim that these diseased and emotionally disabled minorities have such power over the majorities who accuse them.

"TOO MUCH POWER.
TOO MUCH PRIVILEGE."

Over pictures of a large map marked with bold lines showing the spread of Jewish influence around the world, the narrator of *The Eternal Jew* warns: "At the beginning of the twentieth century, the Jews sit at the junction of the world financial markets. They are an international power. Although only one percent of the world's population, with the help of their capital, they terrorize the world stock exchanges, world opinion, and world politics."

Fundamentalist Christians have agreed that lesbian and gay Americans represent only 1 to 3 percent of the population; yet they speak of us as the most powerful and destructive force in America. For example, Jerry Falwell claims that "the militant homosexual minority in America has steam-rolled television and movies, government, education, and the military...all in an attempt to establish themselves and their aberrant lifestyle as normal and natural."[56] "It is no secret that homosexuals have an inside track, through top level White House and cabinet officials, directly to the massive federal bureaucracy." "Make no mistake, these deviants seek no less than total control and influence in society, politics, our schools and in the exercise of free speech and religious freedom...If we do not act now, homosexuals will own America."[57]

D. James Kennedy expresses his similar complaint. "The homosexual community does not fit the bill [of a legitimate minority]. Homosexuals are, as a whole, better educated and better off financially than average Americans. In fact, homosexuals hold a disproportionate number of professional and management positions in our economy!" "...For years now our culture has been engulfed by [their] anti-virtue, pro-immorality message—in the media, in the courtrooms, in the legislative chambers, and even in some churches." "Their political clout is abundantly clear, even to the casual observer."[58]

Remembering the illegal marriages performed for beaming gay and lesbian couples in City Hall, James Dobson declares, "What thousands of homosexuals in San Francisco have achieved represents the collapse of the rule of law, with no legal or governmental official being willing or able to stop it or provide more than a temporary stay." "A revolution of striking proportions now looms before us." "What is at stake here is nothing less than the future of the family—the basic unit of society on which everything of value rests. Chaos would occur...everything of value would quickly unravel, beginning with the welfare of the younger generation. Cultures that have allowed their families to disintegrate have quickly deteriorated or passed from the scene." "This is the climactic moment in the battle to preserve the family, and future generations hang in the balance."[59]

"SINFUL, FALLEN CREATURES CONDEMNED BY GOD"

To eliminate this powerful Jewish threat to the "new Germany," Hitler had to demonize his enemies. It would be easier for German Christians to condemn the Jews if they were certain that God condemned the Jews as well. When an orthodox rabbi appears on the screen with his beard, side curls, leather-thonged tefillin, and fringed shawl, the narrator describes the scene as an example of "...their so-called religion."

The film spends a disproportionate amount of time on gruesome, close-up photos of a calf being slaughtered and drained of blood by a kosher Jewish butcher. Misusing the scene to illustrate the cruelty of all Jews, the narrator insists that "no German would let an animal suffer in that way."

To show that the Jews were not to be trusted—over a political cartoon caricaturing a "money grubbing Jew"—the narrator says, "For example, in Deuteronomy it is written: 'Unto a foreigner thou mayest lend upon usury, but unto thy brother thou shalt not lend upon usury.'" In other words, the Torah gives a Jewish banker, money changer, or even a merchant the right to exploit a German customer while demanding that he treat his fellow Jews fairly.

For the past forty years, fundamentalist Christians have been demonizing gay men and lesbians. If God condemns homosexuality and homosexuals, then fundamentalist Christians can condemn them, as well. They've even used "your so-called religion" language to demonize the Metropolitan Community Church. D. James Kennedy claims that "members of the homosexual community—particularly their nationwide denomination of more than two hundred 'Metropolitan Churches'—have twisted this Scripture and others to justify their sin...the leaders of the Metropolitan Churches are willing to say anything, true or not, in order to sell their position to the gullible and the ignorant."[60]

"Do you believe the Word of God?" Kennedy asks his Coral Ridge Presbyterian congregation. "It clearly states that God condemns homosexuality."[61] In a fund-raising letter to his Faith Partners, Jerry Falwell writes: "I believe homosexuality is a sin. It is against God's plan...a wicked, perverse lifestyle."[62] Pat Robertson even raises the image of the Third Reich to demonize us literally. "Many of those people involved with Adolph Hitler were Satanists," he claimed. "Many of them were homosexuals—the two things seem to go together."[63]

"THE ENEMY"

The Holocaust shows us all too clearly Hitler's final solution for the Jews. He appears only once in *The Eternal Jew*, as a disembodied voice demanding in one of his fiery speeches "the annihilation of the Jewish race in Europe!" Over pictures of German youth training for battle, soldiers marching in the street, crowds cheering, and bands playing, the narrator speaks these ominous words: "Under the leadership of Adolf Hitler, Germany has raised the battle flag of war against the eternal Jew." It is rather apparent by their rhetoric that fundamentalist Christians have raised their own battle flags of war against gay Americans.

"Will you join me in a declaration of war?" Jerry Falwell asked millions of people on his mailing list. "Homosexual groups have a design for a takeover of our country and your family. We must wage spiritual warfare to save America."[64] Sent to millions on his mailing list, the extremely oversized envelope had the words DECLARATION OF WAR printed in bright black letters on the back. "There is no middle ground," Falwell exclaims. "For Christians there can be no peaceful coexistence with these Sodomites whom God has given over to a reprobate mind."[65]

James Dobson calls the United States a place "where the civil war of values rages..." "...the church is marshaling its forces," he adds, "...preparing to meet the challenge [of same-sex marriage]. Evil has a way of overreaching, and that appears to have happened regarding the blatant and lawless assault on marriage and biblical morality."[66]

"Make no mistake about it," says D. James Kennedy. "... we are absolutely involved in a 'cultural war' for the very 'soul' of America. And I refuse to let the anti-virtue extremists win and continue to take our great nation toward the very brink of moral disaster." "We are networking thousands of committed Christian volunteers in the effort to reclaim America for Christ through our Center for Reclaiming America—returning the nation to a Judeo-Christian worldview—the original intent of our Founding Fathers."[67]

"The people who have come into [our] institutions [today]," Pat Robertson claims, "are primarily termites. They are into destroying institutions that have been built by Christians, whether it is universities, governments, our own traditions, that we have...The termites are in charge now, and that is not the way it ought to be, and the time has arrived for a godly fumigation."[68]

Rabbi Abraham Heschel once said, "Speech has power... words do not fade. What starts out as a sound ends in a deed."[69] We don't have to wait to see the consequences of fundamentalist Christian rhetoric. We already know what happens when religious leaders wage war against gay and lesbian Americans. The suffering began centuries ago when the Catholic Church decided that we should be hanged or burned at the stake. The suffering continues today. And it could get worse, much worse, if Pat Robertson and his fundamentalist Christian friends accumulate enough power to begin their "godly fumigation." It happened in Germany in my lifetime. Could it happen again?

In 1944, Vice President Wallace warned Americans to look for gatherings of powerful men and women that represent the dangers of fascism to our country. Wallace defined the "Fascist group" as "a purposeful coalition between the cartelists, the deliberate poisoners of public information, and those who stand for the KKK type of demagogue."[70] In 2006, Mr. Wallace would recognize his "Fascist group" model in the Council on National Policy, a combination of wealthy business executives and bankers, some involved in multinational corporations ("cartelists"); advertising agency chiefs and owners of television, radio, and cable systems ("poisoners of public information"); military and government officials, political power brokers, and religious leaders ("demagogues") who have come together in America to superimpose their fundamentalist Christian values on the rest of us.

According to their mission statement, the seven hundred—plus members of the CNP meet secretly three times a year "to acquaint our membership with those in positions of leadership in our nation in order that mutual respect be fostered" and "to encourage the exchange of information concerning the methodology of working within the system to promote the values and ends sought by individual members." Guests may attend "only with the unanimous approval of the executive committee." In e-mail messages to one another, members are instructed not to refer to the CNP by name.[71]

The membership lists are "strictly confidential" but over the years have included many of the richest Americans (Hunt, DuPont, Ahmanson, Coors, Grace, DeVos, DeMoss, Crowley) gathered in solidarity with the most powerful fundamentalist Christian gay-bashers (Robertson, Falwell, Dobson, Schlafly, Bauer, Wildmon, LaHaye, Robison, Sekulow, Bob Jones III, Weyrich, Viguerie, Phillips, Matrisciana, Monteith, Ankerberg, T Baehr, A. Bryant, even the founder of the Reconstructionist movement, R. J. Rushdoony and his son-in-law, David North) and their political and military allies (Ralph Reed, Jack Abramoff, Congressmen Vander Jagt, Is-took, Kemp, Dannemeyer, Ashbrook; Senators Richardson, Nickles, Lott, Helms, Callaway, Burton, Batchelder, Armstrong; Ambassadors S. L. Abbott and Alan Keyes; Secretaries Watt and Hodel; Attorney General

Meese, Governor Sununu, Lieutenant General Gordon Sumner Jr. (ret.), Major General John K. Singlaub (ret.), Major General George S. Patton III (ret.), Brigadier General Albion W. Knight, Lieutenant General Daniel O. Graham, and Lieutenant Colonel O. North. And that's just the tip of the iceberg, a very brief sampling of influential CNP members, past and present.

The *New York Times* reports that in 1999, George W. Bush addressed the CNP to solicit their support for his presidential campaign. And though it is a strict CNP rule that "the media should not know when or where we meet or who takes part in our programs, before or after a meeting," the Bush visit leaked to the press. Democrat leaders demanded a transcript of his speech. Bush refused. Shortly after the invasion of Iraq, Vice President Cheney and Defense Secretary Donald H. Rumsfeld attended a CNP meeting. Before the 2004 election, Bush administration and campaign officials were CNP guests, and in August 2004, just before the Republican convention, the CNP met at the Plaza Hotel in New York "for what participants called 'a pep rally' to re-elect President Bush."[72]

I admit that I have mixed emotions about the CNP. It is all too easy to make demons of its members (as so many of their members make demons out of us). I'm often tempted to define them as a "Fascist group" or at least a "Fascist group" in the making. At times I even get the urge to compare them to the Nazis who met at Lake Wannsee to plan the final solution for European Jewry. But I can't—at least not yet. More than a dozen CNP members were once my close friends or clients. I had no idea who these men and women were or what they were planning when I was invited to deliver a devotional message to a CNP meeting shortly after the council was founded in 1981. I remember entering the empty hotel conference room a few minutes before I was scheduled to speak. The first man into the room held out his hand and greeted me. "Hello, I'm Paul

Weyrich," he said. "We're delighted that you could join us, Mel." I didn't recognize Weyrich, whose impressive fundamentalist credentials include: cofounder of the Moral Majority, a founder of the Council National Policy, president of Free Congress Foundation, founding president of the Heritage Foundation (launched with a $250,000 donation from Joseph Coors and the Coors Corporation), and founder of the American Legislative Exchange Council.

You might ask, as Gary often does, why *do* I have mixed emotions about the CNP? Along with their most recent offspring, the Arlington Group, isn't this a perfect example of Wallace's cabal of powerful men and women meeting secretly to use the political process (which is their right) to reshape (or even replace) our democracy guided by their fundamentalist beliefs (which isn't their right)? Haven't we already seen that their values match Britt's definition of fascism exactly and don't their supporters across the nation demonstrate all six authoritarian characteristics of a fascist? Are they guilty or potentially guilty of becoming a "fascist group" in our time whose members were defined by Vice President Wallace in his time? "They claim to be super-patriots," Wallace writes, "but they would destroy every liberty guaranteed by the Constitution. They demand free enterprise, but are the spokesmen for monopoly and vested interest. Their final objective toward which all their deceit is directed, is to capture political power..."[73]

Yes, but—and here's where Gary gets really irritated— they are also my fellow Americans, most of them my Christian sisters and brothers who have been deceived by the spirit of fundamentalism. They are victims of misinformation, and in the process they are making victims of us all. I call them "fascists" because their end goals and their tactics for reaching those goals are so much in the spirit of fascism. But when I call them "fascist," it begins a chain of fear, anger, and violence against them exactly like the chain of fear, anger, and violence they have set in motion against me. I may get satisfaction from calling them names but instead of getting closer to a solution, name-calling simply drives us further apart. Therefore, to call them "fascist" is an act of violence against them that leads directly and indirectly to violence against me, as well.

In *Stranger at the Gate*, I described what was happening to me in 1981 at the same time I was leading members of the CNP in their morning devotional (how ironic that looks to me now). For the last year, I had been obsessed with the idea of death. Finally, with the help of my pastor, George Regas, and my psychiatrist, Warren Jones, I decided that even though I was still in the midst of terrible emotional conflict, "it was time to choose life, to admit my desperate needs, to begin the search for a way to meet them, and to trust God's grace for all the rest."[74]

About that moment, the Council on National Policy asked me to lead them in a morning meditation. After I was introduced, I walked to the mike and stood there shaking. I saw a lot of friends staring up at me in silent support. At least one of the billionaires in the room had been my friend for twenty-five years. During the last two decades, I had worked with at least two major publishers in the room and was the close friend of the president of a large media corporation. And of course, as a ghost, I had also established a productive working relationship with many of the fundamentalist television-types who were present. I can't remember a word I said to CNP members that day. But I do remember that my friend with an international media ministry came up at the close of the meeting, invited me to lunch, and, following lunch, to a fancy men's store in the hotel lobby where he insisted on buying me a very expensive winter jacket. He sensed that something was wrong, that I was in emotional turmoil, and he did all he knew to help me feel better.

I still wear that jacket more than twenty-five years later. And when I put it on it reminds me that my enemies were once my friends. I liked those guys. We had fun together finding ways to make films, produce television programs, and write books, pamphlets, and study guides that would teach the world about Jesus. They weren't into politics then, or at least they weren't as consumed by it as they are today. They were crusading for something and not against everything. I have a thousand memories of the good times, the playful times, the late-night dinners and all-too-early-morning breakfasts, the pre- and postproduction meetings, the times on location filming and videotaping in at least forty different countries. I stayed in their homes. I met their families. I knew their strengths and their weaknesses. I remember them as people who were living their lives the best they could and at that time sincerely trying to find and do God's will.

All during those decades that I worked with the men who would become powerful members of the CNP, I thought they were right about homosexuality. Without telling anyone, I was struggling against what they called a "sickness" and a "sin." I had no idea that one day I would see how wrong they are. When that day came, I used *Stranger at the Gate* to tell the world that my homosexual orientation was neither a "sickness" nor a "sin" but a gift from God the same way heterosexual orientation is God's gift. I wrote my old friends and employers to tell them that they were wrong about homosexuality and homosexuals; that their war against gay Americans was having tragic consequences in the lives of my new sisters and brothers; that finally the Spirit of Truth, God's Spirit, had broken through the decades of untruth and set me free and that if they would just consider the evidence they could be set free, as well.

I never heard from one of them again. When they learned I was gay, they just walked away.

Now we stand on opposite sides of an ever-widening chasm. They are shouting "faggot" and we yell "fascist" right back at them. Someone has to be willing to stop this cycle of fear, anger, and violence against one another, because the suffering will not end until we do.

Part Four

RESISTING
FUNDAMENTALISM

EIGHT

RECLAIMING OUR PROGRESSIVE POLITICAL VALUES

*T*he Lincoln Monument in Washington, D.C., is a sacred place for most Americans. In the summer of 1981, when Mike was eleven, we took one of those rare, father-son trips to the nation's capital. It was at least a hundred degrees in the shade with no shade in sight. Our first stop was that marble-and-limestone tribute to our sixteenth president, the gangly rail-splitting lawyer born in a one-room log cabin in Sinking Springs, Kentucky.

No parking space was available, so we walked to the monument from a temporary dirt lot near the Potomac. We could feel the hot pavement through our sandals. I felt like turning back to the air-conditioned comfort of our rental car until I saw that broad limestone stairway topped by thirty-six Doric, white marble columns rising up ninety-nine feet toward the sky like the Parthenon on the Acropolis in Athens or Hadrian's Pantheon in Rome.

Breathing hard and sweating profusely, we walked up the eighty-six stairs, grateful for the shade and silenced by that massive marble statue of Honest Abe gazing out past the Washington Monument across the capitol. When I looked closely at Lincoln's eyes, the president seemed stunned, as he might have looked when General Grant told him that six hundred twenty thousand American men and boys had been slaughtered to save the Union,[1] or during that split second in Ford's Theatre when he looked up to see John Wilkes Booth pull the trigger.

There's something awe-evoking about this place. Great Americans, men and women alike, have addressed the nation from these steps. When Marion Anderson, the African-American contralto, was refused permission to sing in Washington's Constitution Hall, Eleanor Roosevelt arranged for her to perform here before a crowd of seventy thousand people on Easter Sunday, 1939. On August 28, 1963, at the climax of the March on Washington for Jobs and Freedom, Martin Luther King, Jr., delivered his "I have a dream" speech to two hundred fifty thousand spectators from these steps, and on August 23, 2003, the fortieth anniversary of that historic event, I was there when Coretta Scott King stood on these same steps and declared that "dissent and protest are not only right, but obligations of good citizenship."

We must never forget that also on these steps, 460 fundamentalist Christian leaders gathered on July 4, 1986, in "solemn assembly" to sign their *Manifesto for the Christian Church*. Is it possible that these 460 sincere and well-meaning American fundamentalists committed treason that day? What exactly did they mean when they "covenanted with Almighty God" to work toward the day when all the people of this nation would live "in full, serious obedience to all the Bible's commands"?[2]

The U.S. Constitution defines "treason" as "levying war"

against these United States or "in adhering to their enemies, giving them aid and comfort."[3] Simply put, treason is an act that threatens the unity of the nation, and the covenant signed by those 460 fundamentalist Christian leaders is arguably such a threat. On the steps of the Lincoln Memorial, 460 Americans solemnly pledged that they would risk their lives "to promote Biblical obedience, peace, unity, love, joy, and compassion among all men, and to secure for ourselves and future generations the blessing of God Almighty."

Does that language sound familiar? Of course, as it echoes and at the same time it mocks the Preamble to the U.S. Constitution. We learned it as children and were tested on its meaning in twelfth-grade government classes: "We the people of the United States, in order to form a more perfect union, establish justice, insure domestic tranquility, provide for the common defense, promote the general welfare, and secure the blessings of liberty to ourselves and our posterity, do ordain and establish this Constitution for the United States of America."

And though the words of these preambles are fairly similar, the documents are very different in intent. To our forefathers—Christians, deists, masons alike—the U.S. Constitution was the bedrock of our experiment in democracy, the ultimate authority for a government of the people, for the people, and by the people. The signers of the *Manifesto for the Christian Church* were announcing their loyalty to the Bible as the standard by which the nation should be governed. It is a pledge by powerful fundamentalist Christian pastors, professors, authors, publishers, owners of television and radio networks, chief executives of foundations, political and religious organizations, and popular media gurus to replace the U.S. Constitution with their inerrant Bible. Look again at the language they use in their *Manifesto* to describe the role they would have the Bible play in the life of this nation and in the lives of this nation's almost 300 million citizens:

"The Bible is the only absolute, objective, final test...
for all philosophies, books, values, actions, and plans..."

"Whatever statements or values are in opposition to
the statement and values of the Bible err to the degree
of their opposition."

"The Bible States Reality for all Areas of Life and
Thought...in the spheres of law, government, economics, business, education, arts and communication,
medicine, psychology and science."

"All theories and practices of these spheres of life are
only true, right, and realistic to the degree that they
agree with the Bible."

"Those people or nations that live in opposition to
biblical laws and commandments will sooner or later,
be cursed and destroyed."[4]

It staggers the imagination that my fellow Americans—even
worse, my fellow Christians—stood on these steps and signed
a public document expressing their willingness to be martyred
if necessary to see that biblical law (read literally) replaces the
U.S. Constitution as the nation's ultimate legal authority. You
might not be as emotionally involved as I am in this treasonous
act, but these fundamentalist Christians sincerely believe that
the Bible declares my sexual orientation "an abomination," and
that accepting my homosexuality as a gift from the Creator is
an act worthy of death. You may not take these fundamentalists
seriously. I do. There are those who signed the *Manifesto* who
are eager to see the death penalty enforced on homosexuals to

keep this nation from being "cursed and destroyed" by God.

Forgive me for belaboring my growing discomfort with the "absolute" political and moral values of my fundamentalist Christian neighbors. It must be terribly obvious that I am angered and frightened by their misuse of those so-called values to raise money, mobilize volunteers, win elections, get initiatives passed and constitutions amended to deny my right to life, liberty, and the pursuit of happiness. Now, we're left with the most important question a non-fundamentalist can ask. First, what are our progressive political values and how do they interact with the values of our fundamentalist friends?

WE VALUE THE U.S. CONSTITUTION
AS THE BEDROCK OF OUR DEMOCRACY;
therefore we will resist all efforts to put
the Bible in its place.

On Thursday, January 20, 2005, George W. Bush placed his left hand on the Bible, raised his right hand, and repeated these words: "I do solemnly swear that I will faithfully execute the office of President of the United States, and will to the best of my ability, preserve, protect and defend the Constitution of the United States."

The "values" that determine (or that should determine) our president's agenda are enshrined in Article II, Section 2 of the U.S. Constitution, the same Constitution that President Bush swore to "preserve, protect and defend." However, just thirty-four days after our forty-third president took that oath, there was at least one glaring reason to fear that this president's second term in office would be shaped in large part NOT by the U.S. Constitution but by the fundamentalist Christian agenda.

On that day, February 24, 2005, President Bush announced his support for a constitutional amendment that would limit the definition of marriage to one man and one woman and in the process betray the US. Constitution. For the first time since its ratification in 1789, the Constitution would be used to make second-class citizens of millions of loyal, taxpaying gay and lesbian couples. That precious document guarded day and night in the National Archives would be hijacked by Christian fundamentalists to demean our relationships and deny us more than a thousand civil rights and protections that go automatically with marriage. After electing him and then pressuring him to do their bidding, fundamentalist Christians had literally forced our president to ignore his oath, undermine the guarantor of our liberty, and betray the American people.

The problem began during a December 2003 interview with ABC News when President Bush said, "If necessary, I will support a constitutional amendment which would honor marriage between a man and a woman." Those two words, "if necessary," sent shock waves across the fundamentalist Christian world. Suddenly they had reason to worry that the president they elected might not support their obsession with a Federal Marriage Amendment and actually leave to each state how civil marriage would be defined.

One of the fundamentalists' greatest fears is "judicial tyranny." They hate those judges who supposedly by their judicial decisions "make laws instead of enforcing them." They were afraid that judges on a State Supreme Court or the U.S. Supreme Court would overturn a state's decision to define marriage as only between one man and one woman and grant same-sex couples their civil rights. Unlike their president, the fundamentalists had decided that an amendment limiting marriage to one man and one woman was *very* necessary. It would allow them to superimpose their fundamentalist Christian values—based on a literal reading of their inerrant Bible—on the Constitution of the United States of America.

What a thrill that must be to see that their plan is working, that under the ruse of "saving marriage and the family" they are one step closer to replacing Democracy with biblical rule.

Feeling inexorable pressure from the right, Bush announced on January 14, 2004, that he would support a welfare reform law, a kind of compromise with his fundamentalist friends that would "help strengthen marriage" without resorting to a federal marriage amendment. It was not enough. In a press conference, Richard Land, president of the Southern Baptist Convention's Ethics & Religious Liberty Commission, congratulated the president for his efforts to strengthen marriage. "However," he added, "this is not a substitute for supporting a federal marriage amendment to guarantee that marriage in the United States will be only between a man and a woman."[5]

Tony Perkins, president of the Family Research Council (James Dobson's voice in Washington), joined the growing number of fundamentalist Christians pressuring the president. "Efforts to redefine marriage out of existence must be stopped," he said, "and the president's support of a federal marriage amendment would go a long way in making sure that marriage is not only promoted but also protected."[6]

Sandy Rios, president of Concerned Women for America (Beverly LaHaye's organization), scolded the president for "dancing dangerously around the issue of homosexual marriage." On her nationwide radio program, she accused the White House of attempting to pacify conservatives, and she considered the proposed compromise "an insult to all who really understand the issue." Rios made it clear that "those who would lead the president to believe that an initiative to promote marriage among low-income families will be an adequate defense against the destruction of marriage are political fools who will destroy the nation in an effort to mainstream perversion."[7] (Now there's an interesting new way to demonize our struggle for civil rights—"an effort to mainstream perversion." What will they think of next?)

Under this wave of fundamentalist pressure, the president folded. On February 24, 2004, he called a press conference to announce his decision to support the fundamentalist Christian amendment. The words he read from his teleprompter that day might have been taken directly from the transcript of a James Dobson *Focus on the Family* radio show or Pat Robertson's *700 Club.*

"After more than two centuries of American jurisprudence," the president began, "and millennia of human experience, a few judges and local authorities are presuming to change the most fundamental institution of civilization. Their actions have created confusion on an issue that requires clarity. On a matter of such importance, the voice of the people must be heard. Activist courts have left the people with one recourse. If we are to prevent the meaning of marriage from being changed forever, our nation must enact a constitutional amendment to protect marriage in America."[8]

It is ironic that when Pat Robertson speaks of "activist courts" and "judicial tyranny" he is simply quoting his father, Absalom Willis Robertson, the five-term senator from Virginia.[9] In 1956, Senator Robertson and his southern colleagues condemned the Supreme Court for its decision to protect the civil rights of African-American children. In 2004, Pat Robertson and his fundamentalist colleagues were criticizing state courts for protecting the civil rights of gay and lesbian Americans. To keep judges from another "clear abuse of judicial power," they demanded that their president, George W. Bush, support a constitutional amendment that would legalize immorality and deny gay and lesbian couples the rights and protections of marriage.

Fundamentalists flexed their political muscles and the

president's will collapsed. Once again they had demonstrated their power over our president. It's important to remember that those same fundamentalist Christians were flexing those political muscles long before they used state constitutional amendments opposing same-sex marriage to return George W. Bush to the White House.

During his first campaign for office, in 1992, Bill Clinton promised if elected to end the ban on gays in the military. He had no idea that during his first week in office the fundamentalist media machine would generate millions of calls, faxes, and letters to the White House, the State Department, and the Pentagon demanding the ban remain in place. With this nonviolent direct action, fundamentalists used their growing power to close down the nation's capital and exert their will on another American president.

We don't need to be reminded of the power fundamentalist Christians have in enforcing their political values on the executive and legislative branches of government and through their friends in those high places to control the judicial branch as well. So we're left with a dilemma. If our president will not keep his oath to preserve, protect, and defend the U.S. Constitution, then that task is left to us. That's why I have chosen preserving, protecting, and defending the U.S. Constitution as my first progressive political value.

When I speak at a church or a university, I carry a copy of the Bible in one pocket and a copy of the Constitution in the other. When I hold up both documents and ask, "Which is most important, the Constitution or the Bible?" invariably people, even progressive people, answer, "The Bible." That is a most dangerous notion. When it comes to guiding our democracy and running our government, the U.S. Constitution must always trump the Bible, because the Constitution protects our rights to disagree about what the Bible says. It is the only protection we have from the ever-increasing incursion of fundamentalist Christian values into our religious and political lives. The Constitution offers every citizen an umbrella of protection that will guarantee his or her right to read or not read the Bible, to believe in God or to ignore God altogether, to attend or not attend church, synagogue, temple, or mosque.

At the conclusion of the Constitutional Convention in 1778, Benjamin Franklin was asked, "What have we got...a Republic or a Monarchy?" Franklin answered, "A Republic... if you can keep it."[10] Keeping our republic begins by keeping the U.S. Constitution in its place to protect the rights won by blood on battlefields at home and abroad and to confront and condemn anyone who would place the inerrant Bible as the nation's ultimate authority for governance.

Most Americans read the U.S. Constitution in a high-school civics class and never read it again. During those same high-school years that I spent perhaps one week studying the U.S. Constitution, I spent almost every day reading and memorizing the Bible as a member of a Youth for Christ Bible Quiz Team. We memorized full books of the Christian Testament so that we could jump to our feet before the question was finished, state the question, and give the answer, chapter and verse. Now, I realize that as an American citizen I should know the seven articles and twenty-seven amendments of the U.S. Constitution as well as the fundamentalist Christians know the sixty-six books of the Hebrew and Greek Testaments. When someone even begins a statement that might question my civil rights, I should be able to jump to my feet, frame the question, and answer it by quoting from the U.S. Constitution and its amendments.

When I was child, my evangelical Christian parents read Bible stories to me at dinner and at bedtime. I wish I had read at least a few stories to my children of the U.S. Constitution and the wise and courageous Americans who created it. My evangelical pastor preached from Scripture twice on Sunday and once on Wednesday nights. I wish when I was pastor that I had preached an occasional sermon from the U.S. Constitution and even requested prayer for its preservation and protection during those Wednesday night prayer meetings. Almost every Sunday of my life, I got a full dose of Bible from my Sunday school teachers and youth pastors. As a grad school student and seminary professor, I don't remember even hearing the Constitution discussed. I attended a university that began as a Bible college and continued those traditions with a wide variety of required Bible classes, and eventually I graduated from seminary with a doctoral degree, including a strong minor in biblical studies, and yet in my entire life I've never taken a whole course dedicated to the U.S. Constitution and its unique role in preserving and protecting my freedoms.

Whether you are a person of faith or of no faith at all, we dare not begin our search for values—at least not our political values—with the Bible. As Americans, we must begin our search for political values with the U.S. Constitution. Dig out your old copy from civics class or download and print a new replica from "The U.S. Constitution on Line."[11] Memorize at least the Constitution's First Amendment before fundamentalist Christians undermine it completely. Say it clearly and say it often: "Congress shall make no law respecting an establishment of religion, or prohibiting the free exercise thereof; or abridging the freedom of speech, or of the press; or the right of the people peaceably to assemble, and to petition the Government for a redress of grievances."

Personalize the First Amendment. Vow to support NO politician, preacher, or Christian media guru who quotes the Bible and not the U.S. Constitution as the ultimate authority for governing our democracy. Vow to support NO politician, preacher, or Christian media guru who would withhold civil rights from anyone on the basis of his or her understanding of a verse from the "Old" or "New" Testament. Vow to support NO politician, preacher, or Christian media guru who even hints at limiting the free exercise of anyone's faith or lack of faith. Vow to support NO politician, preacher, or Christian media guru who wants to restrict anyone's freedom of speech or anyone's freedom of the press or anyone's right to assemble or anyone's right to petition or appeal or confront the government if it fails in any of these rights and protections.

Leon Jaworski, a special prosecutor during the Watergate scandal, reminds us that "from Watergate we learned what generations before us have known; our Constitution works. And during Watergate years it was interpreted again so as to reaffirm that no one—absolutely no one—is above the Law."[12] That includes our current president and his fundamentalist supporters. Keep a copy of your U.S. Constitution next to your TV's remote control. Judge the newsmakers by its standards. To preserve, protect, and defend the U.S. Constitution is a progressive value worth fighting for and the beginning of the end to that threat fundamentalist Christians pose to the future of this country.

WE VALUE OUR RELIGIOUS FREEDOM;
therefore we will resist all efforts to make this a "Christian nation."

It is very important for each of us to make it clear to our fundamentalist friends and neighbors that this is NOT a Christian nation. Robertson, Falwell, Dobson, and their colleagues disagree. Endlessly on TV, radio, and in print they claim this nation was founded by fundamentalist Christians exactly like themselves. "This country was founded by Christians," Pat Robertson announced on his *700 Club*. "It was founded as a Christian nation. There is no question that in the first 150 or so years of the history of this nation this was considered a Christian nation."[13]

With his juris doctor degree from Yale, Pat Robertson should know that during those first 150 years we weren't a nation, let alone a Christian nation. We were thirteen very different colonies, and although most settlers had Christian ancestry, even in New England there was only one church member to every eight settlers. It is true that early in the 1600s, Anglican leaders in Virginia and Puritan leaders in Massachusetts saw themselves as the agents of Christ come to the new world to set up a new "Christian Israel." And in His name, they established state churches that ruled over the religious and the civil lives of believers and nonbelievers alike. But we must think twice before agreeing to return to those earliest years in American history.

Following biblical law as they understood it, the Puritans established a new tyranny in America that replaced the old tyranny under King James I. In those religion-based colonies, only members of the state churches could hold office or even vote, but everyone was taxed to pay for pastors and for church property. It wasn't enough to call church members "saints" and nonmembers "strangers." Those who disagreed with teachers of the established churches, even fellow Christians, were often forced to pay fines, spend time in jail, flee the state, or face trial and even hanging. I consider myself a Christian, but I don't want to live in a Christian nation, whether a theocracy or a democracy ruled exclusively by "Christians" as defined by fundamentalists who are pushing the country in that direction.

They are just plain wrong. There is ample evidence to support the fact that this is not nor was it ever intended to be a Christian nation. The only mention of God in those early documents upon which our government is based is in the Declaration of Independence, in which God is simply "nature's

God," not defined in any way by the Bible or the Christian faith. There is no further mention of God, let alone Jesus, in the Declaration, the U.S. Constitution, or the Federalist Papers, which have been described as the "working documents of the founding fathers!' The cross, the primary sign of the Christian faith, was not included in our flag, on our coins, or in any other national symbol.

Shortly after the U.S. Constitution was ratified, President Washington began negotiating a Treaty of Peace and Friendship with the Muslim nation of Tripoli that was signed on November 4, 1796, and placed into law by President John Adams in 1797. Article 11 of that treaty gives further evidence that those who signed and those who ratified the U.S. Constitution had no intention of creating a Christian nation.

> As the government of the United States of America is not in any sense founded on the Christian Religion,—as it has in itself no character of enmity against the laws, religion or tranquility of Musselmen [Muslims],—and as the said States never have entered into any war or act of hostility against any Mehomitan [Islamic] nation, it is declared by the parties that no pretext arising from religious opinions shall ever produce an interruption of the harmony existing between the two countries.[14]

There is also an abundance of historic evidence that our forefathers were not all evangelical Christians and that they did not set out to create a Christian nation, let alone a democracy ruled exclusively by "righteous" men. Even Francis Schaeffer, arguably the most influential fundamentalist Christian of the twentieth century, agrees. "Not all the founding fathers were individually, personally, Christians," he admits. It's also important for fundamentalist Christians who admire Schaeffer that his call to "take back America" was NOT a call to replace democracy with theocracy. In his own *Christian Manifesto*, Schaeffer warns, "We must make absolutely plain, we are not in favor of theocracy, in name or in fact." "However," he adds in frustration, "as soon as we begin to talk about the need of re-entering Christian values into the discussion someone shouts Khomeni."[15]

After working eight weeks with Francis Schaeffer on his television series in Switzerland, I am convinced that the twentieth century's number one fundamentalist Christian did NOT call fundamentalists to damage, let alone destroy, the democratic process but to enlighten and enliven the political discussion with their Christian convictions. I am equally convinced that Schaeffer was right to warn us that there is no way to separate our politics from our moral and spiritual values. This is not a Christian nation; nevertheless it is also not a nation where Christians—or Americans of any other or no spiritual tradition—are asked to put their spiritual values on hold when they campaign, vote, initiate legislation, or hold office.

It is ironic that just as I typed that last sentence, a camera crew from a network affiliate in Lynchburg called to ask if I would be available for an immediate interview. The Virginia State Senate has just given their overwhelming approval for amending the Commonwealth's Constitution to limit marriage to one man and one woman and to prevent Virginia from recognizing any relationship "that intends to approximate marriage and from creating another legal status that has the same rights, benefits, obligations, qualities, or effects of marriage."

State Senator Steve Newman from nearby Forest is the chief architect and patron of this amendment. Besides manipulating his constituents by stoking the fires of fear and loathing of homosexuals, Senator Newman is using this amendment to deny gay and lesbian couples living in Virginia hundreds of civil rights that go automatically with marriage. I think he has the long-range goal of driving gay men and lesbians from our state. The current Virginia law that prohibits gay and lesbian couples from even having agreements, contracts, or powers of attorney that might approximate marriage is already causing my sisters and brothers with businesses or children or shared property to pack up and leave Virginia.

So what does this have to do with our second progressive moral value, "This is NOT a Christian nation"? Senator Newman's political patron is the Reverend Doctor Jerry Falwell. I refused to even close my eyes when Senator Newman prayed the "pastoral prayer" in Falwell's massive church on the Sunday before the last election. Newman is a Falwell convert, a personal friend, a staunch supporter. And through Newman, Falwell's "spiritual values" are simply being superimposed on Virginians by Jerry's man in Richmond. These men share the vision for making this a "Christian nation once again." Their political loyalties are to their inerrant Bible, not to the U.S. Constitution, let alone "The Virginia Act for Establishing Religious Freedom," written by Thomas Jefferson, Virginia's favorite son, in 1786, who warned against:

> ...the impious presumption of legislators and rulers, civil as well as ecclesiastical, who, being themselves but fallible and uninspired men, have assumed dominion over the faith of others, setting up their own opinions and modes of thinking as the only true and infallible, and as such endeavoring to impose them on others, hath established and maintained false religions over the greatest part of the world, and through all time...[16]

The Reverend Jerry Falwell, Senator Steve Newman, and their fundamentalist friends have the same right I do to influence the political process with their political and moral values. However, Jerry and Steve are using their political influence to force their inerrant-Bible-based values on the people of Virginia. This is not about honest Americans with deeply held convictions working together to negotiate the compromises necessary for a democracy to survive. These are the politics of Hitler's propaganda minister, Joseph Goebbels, known for hating the Jews and using the "big lie" to destroy their influence and eventually eliminate them altogether.

Falwell's "big lie" (though he believes it) begins with this train of thought: Since this is a "Christian nation," and since as a "Christian nation" it is our duty to obey the Bible (even if it undermines the civil rights and protections guaranteed by the U.S. Constitution), and since the Bible must be read and enforced literally, and since the Bible declares homosexuals an abomination and sentences homosexuals to death, and since that seems a bit outrageous, at least for now, we'll obey the Bible incrementally in ways that won't stir up resistance by first denying them their rights, ending their influence, and driving them back into their ghettos. After that, well, who knows?

To accomplish these goals, Falwell, Newman, and the others follow Joseph Goebbels's most popular axiom: If you tell a lie big enough and keep repeating it, people will eventually come to believe it. The lie can be maintained only for such time as people can be shielded from the consequences of the lie. It thus becomes vitally important to repress dissent, for the truth is the mortal enemy of the lie.[17]

The television crew has just finished the interview and their remote truck is backing up our driveway. I know that tonight's news will not tell our side of this marriage amendment story. Falwell has too much influence on the station. My words will be used out of context, tightened mercilessly, or end up on the cutting-room floor. Whatever happens, Jerry will appear on the screen just after I have spoken to rebut anything I say.

In the interview, I told the truth. But the truth cannot compete with the "big lie" being told by Reverend Falwell. I say "lie" because Jerry can't be dumb enough to believe that my twenty-five-year relationship with Gary Nixon is a threat to his relationship with Macel—yet he says it is. Certainly he must be aware that God will not destroy this nation if our relationship is recognized and our civil rights granted; yet he claims God will. Certainly Jerry realizes that this constitutional amendment against same-sex marriage will not "save marriage and the family," when it is heterosexual couples who have botched up that institution; yet he says it will.

If he really believes these things, he's stupid, and Jerry is as stupid as a fox, but if even he doesn't believe these false charges against us but goes on saying them, he is a liar "and the truth is not in him" (I John 2:4).

We can learn Jerry's secret by looking again at Joseph Goebbels. "The most brilliant propagandist technique will yield no success unless one fundamental principle is borne in mind constantly—it must confine itself to a few points and repeat them over and over."[18] Jerry and his colleagues have repeated their big lie that the U.S. is a "Christian nation and gays are a threat to that nation" until the people believe it. Our task as progressive Americans is to bring truth to that lie and, hopefully, end it.

WE VALUE THE SEPARATION OF CHURCH AND STATE;
therefore we will resist all efforts to bring
down "the wall of separation."

On his *700 Club*, Pat Robertson warned his listeners that "they're trying to sell us this nonsense about separation of church and state. And that's what it is. It's a fanatical interpretation of the First Amendment."[19]

D. James Kennedy sounded much the same when he said, "The great misunderstanding of the 'separation of church and state' (words not found in our Constitution) is [that it is] closer in spirit and in letter of the law of the old Soviet Union than it is to the spirit and the letter of the law, actions and writings of the founders of this country."[20]

James Dobson joins the chorus with, "They've taken those simple [First Amendment] words and twisted them to mean something the Founders had no intention of conveying. The separation of church and state is not in the Constitution. Liberals have had to contrive the basis for these things, and then they talk about them as though they were ensconced in the writings of our forefathers."[21]

Jerry Falwell defines the separation of church and state as "throwing God out successfully with the help of the federal court system, throwing God out of the public square, out of the schools" and then warns that as a result "God continues to lift the curtain and allow the enemies of America to give us probably what we deserve."[22]

Politicians like Congressmen Tom DeLay, former House Majority leader, like to please their fundamentalist Christian patrons by adding their voice to the cacophony. At a luncheon for congressional staff in July 2001, DeLay called President Bush's Faith Based Initiative a way of "standing up and rebuking this notion of separation of church and state that has been imposed upon us over the last forty or fifty years."[23]

The Texas Republican Party Platform, 2002, included this promise: "Our Party pledges to do everything within its power to dispel the myth of separation of church and state." At the Road to Victory Conference sponsored by the Christian Coalition just before the elections in 2002, Alabama Chief Justice Roy Moore termed separation "a fable" and insisted that the phrase "has so warped our society it's unbelievable." Senator James Inhofe (R—Oklahoma) upped the ante, calling concerns about church and state "the phoniest argument there is." But the award for the most vicious attack goes to Joyce Meyer, the TV preacher who co-sponsored the Christian Coalition's national meeting. Meyer lambasted the constitutional concept as "really a deception from Satan."[24]

It's fairly easy to assume why the fundamentalist Christian giants and their political operatives oppose separation of church and state with such fervor. It isn't that the principle denies them their right to be guided by their spiritual and moral values when they do politics. It is that this principle is the only thing standing in the way of forcing their spiritual and moral values on the rest of us.

Fundamentalist Christians are convinced that the First Amendment Establishment Clause—"Congress shall make no law respecting an establishment of religion, or prohibiting the free exercise thereof"—is not adequate to support the "separation of church and state," a guideline shaped by the Constitution's brilliant framers that has managed to keep any one religious sect from dominating our democracy for more than 250 years.

At this moment, that guideline is under siege by fundamentalist Christians who are working hard to turn the American people against it. At the heart of their case is another "big lie." They are trying to get us to believe that the framers of the U.S. Constitution and its First Amendment never intended to separate church and state. Quite to the contrary, they proclaim from platform and pulpit, on radio and television, in books, magazines, pamphlets, and fund-raising letters that our forefathers were at the very least nominally Christian and that they believed that Christians were the only ones capable, worthy, qualified to control the state.

Fundamentalists believe sincerely that they are not trying to replace democracy with theocracy when they call this a

Christian nation (with the Bible as its primary authority and fundamentalist Christians in control). They are saying "we don't want a theocracy we just want our country returned to us." Jerry Falwell puts it perfectly. "The idea that religion and politics don't mix was invented by the Devil to keep Christians from running their own country."[25] His confession is as forthright as it is frightening.

What does the First Amendment mean when it says, "Congress shall make no law respecting an establishment of religion, or prohibiting the free exercise thereof"?

Fundamentalist Christians believe sincerely that this First Amendment clause was meant to be a one-way street protecting church from state without limiting the influence of church over state. Consequently, fundamentalists might paraphrase the Establishment Clause in these words: *Congress shall make no law that threatens or undermines our religious beliefs or prohibits the free exercise of our "absolute political and moral values."*

The ultimate fundamentalist Christian goal is to see their values enforced by the executive, legislative, and judicial branches of government over public schools and libraries, over business and the military, over media, the Internet, entertainment, and on and on until those same "absolute political and moral values" bring down the government of, by, and for all the people that guards our civil rights, guarantees our privacy, protects our religious (or nonreligious) beliefs, and keeps our freedoms in place. Ultimately, if given the chance to govern guided only by their inerrant Bible and unhindered by the U.S. Constitution, I think fundamentalist Christians would give Americans the same opportunity Clovis gave the Franks holding up his sharpened sword: "Be baptized and go to heaven. Or refuse baptism and go to hell."

During the first stages of the current fundamentalist Christian takeover of church and state in America, fundamentalists loved the First Amendment's Establishment Clause ("...Congress shall make no law respecting an establishment of religion, or prohibiting the free exercise thereof"). They used it as a shield to protect their growing influence from laws or rulings that might limit their rise to power. Now that they have a majority in the Congress, they want to withdraw that shield of protection from the rest of us. Now is the time for our side to hold up the First Amendment's Establishment Clause, to claim its protections from a fundamentalist president, a fundamentalist Congress, and a Supreme Court soon to be dominated by fundamentalists and their sympathizers.

We must invoke the Establishment Clause separating state from church to protect us from the so-called "faith-based" initiatives of a president who is rewarding his fundamentalist Christian supporters by using millions of taxpayer dollars to support (or establish) fundamentalist churches and charities.

We must invoke the Establishment Clause separating state from church when the president demands that no federal monies be given to support sex-education programs that talk about safe sex, let alone provide condoms to help stop the spread of HIV/AIDS and other sexually transmitted diseases because "abstinence only is God's way."

We must invoke the Establishment Clause separating state from church when the president enters into wars that fundamentalists consider "holy" or give massive financial and military aid to the side fundamentalists favor.

We must invoke the Establishment Clause when the president cancels environmental programs or refuses to sign international treaties and protocols that benefit all nations just because his fundamentalist supporters believe that "Jesus will return before we run out of natural resources or pollute the skies and seas beyond repair."

And we must invoke the Establishment Clause separating state from church when the president supports the fundamentalist Christian demand (based on an ancient Jewish holiness code) that the U.S. Constitution be amended in a way that demeans and dehumanizes gay and lesbian relationships, denies us our civil rights, and makes us second-class-citizens if not outcasts in our own land.

What does Article VI of our Constitution mean when it reads: "...no religious Test shall ever be required as a Qualification to any office or public trust under the United States"?

Article VI means nothing to fundamentalist Christians. In just one sermon, Jerry Falwell exposes the fundamentalist master plan for the de facto takeover of the nation and the management of their new theocratic state. They will end democracy not by violence but by the legitimate means provided by the same democracy they would overthrow. And they will govern their theocratic version of democracy by the "righteous" men they elect.

Remember that Jerry Falwell said to an audience of millions of Americans who didn't even blink when he said it, "It is my goal that before I die, every national, state, local, school board or board of supervisor election will elect and re-elect men of God into positions of authority...We must elect the righteous into office who will see that righteousness prevails."[26]

There is a growing mountain of evidence that President George W. Bush has broken or at least ignored Article VI time and time again by appointing unqualified fundamentalist Christians into positions of power and authority and by consulting with fundamentalist Christian leaders before any important appointment is announced. Apparently, even the president's Supreme Court nominees are approved in advance by fundamentalist Christian leadership.

The media were stunned by one particularly egregious example. On October 5, 2005, James Dobson announced on a Fox News interview that Karl Rove, perhaps the president's most trusted adviser, had called him in advance about Harriet Miers's nomination to the Supreme Court. "I do know things," Dobson told Brit Hume, "that I'm not prepared to talk about here." Later that day, Dobson told a reporter from the *New York Times*, "Some of what I know I'm not at liberty to talk about."

When Rove called Dobson, it was not an innocent conversation between two old fundamentalist friends. It was the president seeking approval for a Supreme Court nominee from the nation's most powerful fundamentalist Christian. Our president, who signed an oath to "preserve, protect and defend" the U.S. Constitution, violated his oath of office that day when he ignored Article VI by assuring himself that Miers passed Dobson's religious test "given as a qualification to any public office."[27]

When Dobson "leaked" word of that conversation (actually when Dobson used that conversation to illustrate his power with the president), he made front-page news across the country. Can you imagine the millions of people who listened to *Focus on the Family* on October 11, 2005, when Dobson finally revealed his "secret information"?

"What did Karl Rove say to me that I knew on Monday that I couldn't reveal?" Dobson began. "Well, it's what we all know now, that Harriet Miers is an evangelical Christian, that she is from a very conservative church, which is almost universally pro-life, that she had taken on the American Bar Association on the issue of abortion and fought for a policy that would not be supportive of abortion, that she had been a member of the Texas Right to Life." Later in that program, he added, "I know the church that she goes to and I know the people who go to church with her…I know the individual who led her to the Lord."[28]

Fortunately, Dobson's mistake helped undermine Meirs's nomination. However, that lucky break was a rare exception. Always remember that if you aspire to political office in a fundamentalist Christian—backed administration on a city, state, or federal level, you are no longer protected by the Constitution's Article VI. Here is the test you need to pass (he said, tongue in cheek). Have you been saved? Are you now an evangelical (meaning fundamentalist) Christian? Do you attend a conservative church (which translates to a church whose pastor believes in an inerrant Bible and preaches from it and it alone)? Are you pro-life (their covert description of a person who supports the overthrow of *Roe v. Wade* and thus another civil rights loss for women)? I don't know if support for the Federal Marriage Amendment was mentioned when President Bush discussed Harriet Miers with James Dobson; but if you really want approval for public office by the fundamentalist Christians in power, you have to support as well their obsessive crusade to deny gay Americans their civil rights.

Why do we believe that religious leaders can be trusted to cherish and not threaten our freedoms? Why can't we learn that anyone who even suggests removing the wall that separates church from state is a menace to the nation? Why is it so hard for us to recognize that unqualified fundamentalist Christians are being appointed into positions of power and authority in this country based on one criterion—they are acceptable to fundamentalist Christians on the basis of their religious beliefs?

Roger Williams, an English clergyman who migrated to Massachusetts in 1630, was one of the first Americans to tell us why. He left England to escape religious intolerance, only to find that same intolerance had been transplanted to the shores of this new world. And though Roger Williams is unknown to most of us, it was his vision of a wall of separation between church and state that has kept religious tyranny from taking root in American soil. Now fundamentalist Christians are hacking away at those roots.

Roger Williams was in his late twenties when the religious leaders of the Massachusetts Bay Colony recognized the wisdom and intelligence of this young Cambridge-educated cleric. Less than a year after his arrival in Plymouth, Roger Williams was appointed "elder" with both religious and political authority. Four years later, he was banished from Massachusetts and forced to flee the colony because he would not conform to the religious values enforced by government. That story informs this ongoing debate about the separation of church and state. In the life of Roger Williams, we see clearly what happens when religious and political powers unite. Almost invariably those same powers work together to silence dissent and crush all opposition.

It wasn't long after his appointment that their youngest elder became a thorn in the flesh of the Massachusetts Bay Colony and its leaders. He condemned the elders when they were guilty of religious, racial, or political intolerance. He objected when they stole land from the Indians. He protested when they withheld the right to vote from unconverted colonists. He dissented when civil crimes were prosecuted under biblical laws.

If Roger Williams had condemned, objected, protested, and dissented in private, his fellow elders might have simply ignored him, hoping that "with maturity he would conform." Instead, he wrote, preached, and taught "'that no person should be restrained from, nor constrained to, any worship or ministry' except in accordance with the dictates of his own conscience."[29]

In 1635, Roger Williams was excommunicated and banished from the colony. A year later, Williams bought land from the Narragansett Indians and founded a sanctuary for dissenters like himself who refused to live under religious and political oppression. In 1644, Roger Williams's sanctuary was chartered as Rhode Island, and as long as Williams lived that new colony, built on the absolute separation of church and state, continued to be a safe place for all people, including the Narragansett Indians.

Writing from his home in Providence, Roger Williams coined the phrase "wall of separation" 158 years before Thomas Jefferson used the same three words in his 1802 letter to the Baptists in Danbury, Connecticut. Having experienced intolerance and discrimination in England and in Massachusetts, Williams wrote a letter using a simple analogy to describe the necessary distance between garden [church] and wilderness [state] as "a hedge or wall of separation." Williams warns that the garden will be destroyed if a gap appears in the hedge and then adds, "...if He [God] will ever please to restore His garden and Paradise again, it must of necessity be walled in...."[30]

On January 1, 1802, a century and a half later, President Jefferson received word from the Danbury Baptist Association about a widespread rumor that the Congregational Church had been selected as the young nation's official denomination. Jefferson responded immediately with a letter that pleased nineteenth-century Baptists but causes twenty-first-century Baptists to mutter to themselves and squirm with discontent. "I contemplate with solemn reverence," Jefferson wrote, "that act of the whole American people which declared that their legislature should 'make no law respecting an establishment of religion, or prohibiting the free exercise thereof' thus building a wall of separation between Church and State."[31]

Fundamentalist Christians wish with all their hearts that Jefferson had never written those words, because they leave no wiggle room for those who oppose the separation of church and state or state and church on the shaky ground that our forefathers didn't use those exact words in the Constitution. In his letter, Jefferson defines the First Amendment "Establishment Clause" in specific, undeniable, crystal-clear language as "a wall of separation between Church and State." That should settle it for fundamentalist Christians. But it does not. They are too intent on pulling down the wall of separation to be informed by the historic evidence.

In 1785, seventeen years before Jefferson's Danbury letter, James Madison included this warning in his "Memorial and Remonstrance Against Religious Assessments" in Virginia. "Who does not see that the same authority which can establish Christianity, in exclusion of all other Religions, may establish with the same ease any particular sect of Christians, in exclusion of all other Sects?…Whilst we assert for ourselves a freedom to embrace, to profess and to observe the Religion which we believe to be of divine origin, we cannot deny an equal freedom to those whose minds have not yet yielded to the evidence which, has convinced us. If this freedom be abused, it is an offence against God, not against man."[32]

Aye, there's the rub. Even the fundamentalist Christians who are currently enjoying their access to political power and patronage should rush to embrace the First Amendment; for close at hand, just beyond the horizon, another faith movement is waiting to move in and replace them. And there is no question that the neo-fundamentalists could be a worse disaster than the current crop. They mean well, I know, but when they put the Bible before the U.S. Constitution, they risk destroying democracy and the protections it guarantees us. When they deny us our liberties, they begin a process that just might undermine their own.

Enter the Lincoln Monument. Reread the words of our sixteenth president. Remember what happened in his day when the Bible was misused to support bigotry and oppression. For more than two centuries, those who traded in slaves and the wealthy plantation owners who were dependent on slave labor misused biblical texts to support slavery. "The notion that slavery was God's will gained momentum after the Nat Turner slave rebellion of 1831. In hundreds of pamphlets, written from 1836 to 1866, Southern slaveholders were provided a host of religious reasons to justify the social caste system they had created."[33]

Lincoln was assassinated because he read the Bible differently from those who misused it to support slavery. Three years before he shot and killed the president, John Wilkes Booth told his sister, "So help me holy God! My soul, life and possessions are for the South."[34] For millennia, biblical misuse has led to suffering and death. That history is writ large on the limestone walls of the Lincoln Memorial. It is such a shame that the 460 fundamentalist Christians began signing their *Manifesto* on Lincoln's steps before spending time inside the monument looking up and remembering the sage warnings he gave us.

Lincoln's Gettysburg address is carved into the southern wall. The president spoke those deeply moving words while looking out across the field in Pennsylvania where North and South together had suffered thirty-five thousand casualties in one bloody day. A mural depicting an angel of truth stands over the inscription that begins: "Four score and seven years ago our fathers brought forth on this continent, a new nation, conceived in Liberty, and dedicated to the proposition that all men are created equal." The Bible was misused then as it is being misused now to prove that all men and women are not created equal. With North and South each claiming to know God's will, both Union and Confederate troops picked up their Bibles in one hand, their rifles in the other, and plunged the nation into civil war.

Until Gary and I moved from California to Virginia, we had not spent time walking those battlefields. Only then did we begin to grasp the horror of the Civil War. The First Battle of Bull Run, July 1861 (4,900 Americans killed, wounded, captured, or missing); April 1862, the Battle of Shiloh (13,000 of 63,000 Union soldiers dead and 11,000 of 40,000 Confederate troops killed in action); five months later, September 1862, in just one day at Antietam (2,108 Union soldiers killed with 2,700 Confederates also slaughtered on the field and a total of 18,578 men wounded from both North and South); Gettysburg, July 2-4, 1863 (Union casualties numbered more than 23,000 and the South lost 25,000 men).

How quickly we forget Shiloh, Seven Pines, Harpers Ferry, Antietam, Fredericksburg, Chancellorsville, Vicksburg, Gettysburg, Appomatox, and even worse how quickly we forget that the men whose bloody broken bodies littered fields and pasture lay down together and died still clutching their rifles in one hand and their Bibles in another, fully believing right up to the end that God was on their side.

On the northern wall you can read Lincoln's entire second inaugural address, delivered on March 4, 1865, to thousands of people celebrating the very real possibility that the bloody civil war was ending. Noah Brooks, an eyewitness to the speech, said that those who saw it delivered will always remember "that tall, pathetic, melancholy figure of a man who, then inducted into office in the midst of the glad acclaim of thousands of people, and illumined by the deceptive brilliance of a March sunburst, was already standing in the shadow of death."[35]

Everyone is familiar with the dramatic ending of that second inaugural address. "With malice toward none, with charity for all, with firmness in the right as God gives us to see the right, let us strive on to finish the work we are in, to bind up the nation's wounds, to care for him who shall have borne the battle and for his widow and his orphan, to do all which may achieve and cherish a just and lasting peace among ourselves and with all nations."

After reading the text of Lincoln's speech, a reporter for the

London Spectator wrote: "We cannot read it without a renewed conviction that it is the noblest political document known to history and should have for the nation and the statesmen he left behind him something of a sacred and almost prophetic character."[36] What could those words teach 460 fundamentalists who are certain that they know God's will and equally certain that God is on their side as they set out to make this a "Christian nation"? What could we all learn from them?

You can feel Lincoln's anguish as he describes the irony of soldiers from North and South killing one another. "Both read the same Bible," he said, "and pray to the same God; and each invokes his aid against the other." Nothing has changed. The culture war being waged at this very moment is a war between Americans who pray to the same God and invoke God's aid against the other. The fundamentalist Christians pray daily that they will succeed in superimposing their literal biblical view of homosexuality on the nation. I pray daily that they will fail.

In his second inaugural, Lincoln made an almost casual aside that in fact defines the president's understanding of God and God's will. "It may seem strange," he said, "that any men should dare to ask a just God's assistance in wringing their bread from the sweat of other men's faces." Lincoln read the whole Bible. He took seriously that amazing story of a Creator determined to rescue and renew Creation from hatred and intolerance. The president was certain that God is a "just" God who demands liberty and justice for all. President Lincoln fought that terrible civil war to preserve the Union; to overcome the forces of injustice that preserved and protected slavery; to make things equal for those who suffered inequality; to end bigotry, intolerance, and discrimination.

Have we learned nothing? Have millions of our ancestors died in vain? Will it take another civil war to guarantee the civil rights of all Americans? It will unless we decide that fundamentalist Christianity is a real threat to this democracy and that the only way we can confront that threat without bloodshed, resolve our differences, and reconcile with our fundamentalist neighbors is to rediscover the power of relentless nonviolent resistance demonstrated in the twentieth century by Gandhi in South Africa and India and by Martin Luther King, Jr., in America.

NINE

RECLAIMING OUR PROGRESSIVE MORAL VALUES

*W*e turned to the U.S. Constitution to help reclaim our progressive *political* values just as we now turn to the Bible to help reclaim our progressive *moral* values. I can hear you groan. After I've labeled the Bible the most dangerous book in history, I hold it up as a primary source of moral values for progressive people.

I understand your skepticism. One morning, while I was serving time in a Virginia Beach jail after being arrested at the headquarters of Pat Robertson's Christian Broadcasting Network, a guard pushed a Bible through the slot in the solid steel door. Without moving from my very thin mattress I could read the gold letters embossed on the Bible's front cover: *Compliments of the Christian Broadcasting Network*. Needless to say, I didn't know whether to read it or flush it.

Fundamentalists have given the Bible a bad name, and we're are caught somewhere between reading it and ignoring it altogether. While we wait, the Bible gets covered with another layer of dust on a shelf just out of sight. Don't you think it may be time to reclaim the book Lincoln called "the best gift God has ever given to man"?[1]

Thomas Huxley, one of Darwins chief defenders and a progressive to be sure, called the Bible "the Magna Charta of the poor and oppressed. The human race is not in a position to dispense with it." Another progressive, Horace "Go West, young man" Greeley, publisher of the *New York Tribune*, reformer and liberal politician, said, "It is impossible to enslave mentally or socially a Bible-reading people. The principles of the Bible are the groundwork of human freedom." John Ruskin, whose book *Unto the Last* was a transformative influence in the life of M. K. Gandhi, credits the Bible for the role he played in fomenting nonviolent revolution in South Africa and India. "Whatever merit there is in anything that I have written," says Ruskin, "is simply due to the fact that when I was a child my mother daily read me a part of the Bible and daily made me learn a part of it by heart:"

WE RECLAIM THE BIBLE AS A PRIMARY SOURCE
OF OUR PROGRESSIVE MORAL VALUES
And we will resist fundamentalist efforts to
claim the Bible as their own.

Whatever we feel when someone walks by Bible in hand, whatever memories good or bad that may stir up in us, it is time to recognize its wisdom, rediscover its power, and reclaim it from fundamentalist Christians who declare it as their own. Most Americans already credit the Bible as the primary source of their moral values. If you don't agree, spend a day interviewing people on the street, asking them just one question: "What is the final authority in your life for right and wrong?" Invariably (after looking perplexed and a bit embarrassed) they will answer, "The Bible?"

And though 85 percent of Americans polled consider themselves Christian, most have never read the Bible seriously, if at all.[2] Their biblical values are assimilated by osmosis or recalled from verses memorized as children. If you ask Americans to name a biblical value they hold dear, you will probably hear "Thou shalt not kill" from the Ten Commandments, or "God is love" from I John 1:8. Forty percent of all Americans can't recall more than four of the Ten Commandments[3] and a far larger percentage has no idea that the words "God is love" conclude a biblical warning, not a warm and fuzzy slogan. "He who doesn't love [his neighbor] doesn't love God, for God is love."

According to a study cited in *Harper's* magazine, less than half of the Americans polled were able to name even one of the Gospel authors: Matthew, Mark, Luke, or John.[4] And in *The Good Book*, Peter Gomes claims that 38 percent of the people who responded to a questionnaire were certain that the Old Testament was written a few years after Jesus' death; that 10 percent believed Joan of Arc was Noah's wife; and that a considerable number believe the joke that the epistles were the wives of the apostles.[5]

Perhaps most disturbing is the statistic that three-quarters of Americans believe the Bible teaches values like "God helps those who help themselves."[6] This bromide by Ben Franklin is not in the Bible and is in fact just the opposite of the central theme of both testaments: The Jewish Testament describes our Creator hard at work rescuing, reviving, and renewing creation in spite of our indolence. The Christian Testament announces that God's gifts are free and there is nothing we can or should do to earn them.

Rather than calling it "The Greatest Story Ever Told," the Bible should be called "The Greatest Book Never Read."

And yet, from the beginning of our nation's history, that single book has literally shaped the political and moral values of the American people. England's King James must have wondered what made this ancient book so important that the Pilgrims would risk imprisonment and death, leave their homes, and sail the Atlantic on a creaky wooden vessel 25 feet wide and 113 feet long just so that they could read the Bible and apply it freely.

The Pilgrims' powerful loyalty to the Bible was not new to English kings. For centuries, the Bible had posed a serious threat to European kings and popes alike. The Vatican was so afraid that laymen would read the Bible and apply it to their personal and political lives that they sentenced to death anyone who even owned a version not in Latin, a language only the clergy could read.

John Wycliffe was excommunicated for translating the Bible into English in the 1380s, but before the crown could punish him, he died of a stroke in 1384. In 1415, Wycliffe's collaborator, John Hus, was arrested and burned at the stake with pages from Wycliffe's Bible used to kindle the fire. That same year, a church council decreed that Wycliffe's remains should be dug up, his bones burned and his ashes scattered.

During the reign of Henry VIII, William Tyndale, another English scholar, translated the New Testament into common English. The king was so threatened by the fact that his subjects could now read the Bible in their own language that he managed to get Tyndale burned at the stake in Belgium. Tyndale's last words were "Lord, open the king of England's eyes."[7]

Seventy-five years later, Tyndale's prayer was answered when James I, under pressure from the Puritans, ordered the Bible translation that would carry his name. In 1611, oversized copies of the King James Version of the Bible were chained to the pulpits of churches across England, not exactly what Tyndale had in mind, but a start. When the Pilgrims demanded that James I allow them the freedom to read and discuss freely the Bible he authorized, the king determined to silence them, and in 1620 the migration to America began.

For centuries, the Bible has been at the center of this nation's political and moral life. Sometimes fundamentalist reformers, Bible in hand, have plunged the nation into chaos. At other times the Scriptures led to periods of spiritual awakening and social reform. The Bible may be dangerous in unworthy hands, but that same book leads nations to overthrow tyrants and colonialists to demand liberty and justice for all.

During my years as a writer and filmmaker, I have seen the Bible at work in the personal lives of men and women under extreme duress: Captain Howard Rutledge, who spent seven years in solitary confinement in Vietnam sustained by Bible verses he had memorized as a child; Marie Rothenberg reading from the Psalms, watching over her son David's recovery after he was burned nearly to death by his father; Margaret Kaupuni finding her hope restored by the Scriptures during her lifetime as a leper on the Island of Molokai; Ken Medema, born blind, who invents at the piano new ways to sing stories from the Bible that deeply move every audience who hears him; Merrill Womach, a pilot, recording artist, and successful businessman whose face was literally burned off in the fiery crash of his private plane, whose love for "The Word" kept him alive during more than a decade of painful skin grafts. The Bible is their book, too.

I suppose that my own commitment to the Bible as a source of progressive moral values is a result of watching my father read it daily for the past sixty-six years. I will carry forever that image of Dad sitting in his leather chair early every morning reading the Bible after praying that God's Spirit would teach him something new from its well-worn, heavily underlined pages.

My father is ninety-three years old now, with congestive

heart failure, an oxygen tank, a pacemaker, and a string of body parts that are gradually breaking down. My brother, Marshall, and I already dread the day when we will have to do without him. He has never failed to come through for us. In 2003, I was selected grand marshal of the Pride Parade in Santa Cruz, California, our hometown. I asked my father to ride with me in an open car at the head of the parade down Pacific Avenue.

Dad had been mayor of Santa Cruz, director of Urban Renewal, and a leader in the evangelical community there. Supporting me in private was one thing, but joining me at the head of this particular march was something else. He knew what might happen if people saw him riding with his openly gay son in a parade celebrating the lives of lesbian and gay Americans.

Before he answered me, he called his pastor, members of his church and men's prayer group, and a few other close Christian friends to ask their advice. As I remember it, not one person encouraged him to ride with me. In fact, he was warned by several that his "Christian witness" in the community "would be ruined" if he did. Dad heard his friends patiently and then sat down with his Bible in his lap, prayed for God's guidance, and began to read.

One day before the Pride Parade, Dad said, "I'll ride in the parade if you still want me." I almost lost it as I watched him approach the parade route past dykes on bikes, leather men in chaps, and cross-dressers in feathered boas and blue taffeta. He sat down beside me in the backseat of a convertible looking shell-shocked but determined. While we waited for the parade to begin, parents from PFLAG and teachers from GLSEN who knew Dad approached the car to thank him for riding with us. All along the route, old folks in lawn chairs, women with babies in their arms, men holding hands, kids with spiky purple hair and tattoos cheered my father, wishing they, too, had someone like him in their lives. People he knew from almost fifty years of leadership in the community ran up to the car to shake his hand and thank him as we passed. He was stunned by the reception and wonderfully confused by it.

When I introduced my father at the interfaith luncheon immediately following the parade, pastors, priests, and rabbis joined in the standing ovation. As I spoke, I could see Dad's eyes fill with tears. When the luncheon ended and the crowd dispersed, I found him talking to a young lesbian who was holding his hand and crying openly. After waiting and watching from across that empty banquet room, I saw Dad end their conversation with a prayer. The young woman hugged him and walked away.

My father was shaken by the experience. En route to our family's home in Scotts Valley, he finally broke the silence. "She told me that when her father learned that she was gay, he rejected her." Dad spoke haltingly as though it hurt to even say the words. "He rejected her and he was a Christian," Dad said, shaking his head in disbelief. "I don't know how anyone could possibly reject his own daughter for any reason," he whispered, "let alone a man who calls himself a Christian." I didn't even try to explain how many lesbian and gay children are rejected by their "Christian parents" or the suffering fundamentalist Christianity was causing literally millions of my sisters and brothers. I just waited for Dad to talk it out. "She asked me," he said, "if I would be her father." It was obvious that her request had moved him deeply. "What did you say?" I asked, knowing what his answer would be. "I said, 'Yes!' of course." Then he paused again. "She called me her hero. Can you imagine that?"

Oh, yes, Dad, I can imagine that. You are my hero, too. You would have broken my heart if you had decided that your "Christian witness" was more important than riding with your son. In fact, that decision might have ruined your Christian witness for me. However, instead of listening to your friends, you sat down with the Bible, listened for God's advice, and rose up to ride beside me on that long, risky ride down Pacific Avenue.

So I begin reclaiming our progressive moral values with the Bible. If we truly value it, we better start reading it again.

WE RECLAIM OUR FAITH TO HELP EMPOWER
& INFORM OUR PROGRESSIVE MORAL VALUES
And will resist any fundamentalist efforts to define God for us.

Okay. Now I am in real trouble. Progressive folk have good reason to avoid "god talk." It often divides us. There are agnostic, pagan, and atheist progressives. Some represent Catholic, Protestant, Orthodox, or Jewish traditions while others are Muslims, Buddhists, Hindus, or Sikhs. Each has a different picture of God and a whole range of names to describe the deity: Yahweh, Jehovah, Allah, Goddess, Force, Higher Power, Spirit of Truth, Holy Spirit. One scholar lists 603 biblical names for God, including both the feminine "Mother Eagle" and the masculine "Almighty Father."[8]

As a teenager, I was convinced that anyone who disagreed with my evangelical picture of God was "lost." Now, with my boyhood hero Billy Graham, I say, "I'm going to leave that to the Lord. He'll decide."[9] However, fundamentalist Christians, Muslims, and Jews still believe that they have an exclusive franchise on truth and see the rest of us as "godless."

That kind of arrogance is the primary reason for genocide, civil wars, and bloody international conflicts.

And yet from my earliest Sunday school days, I was taught that Jesus' death and resurrection provided the *only* way of salvation, and that if we didn't accept Jesus as Lord and Savior we would spend eternity in hell. In my adolescence, that belief was not "arrogant." It was simply true, and a truth so important that it must be shared with everyone we knew. The fate of their souls was in our hands, and if we failed to "witness," our friends would be "lost" and our own salvation placed in jeopardy. That's quite a trip to lay on a kid in junior high school (or on anyone else, for that matter).

The first "Christian" film I remember seeing at a Youth for Christ rally in San Jose, California, was *Silent Witness*, the so-called true story of two young men: a high-school senior who was THE big man on campus and a nerdy little Christian freshman. As I remember, the senior had perfect grades, lettered in every sport, was certain to be voted unanimously the graduate "Most Likely to Succeed," and, I'll confess, was about the cutest boy I'd ever seen on the big screen. But he didn't know "Christ as Savior and Lord" and thus was "lost for all eternity."

So the poor nerdy little freshman decided it was his responsibility to "win to Christ" that bright, athletic (and very handsome) senior. However, every time the nerd tried to share his faith, something or someone intervened. Actually, it was fear that got in the way. No wonder—this poor kid had nothing in common with Superhero; besides, in my day freshmen couldn't teach seniors anything, and when Superhero was killed in an automobile wreck that poor little nerd almost died himself from guilt and fear. His "Silent Witness" had caused a classmate to spend eternity in hell.

After watching *Silent Witness* two or three times (and you can decide why I was so eager to repeat it), I determined that I would never again be silent about my faith and that no one would ever have to spend eternity in hell because of me. Then one day during my own senior year, E. Stanley Jones, a famous evangelical author, statesman, and evangelist, came to town. I sat in the front row every time he spoke, absolutely enthralled by his stories of India and of M. K. Gandhi, a Hindu who loved and respected the teachings of Jesus but remained a Hindu. In fact,

Dr. Jones admitted that he had learned things about Jesus from this Hindu, who carried a stick and wore sandals and a simple white piece of cloth. Although I've never found the source of this Gandhi quote, it still causes me to smile in recognition when I hear it. I think it was Jones who asked Gandhi, "What makes you different from the average Christian?" and Gandhi, as I remember it, replied, "I think Jesus meant it."

In the introduction to that biography, Jones repeats a statement that he made during his meetings in my hometown. It confused me then. Now the words are a source of liberation. "I am still an evangelist," Jones said. "I bow to Mahatma Gandhi, but I kneel at the feet of Christ and give him my full and final allegiance. And yet a little man, who fought a system in the framework of which I stand, has taught me more of the spirit of Christ than perhaps any other man in East or West."[10]

Gandhi and Jones, Hindu and evangelical Christian, helped me understand that people of very different faiths can and must learn to live with one another in shalom, especially in a democracy committed to protect everyone's sacred right of belief (or disbelief) and that my determination to "win to Christ" everybody I met was not only futile, it was un-American.

I may feel compelled to share my faith, but I am equally responsible as a member of the world's oldest democracy to listen to others as openly and as honestly as I hope they will listen to me. Once we become determined to convert everyone we meet, the dialogue ends and the danger of bloody religious wars begins.

E. Stanley Jones once asked Gandhi to describe how evangelical Christians in India could be more effective in sharing their faith in Christ. Gandhi answered, "First, I would suggest that all of you Christians must begin to live more like Jesus. Second, practice your religion without toning it down. Third, emphasize love and make it your working force, for love is central in Christianity. Fourth, study the non-Christian religions more sympathetically to find the good that is within them, in order to have a more sympathetic approach to the people."[11]

Gandhi and Jones taught me how to be entirely "out" as a Christian and at the same time be totally accepting of anyone who disagrees, trusting that the Spirit of Truth will teach us both in the process. In 2000, 250 or so Soulforce volunteers surrounded a United Methodist Convention that was about to deny us one more time the rights of ordination and of marriage. We carried signs saying "Stop Spiritual Violence." Our T-shirts proclaimed that "We Are God's Children, Too!" I was standing in the vigil line when a young woman approached me and asked quietly, "Can I join your vigil?" I answered, "Of course. Why shouldn't you?" She paused for a second and then said, "I'm a Wicca. Do you let Wiccas stand with Soulforce?"

I knew little or nothing about a Wicca. I had heard Wiccas described as members of a "neo-pagan, earth-centered" religion. I didn't know much more than that, but one thing I did know for certain. I was an evangelical Christian. She was a Wicca. Each of us was on our own unique spiritual journey. We only had one choice to make. Could we walk together on our different journeys? Of course! If democracy is to prevail over theocracy, we must find ways to hold faithfully to our beliefs and at the same time allow others to hold faithfully to theirs.

Unfortunately, this means dialogue, and, as the well-known language theorist Stanley Fish has said, a fundamentalist "doesn't want dialogue about his beliefs; he wants those beliefs to prevail. Dialogue is not a tenet in his creed, and invoking it is unlikely to do anything but further persuade him that you have missed the point."[12] I am not a fundamentalist Christian who is determined to see his beliefs prevail. I am an evangelical who is inspired and informed by the life and teachings of Jesus. And though I admit that down in my heart I hoped that young Wicca would one day be equally inspired and informed by the Christian faith, until that day my responsibility was not to convert her but to love her just as Jesus would love her, giving her all the rights and freedoms that kind of love (and democracy) demand and to learn from her in return.

I took her hand and led her to a place beside me in the vigil line. When I turned to see how she was doing, she smiled and squeezed my hand but tears were streaming down her face. Later, I learned her father was a Methodist minister who had rejected her because she was a lesbian. For a while she had given up on God. Now she felt loved and accepted by her Goddess and by her new friends at Soulforce.

I don't want to alienate anyone because I'm making a pitch for progressives to think seriously about their own spiritual journey. And I'm certainly not trying to convert you to Christianity as I know it. I probably have as much tension with the Christian church as you have, maybe more. I have many close, personal friends, allies, and coworkers who are not Christians and others who are victims of the Christian church and find themselves in a rather uncertain spiritual shift. Some call themselves "Recovering Baptists" or "Catholics in Transition." Others belong to "Evangelicals Anonymous" or see themselves now as agnostics, atheists, or pagan. Some attend Buddhist temples or practice Hindu yoga. Others are at least temporarily among the spiritually homeless, wandering, waiting, hoping for something that will renew their faith and help them believe again.

Although I claim to be a Christian, I live at a moment in time when the Christian faith is being defined by fundamentalists who have dishonored Christ and are in the process of destroying His church. Given the current state of the "Christian" religion, Catholic and Protestant alike, I refuse to wear the "Christian" label without redefining it.

After my keynote address to more than a thousand young gay and lesbian activists at a Creating Change Conference, the civil rights activist Urvashi Vaid asked me, "With all they've done to you and to us, how can you consider yourself a Christian?" I answered with a question. "What is a Christian to you, Urv?" She replied, "Like Robertson, Falwell, and the others." "Then I am not a Christian," I had to admit. "I'm a mediocre follower of a first-century Jewish carpenter." She paused for a moment and then said softly, "I can live with that."

What bothers me most these days is the large number of my sisters and brothers who have been so damaged by religion they have stopped their spiritual journeys altogether. They confuse religion and spirituality. Because the church rejects them they think they are rejected by God as well. Consequently, they walk away from the offending church and never think to find a "Welcoming and Accepting" congregation or a Metropolitan Community Church where their spiritual wounds can be healed and their faith in God take root again. And out there alone, apart from any community of faith or any individual strategy to keep faith alive, spirits shrivel and faith dies. The death of faith in the gay and lesbian community has serious consequences for the future of our liberation movement and consequences that are equally dire for progressives who have quit religion and at the same time abandoned the spiritual journey.

When I talk of "reclaiming faith," I use Gandhi as the model. His people, too, had been beaten down by Christians from England who carried the Anglican *Book of Common Prayer* into battle as they subdued the Indian people and colonized their nation. Gandhi demonstrates the perfect model for stating how faith might be reclaimed in a democracy. For example, Gandhi doesn't give God a name. "There are innumerable definitions of God." he says, "because His manifestations are innumerable. So no description of God is adequate."[13]

The closest Gandhi comes to describing God is "Truth." His definition helps us overcome Michelangelo's vision of God as a long-haired, bearded, white man reaching toward Adam way above us on the ceiling of the Sistine Chapel or the paintings of the meek and mild Jesus with long blond curls, blue eyes, and a Kirk Douglas chin.

At first I rebelled when I heard Gandhi say, "God is Truth. Truth is God." Then I began to remember the role Truth plays in my own faith. John the Baptist came to "bear witness unto the Truth" (John 5:33). John the disciple described Jesus as "full of grace and Truth" (John 1:14). Jesus identified himself with Truth (John 14:6) and promised that the Spirit of Truth would come "to guide them into all Truth" (John 16:13).

Gandhi called his autobiography *The Story of My Experiments with Truth*. He named his nonviolent liberation army *Satyagraha* ("truth force") and his nonviolent warriors *Satyagrahis* ("disciples or doers of Truth"). When Gandhi saw in his own life and in the life of his followers what happened to the souls of those who were open to Truth, or as Jesus said, being "set free" by Truth, he renamed his movement "soul force." He saw that genuine faith in God frees and empowers the soul and gives life new direction and new meaning.

Gandhi describes two stages in knowing God. "The first is faith and the second and ultimate stage is experience-knowledge arising from it (faith)."[14] He sees no conflict between what we learn from empirical data and what we learn from faith. If only fundamentalists could understand that evolution (empirical data) and a Creator (what we learn from faith) are not in conflict. The formula Gandhi prescribes is "rejection of every demand for faith where a matter is capable of present proof" and "un-questioned acceptance on faith of that which is itself incapable of proof except through personal experience."[15]

Gandhi's faith is not academic, a concept long ago and far

away. When Gandhi was troubled by a very difficult decision—when to start the Salt March or when to end his fast against the Hindu-Muslim conflict—he prayed, mediated, and waited for "the visible finger of the invisible God" to point the way.[16] In an interview when asked if he had any mystical experiences, he said, "If by mystical experiences you mean visions, no...But I am very sure of the Voice which guides me."[17]

There are many reasons that Gandhi saw faith in God as necessary and not just for the person involved in a nonviolent liberation movement. Gandhi saw faith as a powerful and positive force in our daily lives. His personal faith was hammered out of blood and tears when his nation was on fire, the arsonists were Anglican Christians, and faith in any God was rapidly giving way to faith in the weapons of violence and destruction. His call to "Reclaim faith" then seems appropriate for our call to reclaim faith today.

"We have become atheists for all practical purposes," Gandhi laments, "and therefore we believe that in the long run we must rely upon physical force for our protection."[18]

"Without faith in God," Gandhi says, "man can have faith neither in himself nor in others...The finite cannot be understood unless we know it is rooted in the Infinite."[19]

Without faith in God, a personal value becomes "a lifeless thing and exists only while it is a paying proposition. So are all morals," he says. "If they are to live in us they must be considered and cultivated in their relation to God. We try to become good [keep our moral values] because we want to reach and realize God."[20]

Without faith in God, our values are "likely to break down at the critical moment."[21]

"God is a living Force," says Gandhi, "and our life is of that force. That Force resides in us, but is not the body. He who denies the existence of that great Force, denies to himself the

use of that inexhaustible Power and thus remains impotent…
like a rudderless ship which tossed about here and there perishes
without making any headway."[22]

Without faith in God "we won't have the courage to die
without anger, without fear and without retaliation. Such
courage comes from the belief that God sits in the hearts of all
and that there should be no fear in the presence of God."[23]

The "shield and buckler" of the nonviolent person, Gandhi
promises, "will be his (or her) unwavering faith in God."[24]

"Great as the other forces of the world are…soul-force is
the greatest of all."[25]

Martin Luther King, Jr. sounds so much like Gandhi at the
funeral of the little girls who were killed by a bomb after Sunday
school on September 15, 1963:

> Never forget that God is able to lift you from fatigue
> of despair to the buoyancy of hope, and transform dark
> and desolate valleys into sunlit paths of inner peace.[26]

On April 4, 1967, Dr. King linked the war in Vietnam to the
civil rights movement for the first time in a historic sermon at
the Riverside Church in New York City:

> When I speak of love, I am not speaking of some sen-
> timental and weak response. I am speaking of that
> force which all the great religions have seen as the su-
> preme unifying principle of life…This Hindu-Moslem-
> Christian-Jewish-Buddhist belief about ultimate reality
> is beautifully summed up in the first epistle of Saint
> John: "Let us love one another; for love is God and ev-
> eryone that loves is born of God and knows God. He
> that loves not knows not God; for God is love. If we love
> one another God dwells in us, and his love is perfected
> in us.[27]

On Christmas Eve 1967, the Canadian Broadcasting Corporation aired Dr. King's "A Christmas Sermon on Peace."

The next thing we are to be concerned about if we are to have peace on earth and good will toward men is the nonviolent affirmation of the sacredness of human life. Every man [and every woman] is a child of God. And so when we say, "Thou Shalt Not Kill," we're really saying that human life is too sacred to be taken on the battlefields of the world...Man is a child of God, made in His image, and therefore must be respected as such. Until men see this everywhere, until nations see this everywhere, we will be fighting wars.[28]

"I See the Promised Land" was Dr. King's last sermon, delivered in Memphis on the eve of his assassination.

I would like to live a long life. Longevity has its place. But I'm not concerned about that now. I just want to do God's will. And He's allowed me to go up to the mountain. And I've looked over. And I've seen the promised land. I may not get there with you. But I want you to know tonight, that we, as a people will get to the promised land. I'm happy, tonight. I'm not worried about anything. I'm not fearing any man. Mine eyes have seen the glory of the coming of the Lord.[29]

WE RECLAIM THE VALUES OF THE
JEWISH PROPHETS: JUSTICE AND MERCY
Therefore we will resist injustice and seek to be more merciful to those who suffer injustice.

Roughly seven centuries before Christ, a wiry, bearded, sunbaked little man appeared in the city of Jerusalem and made quite a stir. He came from a poor village halfway between the capital and Gaza and set up shop directly in front of the palace of the Judean King, Hezekiah. If the little man hadn't been naked, there would be no way to pick him out of the crowd of farmers and shepherds who came to town to trade in produce, livestock, and gossip. But naked and probably shouting, it was very difficult to overlook Micah, the Jewish prophet who entered the city to announce the moral values of Yahweh and denounce the materialist values of King Hezekiah and the people of Judah.

The bemused city folk gathered around Micah and listened with growing insolence as he warned them of the consequences of their wicked ways. Apparently, Micah's countrymen and women were in the habit of worshipping Yahweh on the Sabbath with a veritable parade of priests in elegant vestments, animals to be sacrificed, oil to be poured on the sacred altar, loud singing, and pompous preaching from the Torah. But the rest of the week they forgot the ways of Yahweh, ignored the poor, the hungry, the outcast, and the victims of intolerance and injustice.

Right in the middle of Micah's jeremiad, someone had the temerity to interrupt. "So, what does the Lord want from us?" We progressives might paraphrase the question: "What are the moral values being preached by the Jewish prophets and what have they to do with us today?"

When you read Micah's response, you get the idea from his hyperbole that he was probably shouting when he said, "Do you really think the Lord is pleased when you sacrifice thousands of animals and pour out ten thousands of rivers of oil?" Then perhaps his voice grew quiet and threatening. "You know what is good. God has told you many times. And I will repeat it now Are you listening?" I imagine about that time his voice rose suddenly in pitch and volume as he said, "This is what the Lord values. Do justice. Love mercy and walk humbly with your God."

A Christian historian writes, "All the great conceptual discoveries of the human intellect seem obvious and inescapable once they had been revealed, but it requires a special genius to formulate them for the first time. The Jews had this gift... To them we owe the idea of collective conscience and so of social responsibility..."[30]

Over the centuries, Jewish prophets have appealed to the "collective conscience" of their nation to take "social responsibility" for widows and orphans, the poor, hungry, and naked, the victims of neglect and of injustice. As history goes, that matched pair of values—justice and mercy—was a rather new idea. It must have been jarring to hear that we have been created for the express purpose of assisting the Creator in providing mercy for those in need and demanding justice for those who suffer injustice and discrimination. Being both merciful and just may have been a new idea then. It is no longer a new idea and yet generation after generation we forget the consequences of greed and injustice. We need to hear those prophetic words again.

MICAH: "This is what the Lord requires: do justice, love mercy, and walk humbly with your God" (Micah 6:8).

ISAIAH: "Quit doing evil and learn to do good. What is good? Seek justice. Relieve the oppressed. Care for children without fathers and women without husbands" (Isaiah 1:10-18).

AMOS: "I hate, I despise your feast days. I will not smell the incense in your holy assemblies. Though you bring me offerings, I will not accept them. Shut up your noisy singing. I will not listen to the music of your orchestras and choirs. Instead, let justice run down as waters, and righteousness as a mighty stream" (Amos 5:21-24).

JEREMIAH: "...execute righteousness & justice in the earth. In that day you'll be saved" (Jeremiah 7:22-23).

HOSEA: "What shall I do unto thee, O Judah? Your goodness is as a morning dew that disappears with the first light...I desired mercy, and not sacrifice. I wanted you to know me, not bring burnt offerings unto me" (Hosea 6: 4-6).

JESUS: "Too bad for you, scribes and Pharisees, you hypocrites! You know how to tithe the spices in your gardens, but you have neglected the weightier matters of the Law: Justice, Mercy, and Good faith" (Matthew 23:23). "I was hungry, and you gave me no meat. I was thirsty, and you gave me no drink. I was a stranger, and you took me not in. Naked, and you clothed me not: sick, and in prison, and you visited me not...I say to you, since you did it not to one of the least of these, you did it not to me. And these shall go away into everlasting punishment, but the righteous into life eternal" (Matthew 23:42-46).

In his classic poem "The World Is Too Much with Us," William Wordsworth explains exactly why we have no time to "do justice" or "love mercy." "The world is too much with us; late and soon, Getting and spending, we lay waste our powers; Little we see in Nature that is ours; We have given our hearts away, a sordid boon!"

Once again we turn to Gandhi. The words "mercy" and "justice" took on a whole new meaning for me when he defined them in such a simple, powerful way. For Gandhi, "mercy" means helping those who suffer, and "justice" means cutting off that suffering at its source. Deitrich Bonhoeffer, the young German pastor who was hanged by the Nazis, explained "mercy" and "justice" this way: "...our role is NOT just to bandage the victims pulled out from under the wheel [mercy], but to put a spike in the wheel itself [justice]."[31]

How you apply these two progressive moral values—
"mercy" and "justice"—is your business; however, I hope I can
persuade you that lesbians and gays are in desperate need of
both mercy and justice, and that the struggle for "gay rights"
is the next stage in the broader struggle for civil rights in this
country.

I wish that wiry, bearded, sunbaked little man would
appear suddenly out of the past and convince our community
to create a massive liberation movement that would end all
this. Unfortunately, it can't happen until we first convince
that wounded generation that they are not "sick" or "sinful,'
that God created them, and that God loves them exactly as
they are. That won't happen until those who have been so
damaged by fundamentalist Christianity see that Jesus was not a
fundamentalist nor did he hold to fundamentalist beliefs.

WE RECLAIM THE PRIMARY VALUE
OF JESUS LOVE (AHIMSA)
Therefore we will resist thoughts, words and actions that
are unloving and put nonviolence into practice
with our friends and enemies alike.

In the fall of 1994, when *Stranger at the Gate* was published,
I began a tour of the country to promote my autobiography
and to tell the story of my own gradual realization that God
created me a gay man and loves me exactly as I am. On my
first stop at Texas A&M in College Station, Texas, I finished
my presentation, fielded questions from the audience, and was
about to be escorted to a reception by the host committee when
I passed a first-year student standing at the stage door with tears
in her eyes. I excused myself from my student guide, walked up
to the young freshman, and asked quietly, "Are you all right?"

Unable to speak, she just looked up at me and whispered, "No" Then, after a pause, she shared her fears with one simple question. "How can you be sure that God loves you, too?"

For the past fifteen years, I have been asked that question by lesbian and gay people who approach me cautiously, their eyes turned downward, their voices low. With their dignity and self-esteem battered by religion, they whisper the question, afraid even to say it aloud. They have been so abused by false teachings, so overwhelmed by the toxic rhetoric, so terrified by the promise of eternal damnation that accepting their sexual orientation as a gift from God seems almost incomprehensible.

Their question can't be answered by a review of the latest scientific, psychological, historical, personal, or even biblical data. That comes later. These are victims of fundamentalist Christianity. They grew up singing "Jesus loves me. This I know. For the Bible tells me so." Now, to make it simple, they're afraid that Jesus doesn't love them anymore. The only way to answer their question is to help them see Jesus in a new light.

Fundamentalist Christians have emasculated Jesus. They have broken his new covenant of love and grace and tacked up in its place the old covenant of law and order. They aren't singing about "the love that will not let me go." Instead, they are chanting verses from Leviticus and looking for someone to punish. They are obsessed with Jesus' death on the cross and overlook his life and teachings almost entirely. All too often, they forget that he was flesh and blood and lived among us. He experienced life and understands the hard decisions life asks of us. He showed us that God knows our failures and loves us anyway. Therefore, the best way to answer that young lesbian's question—"How can you be sure that God loves you, too?"—is to let Jesus speak for himself.

When a Pharisee asked Jesus which of their 613 laws was "the great commandment," Jesus answered, "Love God with all your heart, soul, mind and strength and love your neighbor as yourself." On the night he died, Jesus boiled it down to what he called "a new commandment." "Love one another as I have loved you." It wasn't new at all. He just wanted to be sure that his slow-witted disciples (then and now) would remember that love was at the very heart of his life and ministry.

It is almost incomprehensible that the followers of Jesus—entrusted with the task of bringing a new kind of love into the world—have instead caused so many people to ask "How can I be sure that God loves me, too?"

Instead of feeling love from their Christian families and their Christian churches, they are treated as outcasts. Fortunately, the story of Jesus assures us that God loves outcasts best.

You don't have to be gay or lesbian to feel like an outcast. Fundamentalist Christians have made people outcast by the color of their skin, by their race and religion, by their sex, their sexual orientation, and their gender identity. When I was a child my home church made outcasts out of smokers, drinkers, dancers, rock-and-roll listeners, moviegoers, television watchers, longhairs, hippies, divorcées, unmarried bachelors and spinsters, Roman Catholics, liberal Protestants, pagans, atheists, and agnostics. Even those families who missed church by spending an occasional weekend at their mountain cabin were made to feel like outcasts when they returned the following Sunday.

Fundamentalists in the twenty-first century are the equivalent of the first-century Pharisees, who knew the law by heart but had forgotten that love is the heart of the law. From the very first sermon he preached, Jesus condemns the Pharisees as he would condemn contemporary fundamentalist Christians for their success at legalism and their failure to love. From the beginning, he ignored all the fundamentalists' precious rules and it drove them crazy.

"You eat foods that are not pure," they charged him. "It's

not what enters into the mouth which defiles a person," Jesus replied, "but that which comes out of it."

"You disregard the traditions of the elders," they accused. "For the sake of your tradition," Jesus answered, "you have rendered useless the word of God."

"You disobey God's laws," they warned. "And you honor God with your lips," he said, "but your hearts are far from him."

If a fundamentalist Christian in your life makes you feel like an outcast, tell him or her to read Jesus' story again from the top.

I think God was trying to make a point when Jesus was born by human standards an "illegitimate" baby, delivered without a doctor or a midwife to an unwed teenage mother, not in a mansion but in a barn, wrapped in rags and placed in a hayloft surrounded by bleating animals and the stench of urine and manure.

I think God was trying to make a point when Jesus was born a person of color, to a conquered people in a backwater, third-world nation; that he was adopted and knew from infancy what it meant to be poor and homeless, an illegal alien, a war refugee living with other refugees in an Egyptian refugee camp.

I think God was trying to make a point when at twelve years old Jesus was headstrong and disobedient, already arguing with the male elders; that he was baptized in a muddy little river by a renegade preacher who wore leather; that he was an apprentice in his father's carpentry shop with no official record that he ever graduated from high school, let alone college; that he studied theology in the desert, where he argued not with esteemed professors from many different academic fields but with the devil himself.

I think God was trying to make a point when Jesus' first miracle was changing water into wine at a wedding party after the guests had finished off their host's supply. The evening was young. This was the celebration of *eros* at work in the lives of two young people, and God was there in the midst of this sensual, joyous occasion and didn't want the party to end.

I think God was trying to make a point when Jesus didn't choose one clergy-type to be his disciple; that he was known for the bad company he kept: Jews who collected taxes for the Romans, women of ill repute, foreigners, half-breeds, children; and that Jesus had one special friend among the disciples, the one they say he "loved," who after supper lay against Jesus' chest and that the one Jesus loved was the only disciple at the foot of the cross when he died.[32]

I think God was trying to make a point when Jesus would not conform to religious norms but confronted the Pharisees and the other religious fundamentalists on a regular basis with very tough language: "fools and blind," "hypocrites," "serpents and vipers," "clean bowls on the outside filled with extortion and excess," "magnificent looking graves filled with dead men's bones."

I think God was trying to make a point when Jesus, though innocent, was tried, convicted, and put to death by officials from both church and state for demanding justice and mercy instead of business as usual; that Jesus was condemned by the crowd, tortured by sneering soldiers, executed between two felons, and buried in a borrowed tomb; that one of the twelve betrayed him and the others slept through his agony, then denied and deserted him; that on the cross Jesus felt abandoned even by his Creator when he cried out, "Father, why have you also forsaken me?"

What is the point? If there is any one message the Bible delivers, it is the message that God loves outcasts and that Jesus was born into the world an outcast to rescue and renew outcasts from religion gone bad. He was born poor and died poor, yet the legacy of love he left us, the legacy of inclusion and acceptance and understanding, will endure forever.

If you're still not convinced, look closely at the miracle stories. Jesus' love for the outcast leper caused him to hug the "untouchable" even before healing him. Jesus' love for the outcast Samaritan caused him to share a drink of water with a woman despised even before he sent her on her way rejoicing. Jesus' love for the outcast woman with the flow of blood considered "unclean" by the religious leaders…Jesus' love for the outcast prostitute caught in the act of adultery…Jesus' love for the man considered sinful since he was blind from birth…Jesus' love for the lunatic rejected by his family living in a graveyard…Jesus' love for the widow whose child lay dead at his feet…Jesus' love for his friend Lazarus…Jesus' love for every outcast that crossed his path. What will it take to help lesbian and gay people to realize that they, too, are loved unconditionally and that the fundamentalists are the ones who should be asking the question "How can I be sure that God loves me, too?"

Needless to say, my favorite miracle is the healing of the outcast Roman centurion's "special servant," It is well known that the wives or lovers of Roman centurions were allowed to accompany them on their journeys. A Gentile and a member of the occupying force, the centurion was an outcast in Jerusalem, and his "special servant." almost certainly gay, was an outcast for a whole other set of reasons; yet when that centurion cried out to Jesus to heal his young lover, Jesus said, "Right. Take me to him." The centurion, knowing that the pictures on his desk might give them away, responded, "Could you heal him long distance?"

Jesus must have smiled to himself knowing that the centurion and his lover had no reason to be embarrassed or ashamed. He knew why they hid their loving relationship from the local religious authorities and the gossips on the street, but they had no reason to hide their relationship from God, who created them and loved them exactly as they were. Instead of taking that risk, Jesus healed the outcast lover on the spot. I wish I could have witnessed that moment when Jesus looked into the eyes of the centurion and without a word passing between them said, "Now, friend, let your own guilt and fear be healed as well."

Love is God's gift demonstrated by Jesus in an unloving world. When that legacy of love is discovered by the young lesbian at Texas A&M who had been brainwashed by her Baptist church and rejected by her Christian parents, she will never need to ask the question again "How do I know that God loves me, too?" Because God proved through Jesus' life, death, and resurrection that God loves outcasts best. When you stand with the outcasts, you stand with Jesus, and when you despise the outcast, you despise Jesus, as well.

Once you realize that you are loved, that the fundamentalist Christians are entirely wrong about you, that you are not "sick" and "sinful" but in fact a child of the Creator who loves you exactly as you are, then (and only then) can you start thinking about putting that love into action on behalf of other outcasts who still feel unloved. Becoming an activist is simply a matter of putting love into action. For activists, love is something you do, not something you just talk about, and that's when the fun begins.

TEN

DISCOVERING SOUL FORCE

*M*y short, frantic life as a "gay activist" began accidentally in 1994 with the release of my autobiography, *Stranger at the Gate: To Be Gay and Christian in America*, with Morley Safer's *60 Minutes* interview and my appearances on *Larry King Live*. Reporters were fascinated—and many gay activists were appalled—by my former life as a ghostwriter for leaders of the so-called radical right. A media blitzkrieg followed. Suddenly and without adequate preparation, my partner, Gary, and I found ourselves in the front lines of a war that religious and political leaders were waging against gay and lesbian Americans.

We moved to Dallas, Texas, so that I could become the volunteer dean of the Cathedral of Hope (a Metropolitan Community Church). I will never forget the exhilaration and the relief I felt at my installation service on Pride Sunday, June 26, 1993. The thirty-year struggle "to overcome" my sexual orientation, the endless and totally ineffectual "reparative" therapies, the electric shock, the exorcisms, the guilt, the fear, and the self-loathing were over at last. Trembling with gratitude and excitement, I stood in the cathedral before one thousand lesbian and gay Christians and announced without fear or doubt: "I'm gay. I'm proud. And God loves me without reservation." My new sisters and brothers got to their feet, cheering and applauding, forgiving me my past and launching me into a totally unexpected future.

During the next twenty-four months, I was invited to speak in at least a hundred different cities: at pride celebrations, black-tie dinners, and human rights rallies, at conventions, banquets, and debates, at churches and synagogues, on campuses from Yale to the University of Colorado at Boulder, even at a congressional briefing. I marched, demonstrated, organized, argued, shouted, preached, and prayed in thirty-five different states. I confronted the false and angry rhetoric of Christian extremists on more than three hundred television and radio talk shows. I was interviewed endlessly by the media, threatened by kooks and crazies, arrested and tossed in jail.

Then, after representing the Cathedral of Hope MCC across the nation for two wonderful, exhausting years, the Reverend Elder Troy Perry, founder of the Universal Fellowship of Metropolitan Community Churches, asked if I would join his national staff (again as a full-time, unpaid volunteer), this time in the newly created position of minister of justice and reconciliation. It would be my task to help represent UFMCC's three hundred congregations and 250,000 congregants in thirty-six American states and seventeen countries in the front lines of the battles for justice, not just for gay Americans but for all people who suffer injustice, regardless of their sexual orientation, race, or religion.

Religious fundamentalists with their urge to purge were stalking God's homofolk especially, not just in the United States but in every nation where fundamentalism flourished. From our home just south of Dallas, Gary and I were monitoring the progress of the fundamentalist war against us. From morning until night the telephone rang and the fax machine buzzed. With as many as one hundred incoming e-mail messages a day, checking our address on the Internet became a frustrating experience. Night and day, our audio and video recorders taped miles of false and inflammatory antigay rhetoric. Manila envelopes from other monitors filled our post office box with alarming new print and tape data.

The closer we monitored the antigay rhetoric and antigay political actions of the so-called radical right, the angrier I became. In bright, banner headlines my client Jerry Falwell had declared "war on homosexuals." Then as now, he and his fundamentalist colleagues were regularly accusing us (quite falsely) of "demanding special rights," of "undermining the American family," of "threatening traditional values," and of "molesting, abusing, and recruiting children."

On videotape, we recorded *700 Club* host Pat Robertson saying that earthquakes in California and floods on the Mississippi River were due in large part "to the nation's tolerance of homosexuality and other sinful behaviors." And my old film client, televangelist D. James Kennedy, supported the ban on gays in the military because "your grandson in the army shouldn't have to face the enemy in front at the same time fighting off the enemy coming up from behind."

These ugly and totally false claims against us by fundamentalists in America and abroad were growing more and more outrageous and inflammatory. Their antigay ballot initiatives and proposed antigay constitutional amendments were legalizing discrimination against us. Their false words and discriminatory actions were creating a hostile climate for gays and lesbians across America, and in almost every state, the intolerance had turned to violence. In fact, we were becoming the number one victim of hate crimes in small towns and large cities alike. During my first year in Texas, the hate-crime statistics came painfully to life.

In 1993, just six months after my installation as dean of the cathedral in Dallas, Nicholas Ray West was murdered in nearby Tyler, Texas.

Nicholas was a twenty-three-year-old Southern Baptist singer who was kidnapped, tortured, and executed in a gravel pit simply because he was gay. Speaking at Nick's memorial service was my first close-up encounter with the rash of antigay hate crimes breaking out across the nation.

Just a few weeks later, in January 1994, the body of another innocent gay Texan, Michael Benishek, was found in San Antonio. The coroner wasn't sure if Michael had been killed by the severe blow to his head by some blunt instrument or if he had bled to death from the knife slash across his throat.

The very next month, in February 1994, Tommy Musick, a forty eight-year-old gay hairstylist in Midland, Texas, was shot four times in the back of the head. The jury found his eighteen-year-old killer, Ramsey Harrell, guilty of murder but sentenced him to just twelve years in prison for the crime. "The jury allowed Harrell to have the lesser charge because of their prejudice against gay people," said Billy Cawley, a local pastor. "Tommy Musick got no justice. This sends a clear message that if you kill a gay person in West Texas, you will not be punished."

In March 1994, just a few weeks after Musick's murder, police in El Paso, Texas, found the body of Joe Trevino, another gay man, who had been brutally murdered in his home. Apparently, Joe was strangled and bludgeoned to death by teenagers who had already killed one or two gay men in El Paso before slaying Trevino.

The very next month, April 1994, a sixteen-year-old San

Antonio youth took a rifle out of his truck and shot to death another gay man, twenty-six-year-old John Anthony Burwell. The teenage killer dragged Burwell's body to his pickup truck, drove to a nearby creek, and dumped the corpse off a bridge forty feet above the water, where it lay facedown on a mass of rocks until discovered.

In June 1994, Paul Quintanilla, a young man from Ennis, the same little town south of Dallas where Gary and I lived, was found murdered in a field near Dallas. He had been stabbed a dozen times and his throat and genitals had been slashed.

Toward the end of that year, the *New York Times* reported that 60 percent of the murders involving gay or lesbian victims were called "overkill" because they involved four or more gunshot or stab wounds, repeated use of blunt objects, or the use of more than one killing method. "The bias related slayings of gays and lesbians," said the report, "are often gratuitously violent and many go unsolved."

Pat Robertson, Jerry Falwell, James Dobson, D. James Kennedy, and other fundamentalist Christian leaders did not mean for people to suffer or to die. But the hostile climate in which the suffering and death take place was largely created by the toxic misinformation that flowed into the national environment through their antigay fund-raising letters and their emotional antigay radio and television appeals. Their demonizing claims against gay and lesbian Americans made people who don't know the truth about us angry and afraid.

The dangerous and deadly untruths trickled down into the homes and churches of America from the media pulpits and through books, magazines, pamphlets, videotapes, and fund-raising letters. Fear and anger grew. Every local pastor, parent, teacher, and city council or school board member who heard their untrue reports or viewed their false and malicious videos like *The Gay Agenda* became conduits through which the untruth was spread and even exaggerated. Teenagers saw and heard a steady diet of the untruths about gay and lesbian people from the authority figures in their lives. Nobody thought these untruths would lead to murder. Then, on a Friday night, after the football game and a few beers, teenagers with nail-studded baseball bats went looking for queers to bash, thinking they were doing the community (and even God) a favor.

With every gay bashing or gay murder that we monitored, I became more and more desperate to talk to my old clients who were using the imaginary "gay threat" to raise money and mobilize volunteers. For more than two years, I tried to meet with them. I didn't have much hope that they would sit still long enough to hear, let alone to discuss, the new psychological, medical, scientific, and biblical understanding of sexual orientation.

I wasn't going to argue those six biblical verses used to clobber us or try to convince them that God loves homosexuals, too. I just wanted to show them specific examples of the half-truths, hyperbole, and lies they were spreading about us. I wanted to show them, case by case, how their misinformation led directly and indirectly to suffering and death. They refused to meet with me. They wouldn't even respond to my letters or faxes.

Finally, on November 24, 1994, feeling a growing sense of anger and helplessness, I sent a Christmas letter to four hundred friends and supporters across the country. "I'm finished trying to talk to the fundamentalists," I said, confessing my failure to get through to my former employers. "They're hopeless. I'm giving up on them."

Just days after I mailed my letter, I received a reply from the King Center in Atlanta. Coretta Scott King's assistant, Lynn Cothren, wrote to express his concerns about the "new direction" my life seemed to be taking. Lynn is a gay Christian activist, a leader in Queer Nation's fight against discrimination in the Cracker Barrel restaurants. Though Lynn is young and white, his southern roots are planted deep in the civil rights soil tilled by Dr. Martin Luther King, Jr. Lynn read my letter with the perspective of a seasoned nonviolent activist, and he wasn't happy with what he read. He was even more concerned about what he read between the lines.

"I've been following your progress since I read about you in the *Southern Voice*," he said, "and until your recent letter I liked what I saw. But your angry decision to break off communications with the radical right signals a turn toward violence. I hope you will seriously reconsider."

I was stunned. I read and reread both his letter and mine. I couldn't understand what seemed "violent" to Lynn about what I had written. Finally, after stewing for several days, I called him in his office at the King Center.

"What did you find violent about my Christmas letter?" I asked him.

"When was the last time you read Dr. King's *Where Do We Go from Here: Chaos* or *Community?*" he replied.

"In college," I answered sheepishly, "thirty-two years ago."

"Read it again," he said, "and you will understand."

To be honest, I don't think I had ever read that powerful and prophetic booklet by Martin Luther King, Jr. I went to our little library in Ennis, found *Where Do We Go from Here?* (published in 1967), and read it in one sitting. Dr. King had struggled twelve long years to end segregation and "bring in the beloved community." Black Americans were tired of waiting for equal rights. Dr. King's insistence on nonviolence was under siege by Stokely Carmichael and other more radical African-Americans whose chant for "black power" was growing louder than Dr. King's quiet, persistent promise, "We Shall Overcome."

When James Meredith was shot during the Mississippi

Freedom March in June 1966, violent, black power protests threatened to divide, if not destroy, the movement. King joined the Mississippi march and in *Where Do We Go from Here?* reported hearing comments like these all along the way.

"I'm not for that nonviolence stuff anymore," shouted one of the younger activists in King's hearing.

"If one of these damn white Mississippi crackers touches me, I'm gonna knock the hell out of him," shouted another.

"This should be an all-black march," said one man to King during a late-night debate. "We don't need any more white phonies and liberals invading our movement. This is our march."

In one late-night discussion, a marcher told Dr. King they should discard the movement's theme song altogether. "Not 'We Shall Overcome,' he suggested, but 'We Shall Overrun?'"[1]

Where Do We Go from Here: Chaos or *Community?* was Dr. King's response to this angry support for violence in the civil rights movement. He condemned a violent confrontation in Mississippi on pragmatic grounds as "impractical" and "disastrous." He went on to defend nonviolence on principle as he had for almost a dozen years. And he made it clear that giving up on an opponent was an act of violence against him. He is our brother. We are children of the same Creator. We are in need of reconciliation, and reconciliation will never happen if we call them "hopeless" and walk away.

"We have inherited…a great 'World House,'" King wrote, "in which we have to live together…a family unduly separated in ideas, culture and interest, who, because we can never again live apart, must learn somehow to live with each other in peace."[2]

As I read, I realized the spirit behind my own, short-lived activism was turning sour. When I thought of Robertson, Falwell, Kennedy, Dobson, and the others, I felt waves of anger and frustration. I couldn't imagine ever living in the same "World House" with these fundamentalist leaders, and my rage was exacerbated by their steady refusal to even consider the truth about us.

They had ignored my pleas for dialogue. So, like a petulant child, I was about to take my toys and go home. Even worse, I was feeling more and more like blowing up the playground. Although I couldn't see it, anger was crippling my spirit; and though I would have denied it then, that same anger was leading me slowly but surely toward violence.

At that moment, Lynn Cothren urged me to read Dr. King's book *Where Do We Go from Here?* I had forgotten, if I had ever really known, the power and the eloquence of King's prophetic words. In 1958, for example, in an article for *Jubilee* magazine, Dr. King looked back on Rosa Parks and the 381-day bus boycott in Montgomery, Alabama, that launched King's era of leadership in the centuries-long struggle to end discrimination against African-Americans:

> From the beginning a basic philosophy guided the movement. This guiding principle has since been referred to variously as nonviolent resistance, non-cooperation, and passive resistance. But in the first days of the protest none of these expressions was mentioned: the phrase most often heard was "Christian love." It was the Sermon on the Mount, rather than a doctrine of passive resistance, that initially inspired the Negroes of Montgomery to dignified social action. It was Jesus of Nazareth that stirred the Negroes to protest with the creative weapon of love.[3]

From childhood I had heard Jesus' words "Love your enemies. Bless them that curse you. Do good to them that hate you. And pray for them which despitefully use you, and persecute you."[4] Love was at the heart of his first "Sermon on the Mount," and love was the theme of his last words to them on the night of his betrayal and arrest. "These things I command you," Jesus said moments after Judas hurried away on his errand of betrayal, "that you love one another."[5]

Almost two thousand years later, the writings of Dr. King were calling me to quit talking about love and begin putting it into practice. But how could I love the fundamentalists? How could love stop the flow of misinformation and end the suffering? How could love be the principle that guides us in resisting the oppression?

Dr. King credited M. K. Gandhi for helping him understand how love could become a force for liberation. When he first read the Sermon on the Mount, Gandhi was particularly impressed by Jesus' call to "Love your enemy, bless those who curse you, do good for those who hate you." But it bothered him that so many people associated the active love of Jesus with passivity, acquiescence, silent and helpless suffering. Gandhi was convinced that Jesus' "law of love" had two sides: "to cooperate with all that is good" and "to non-co-operate with all that is evil."[6]

Jesus' call to "non-co-operation" was not, however, a call to violence. Gandhi believed that Jesus' plan was "that the Jews should give up ideas of violence and convert enemies into friends by his technique of love and nonviolence and thus help in realizing the kingdom of his vision."[7]

Dr. King defined Jesus' call to love as *agape* love, "Understanding, redeeming good will for all men [and women], a willingness to go to any length to restore community."[8] Gandhi used *ahimsa*—a Sanskrit word meaning nonviolence— to describe *agape* love. *Ahimsa* or *agape* to Gandhi means "the largest love, love even for the evil-doer. It however does not mean meek submission to the will of the evil-doer. On the contrary it means putting of one's whole soul against the will of the tyrant. Evil, however, cannot be overcome by evil, by violence and retaliation. To use violence against the evil-doer is to deny spiritual unity with him."[9] To both men love is something you do!

Christians often talk of love, but Gandhi created *Satyagraha* ("truth force" or "soul force") as a plan for putting love into action. He recruited, trained, and mobilized the masses to resist injustice through relentless nonviolent resistance. Looking back on the success of the bus boycott in Montgomery, Dr. King described the effects of Gandhi's "soul force" principles on the marchers:

> I had come to see early that the Christian doctrine of love operating through the Gandhian method of nonviolence was one of the most potent weapons available to the Negro in his struggle for freedom... Nonviolent resistance had emerged as the technique of the movement, while love stood as the regulating ideal. In other words, Christ furnished the spirit and the motivation while Gandhi furnished the method.[10]

Even while I read Dr. King's explanation of *agape* love, I remembered a rare and transforming moment in my own life in May 1994, when Tim McFeeley, then president of the Human Rights Campaign Fund (now HRC), asked me to address their Annual Leadership Conference in Washington, D.C. I was a fledgling activist at best. In that large conference room would be assembled seasoned activists from across the country. What could I say to them out of my short experience that would make any kind of difference in their lives?

The suffering and death of innocent gays and lesbians was not a new phenomenon in this country. And for decades, courageous activists, like those men and women I was about to address, had taken their stand against our oppression. Most of them would trace their activist roots to Stonewall, June 28, 1969, the night a handful of courageous transvestites resisted police harassment at New York's Stonewall Inn.[11] Those courageous, angry people launched the latest era in the American struggle for lesbian and gay rights, but there were activists who risked their lives to resist oppression many years before Stonewall.

In my rush to catch up on the history of gay and lesbian liberation in this country, I discovered the Mattachine Society, the Daughters of Bilitis, *One* magazine, the early chapters of the Gay Liberation Front in Los Angeles and New York City, San Francisco's pioneering Council on Religion and the Homosexual, and Chicago's Gay Alliance. I learned the names of the mothers and fathers of the current struggle for gay liberation in America, names I had never heard or read.

Eliminating our heroes and sheroes is just one more example of how oppression works. And until the truth is written about those early days, the few courageous activists we do remember must represent them all: Morris Kight, Barbara Gittings, Harry Hays, Troy Perry, Jim Kepner, Malcolm Boyd, John McNeil, and thousands of gay and lesbian foot soldiers from the past, soldiers like Karen Harrick, who was charged with obstructing traffic during a demonstration against discrimination in San Francisco in 1969 because "she was lying on the sidewalk while she was being clubbed by police."[12]

I spent the week before that Human Rights Campaign Fund conference reading every book or article I could find on gay and lesbian activism in America. And though I had written a speech, I still didn't know what I should say to the activists who would gather there.

My plane was leaving the Dallas-Fort Worth airport for Washington, D.C., at noon on May 6, 1994. Early that morning, with my bags packed and my speech manuscript in hand, I took my regular morning walk with our farm dogs, Bud and Maggie. I prayed that morning, rather desperately, I admit, for something to say beyond my usual theme: "What can we do to keep the radical right from doing more wrong?"

As I walked the isolated country road, hoping for some kind of insight to boil up out of the overload of information stewing in my brain, I sensed the presence of others walking on the road beside me. Often, on my walks down that long farm-to-market road, I pictured Jesus walking with me as a kind of meditation technique. But this time, I sensed his spontaneous presence in a unique and rather inspiring way.

And Jesus wasn't alone. I imagined all my heroes and sheroes walking with him: Moses, other Jewish poets and prophets, Gandhi, Dietrich Bonhoeffer, Dorothy Day, Dag Hammarskjold, Oscar Romero, Audre Lorde. I couldn't see them with my eyes and knew I was just imagining them, but the sense of their presence was very real. I could see them in my soul, and the look on each face was exactly the same. It was the look a kindly professor gives you when you ask a dumb question. "What should I tell these activists?" I had mumbled to myself. And these ancient and modern-day activists, who suddenly appeared beside me, were obviously embarrassed by my question. Now, looking back, I realize they were groaning with impatience that I would finally discover for myself the answer that had been buried in my heart since childhood.

I felt excited and encouraged by this sudden sense of their presence; so I asked the question once again, "What should I say to these activists that will make some small difference in their lives? They're out there on the front lines fighting for justice. What new insight can you give me that will help inspire and inform their work?"

Surrounded by the smiling, impatient, slightly irritated spirits of these men and women who had suffered in the course of seeking justice for their own oppressed peoples, suddenly I knew the answer they would give.

"Tell them," they would say in one strong voice, "that we must learn to out-love our enemies."

With that sudden insight, they were gone and I was alone on the road again. "Out-love our enemies?" The words were clear. But I knew, or at least I thought I knew, how that line would play with a crowd of battle-weary gay activists.

"You tell them," I wanted to shout at the disappearing spirits. "They'll laugh me off the platform."

On the long flight to D.C. that day, I pictured what might happen when I spoke of love to this generation of current activists from the Human Rights Campaign Fund, the National Gay and Lesbian Task Force, the Gay and Lesbian Alliance against Defamation, Act-Up, Queer Nation, the Lesbian Avengers, and others. These activists had been the victims of the rhetoric and the antigay political actions of fundamentalist Christianity. They had seen their own families divided, their best friends alienated, their closest allies exhausted and struck down, their towns, counties, and states turned into battle zones by fundamentalist Christians carrying ugly signs and shouting false accusations. And I was supposed to say, "We must learn to out-love our enemies"?

Late that afternoon, after a long ride from Dulles Airport, I sat in the conference center waiting my turn at the lectern. Congressman Barney Frank ended his brilliant survey of the war being waged against us in the Congress and the courts and then he introduced me. I had never felt less prepared to give a speech.

After bringing the activists up to date on the current antigay rhetoric and political actions of my old fundamentalist Christian clients, I told them the story of that morning's walk on a country road. My palms were wet with perspiration. My voice cracked. I knew that I was about to make a fool of myself. But I offered that simplistic solution anyway: "We must learn to out-love our enemies"

For a moment there was silence. In the center of the room, I saw tears in the eyes of an older lesbian, obviously a veteran activist who had seen years of front-line duty. A younger woman, her eyes also wet with tears, put her arm around her friend in solidarity. I could see around the room that others were struggling with their own deep feelings. A young man in the front row stared up at me, applauding enthusiastically, understanding what I had said but shaking his head in obvious ambivalence.

I walked down from the platform and was immediately surrounded by activists, each anxious to share her or his own stories. It was then I learned for the first time what would be demonstrated time and time again in the days ahead. A large proportion of my sister and brother activists are preachers' or rabbis' kids or the sons and daughters of genuinely religious Catholic, Protestant, and Jewish families. Their interest in doing justice comes from hearing that call when they were still children from the Torah and the Hebrew prophets or from the life and teachings of Jesus. Urvashi Vaid, one of our leading lesbian author/activists, was there. Though "Urv" considers herself a "lapsed Hindu," her activist roots grow deep in the understanding of dharma passed on to her by her Hindu parents.[13]

In the long line of activists who came up to me that day in Washington, D.C., there was an ex-choir director from a Southern Baptist church, an organist who also played regularly at Billy Graham crusades, several ex-Catholic altar boys, at least two ex-pastors, one ex-priest, and five or six former seminarians who in their determination to be honest gave up their call to Catholic or Protestant ministry.

Instead of laughing me off the platform, as I had feared,

these activists agreed with my basic premise but wanted to hear more. Unfortunately, I didn't have more. They, too, knew that we needed to learn to out-love our enemies, that love, effectively applied to our oppressors, would help end our oppression, but they didn't know exactly how to do it, and neither did I. No one seemed to know exactly how to translate that exalted principle into practical, grassroots strategy for resisting oppression. Ironically, while I taught, preached, and argued "try love," my growing anger against the leaders of the "radical right" was leading me to "give up on them."

About that time, Lynn Cothren read my angry letter. In his response, Lynn put his arm around my shoulder and suggested that I would find how love works in resisting oppression through the writings of Martin Luther King, Jr. Although Dr. King and the Montgomery bus boycott were motivated by Jesus' call to love, it wasn't long until King, too, discovered that the call to love was not enough. Love needed to be translated into action.

King was twenty-six years old when he became an activist. The Dexter Avenue Baptist Church in Montgomery, Alabama, was his first pastorate. Just twelve months earlier he had moved into the small parsonage with his bride, Coretta Scott King, a gifted singer who cut short her studies at the New England Conservatory of Music to support her husband's ministry.

Martin Luther King was by nature more the preacher-scholar than the political activist. He had just completed his Ph.D. in theology, commuting back and forth to Boston from Montgomery, when he was selected by the city's ministers in December 1955 to lead the Montgomery bus boycott.

No one could be adequately prepared to direct the historic protest that erupted almost spontaneously after the arrest of Rosa Parks. From the beginning of his ministry, Dr. King was committed to Jesus' teachings about love. But he credits a stranger for reminding him during the first days of that amazing protest how love was being translated into effective political action half a world away.

Just one week after the Montgomery protest started, Miss Juliette Morgan, a sympathetic white woman, wrote to the editor of the *Montgomery Advertiser* comparing the bus protest to the protest movement led by Mahatma Gandhi in South Africa and in India. I was fascinated by Dr. King's brief description of this unknown woman and her timely influence on his life and on the life of the civil rights movement.

"Miss Juliette Morgan," King wrote, "sensitive and frail, did not long survive the rejection and condemnation of the white community, but long after she died in the summer of 1957 the name of Mahatma Gandhi was well known in Montgomery. People who had never heard of the little brown saint of India were now saying his name with an air of familiarity."[14]

Dr. King had studied the life and teachings of Mahatma Gandhi at Crozer Theological Seminary and at Boston University. But it was that brief letter to the editor by Miss Juliette Morgan that reminded the brand-new activist where he might turn for practical guidelines for transforming love into powerful, political action for his own protest movement in Montgomery.

At first, Dr. King and his fellow pastors guessed that the boycott would be a symbolic protest, lasting just a day or two. Then King read Gandhi, who was very clear: Never begin a protest if you're not going to take that protest all the way. For 381 days, the black citizens of Montgomery continued their walk to end segregation on the city buses. Through a long, hot summer, and a cold, rainy winter, they walked. Finally, a full year and several weeks later, the Supreme Court ended the segregation of Montgomery's city buses.

In a July 1959 article for *Ebony* magazine, Dr. King gives Gandhi credit for the successful protest in Montgomery that launched the modern civil rights movement in America: "While the Montgomery boycott was going on, India's Gandhi was the guiding light of our technique of nonviolent social change."[15]

I hadn't thought seriously about Gandhi since learning about him from E. Stanley Jones during my senior year in high school. I had seen Richard Attenborough's Academy Award— winning film *Gandhi* during its premiere run in Los Angeles in 1982, and I had Gandhi's autobiography, *My Experiment with Truth*, molding in the garage in a dusty box of books from my days at Fuller Theological Seminary. Lynn Cothren said, "Read King." Now King himself was urging me to read Gandhi.

"As I read his works," King recalled in his 1960 book, *Stride Toward Freedom*, "I became fascinated by his campaigns of nonviolent resistance. The whole Gandhian concept of *Satyagraha* was profoundly significant to me. As I delved deeper into the philosophy of Gandhi my skepticism concerning the power of love gradually diminished, and I came to see for the first time that the Christian doctrine of love operating through the Gandhian method of nonviolence was one of the most potent weapons available to oppressed people in their struggle for freedom."[16]

After digging out and dusting off my ancient paperback copy of Gandhi's autobiography, I began to read it again with a new hunger. What was "Satyagraha" and why had it become so "profoundly significant" in the life of Dr. Martin Luther King? How did it transform Jesus' rather generic command "to love your enemies" into an effective method for resisting oppression? Finally, after reading the first 318 pages of Gandhi's *My Experiments with Truth*, I discovered a two-page chapter entitled "The Birth of Satyagraha."

"None of us knew what name to give to our movement," Gandhi recalled. He didn't like the term "passive resistance" and he was embarrassed "to permit this great struggle to be known by an English name." So he offered a small prize in *Indian Opinion*, Gandhi's newspaper, to anyone who might suggest the appropriate name for their new liberation movement. His friend Shri Maganlal Gandhi suggested the word "Sadagraha," meaning "firmness in a good cause."

"I like the word," Gandhi recalled, "but it did not fully represent the whole idea I wished it to connote." He then corrected the word to read "Satyagraha." "Truth (Satya) implies love," Gandhi explained, "and firmness (agraha) serves as a synonym for force. I thus began to call the Indian movement 'Satyagraha,' that is to say, the Force which is born of Truth and Love."

A few lines later, Gandhi recalls that moment in a debate in South Africa when he added one more dimension to the newly coined name Satyagraha. "Satyagraha is soul force pure and simple," he explained, "and whenever and to whatever extent there is room for the use of arms or physical force or brute force, there and to that extent is there so much less possibility for soul force."[17]

"Soul force!" I loved the sound of it. All my life I had heard the call from my parents, pastors, and teachers to "follow Jesus." But when I asked what it meant to "follow" him in these modern times, all too often they answered with three vocational choices. I could be a missionary (the most noble option), an evangelist (the second best), or a pastor/preacher. I don't remember much talk about the difficult moral and ethical decisions that Jesus asked his followers to make or any clear instructions as to what "take up your cross and follow" meant in terms of the tragic twentieth century. Suddenly, in Martin Luther King, Jr. (the Baptist preacher), and M. K. Gandhi (the Hindu lawyer) I was discovering a whole new way to understand the life and teachings of this first-century Jewish teacher whom I had loved and admired from my childhood.

During his early years as an attorney in South Africa, Gandhi was greatly influenced by the teachings of Jesus, Thoreau, Tolstoy, and Ruskin. "The Sermon on the Mount," says Gandhi, "went straight to my heart."[18] Determined to reduce "principles into practice," Gandhi created Satyagraha: a plan of action for the development of our inner lives and for the transformation of society. Gandhi refined his "truth force" or "soul force" principles while leading justice movements in South Africa (1893-1915) and India (1915-1948). Then Martin Luther King, Jr., discovered Gandhi's "soul force" rules and used them to shape his own nonviolent civil rights movement in America (1955-1968).

Actually, neither man had time to systematize the "soul force" principles of relentless nonviolent resistance. They were too busy discovering how love works when it is applied against the overwhelming forces of violence lined up against them. Fortunately, there are men and women far more qualified than I who have spent their lives practicing relentless nonviolent resistance who have written about Satyagraha or "soul force" in ways that both inspire and inform. Dr. King summarizes his five basic beliefs about nonviolence in an article he wrote in 1958, "Out of the Long Night of Segregation."

"First, this is not a method of cowardice or passivity," King writes. "It does resist; second, it does not seek to defeat or humiliate the opponent, but to win his friendship and understanding; third, the attack is directed to forces of evil, rather than persons caught in the forces; fourth, it not only avoids external physical violence, but also internal violence of spirit; fifth, it is based upon the conviction that the universe is on the side of justice."[19]

In a 1962 address to the National Press Club in Washington, D.C., King summarizes "soul force" in the following simple terms. "We will take direct action against injustice without waiting for other agencies to act. We will not obey unjust laws or submit to unjust practices. We will do this peacefully, openly, cheerfully because our aim is to persuade. We adopt the means of nonviolence because our end is a community at peace with itself. We will try to persuade with our words, but if our words fail, we will try to persuade with our acts. We will always be willing to talk and seek fair compromise, but we are ready to suffer when necessary and even risk our lives to become witnesses to the truth as we see it."[20]

The discovery of the "soul force" principles has revolutionized my life as an activist and as a human being. I don't know if Lynn Cothren had it all planned when he pointed me gently toward the writings of Dr. Martin Luther King, Jr., but I do know that discovering King and Gandhi has led me to a time of personal renewal and discovery that has only just begun.

While I was in grad school, I read Dr. King's historic letter written from a Birmingham jail, April 16, 1963. Unfortunately, I wasn't ready to hear or understand his words until thirty-two years later. Both King and Gandhi were dead and I was taking my first awkward steps down that long, lonely road toward justice that they call us all to travel. I was a baby activist, desperate to know how to put Jesus' love into action, when I read King's letter once again.

From the jail in Birmingham, King describes "soul force" in four steps: First, gather the evidence. See where injustice prevails and make your strong case against it; second, meet with your opponent to negotiate an end to the injustice; third, if negotiations break down or are used to delay justice, recruit, train, and equip people of good faith in the principles of relentless nonviolent resistance; fourth, with people committed to nonviolence of the heart, tongue, and fist, plan and carry out nonviolent direct actions that prove to your opponent that you will not be satisfied until justice is done.[21]

King explains that demanding justice begins only when we open serious negotiations with our opponent. Yet in my letter of 1995, I had threatened to end my efforts even to talk to my old clients on the radical right. Without even knowing it, I was breaking a cardinal rule of "soul force." Now, in 2006, I can look back on almost a dozen years attempting to negotiate an end to the violent words and actions against us by fundamentalist Christians, Mormons, and Roman Catholics. Our negotiations with bishops, televangelists, moderators, elders, clergy, and laity alike have failed. It is time to move on to serious nonviolent direct action.

Nobody likes to see the oppressed demanding justice in the streets. When King led the march in Birmingham, he was thrown into jail. Even liberal white church leaders turned against him. They wanted him to wait. Wait for the Congress. Wait for the courts. Wait for the president, the governor, the mayor, the police chief, or the sheriff. "This 'wait,'" King wrote, "has almost always meant 'Never.'"

> You may well ask: "Why direct action? Why sit-ins, marches and so forth? Isn't negotiation a better path?" You are quite right in calling for negotiation. Indeed, this is the very purpose of direct action. Nonviolent direct action seeks to create such a crisis and foster such a tension that a community which has constantly refused to negotiate is forced to confront the issue. It seeks so to dramatize the issue that it can no longer be ignored....We know through painful experience that freedom is never voluntarily given by the oppressor; it must be demanded by the oppressed.[22]

I am so grateful to our activists (past and present) for the creative and courageous work they have done and are doing to win justice for all. But our current approach to activism is not enough. Lobbying is very important, but King demonstrated how the legislative process is sped up when there are people in the streets demanding justice. Signing petitions, e-mailing officials, sending letters, and making telephone calls are good but not enough. One-day marches, rallies, or demonstrations inspire us, but they do not convince our adversaries that they are tragically misinformed. (In fact, too often our public actions convince them they are right about the "gay threat to traditional family values.") Candlelight vigils always move us, but seldom move them. All too often, media debates, sound-bite wars, and dueling press conferences do not lead to understanding and reconciliation. Gary and I continue to support our national and state organizations working for justice, and encourage our friends to do the same; but we no longer believe that what happens in the Congress, the courts, or the White House will change the minds and hearts of our adversaries or lead to the understanding and acceptance we seek. That begins when we take it to the streets. I believe that the "soul force" principles of relentless nonviolent resistance offer us the most effective way to bring spiritual renewal to our community; to change the minds and hearts of our adversaries; and to bring hope and healing to our society.

Frankly, I am embarrassed to admit that the religious institutions I once trusted to bring hope and healing to our society have not only failed, they have turned against us. The people God has called to "love mercy" and "do justice" have become the source of our oppression. As a result, the Christian faith that I once knew is gone forever. But from the ruins, I am piecing together a whole new picture of Jesus.

The activist Jesus is largely ignored by fundamentalist Christianity. Mel Gibson's movie *Passion of the Christ* features his bloody death while his fiery speeches about justice and mercy ended up on the cutting-room floor. Not one scene was left to explain why the religious and political leaders conspired to silence him. Jesus was sentenced to death because he condemned their misuse of wealth, confronted their abuse of power, and called them to do justice, love mercy, and seek truth. He was determined to put a spike in the wheels of injustice and instead they drove spikes through his hands, feet, and side. His values conflicted with their values, and it cost him his life.

Unfortunately, fundamentalist Christians have turned his death into a simple formula for "getting saved." And doing justice and loving mercy have been boiled down to leading a neighbor in "the sinner's prayer" or distributing little pamphlets (tracts) with pictures illustrating hellfires and escape routes. How do Christians reshape the Good News when our nation is awash in what Bonhoeffer calls "cheap grace"? How do we rediscover, reclaim, and restate the core of Christian faith when that faith has been hijacked by fundamentalist Christians whose understanding of the Gospel leads directly and indirectly to suffering and death across the Middle East, to intolerance toward people of other faiths or worldviews, to subtle and not-so-subtle discrimination against the poor and less privileged, to the destruction of the environment, to denial of the civil rights of women, of Muslims and other "suspicious" citizens, and a Federal Marriage Amendment that would debase our relationships and deny us our rights?

If we are called to do justice and love mercy, shouldn't proclamation of the Gospel include protests of an unjust war, even nonviolent protests at the White House and the Pentagon? Isn't it part of our witness to demand that Congress end boycotts that prevent medicines and foodstuffs from reaching the poor and needy in other even hostile nations? Doesn't the Good News insist that our president support the protocol banning land mines that go on killing women and children long after the war is over? Can't preaching Good News to the poor include taking a stand against the billions spent on the military to use at least part of those funds to provide food, clothing, housing, and medicines to those in need?

Doesn't proclaiming freedom for the prisoner include working to make the court system more just and prisons more conducive to reform? Doesn't offering release to the oppressed mean that we stand against Christian fundamentalists like Jerry Falwell, who exclaim on national television that terrorists "should be blown away in the name of the Lord"? Doesn't bringing Good News to the downtrodden also mean demanding justice for Palestinians as well as Jews and mercy for Muslims held without access to lawyers or contact with their families? Doesn't the Gospel include working actively to protect and preserve the fragile, wounded earth we call home? Doesn't our proclamation of the Christian faith include defending the civil rights of all Americans, including lesbian and gay Americans? This kind of love will cost us.

Those who marched with King sang, "Freedom is never free." As those young African-Americans taught us, the oppressed must pay a high price to win their rights from the oppressor. They were harassed, beaten, bloodied, arrested, and thrown in jail. Their Freedom Rides were interrupted by angry crowds, and one bus was torched with near-disastrous results. During "Freedom Summer" in 1964, James Chaney, twenty-one, Andrew Goodman, twenty, and Michael Schwerner, twenty-four, were terrorized, beaten, shot, and buried in an earthen dam. At the beginning of the Selma-to-Montgomery march on "Bloody Sunday," March 7, 1965, sheriff deputies charged on horseback beating marchers back across the Edmund Pettus Bridge, and on March 25, 1965, just as the march was ending, Viola Liuzzo, a volunteer from Michigan driving marchers back to Selma, was killed by a volley of bullets fired from a passing car.

Gandhi proved with his own life that doing justice required this kind of "voluntary redemptive suffering." In similar words, Dr. King says, "I have lived these last few years with the conviction that unearned suffering is redemptive."[23] "Our God is a suffering God," Bonhoeffer wrote in 1944 from Tegel Prison, "and we are summoned to share in God's suffering at the hands of a godless world."[24] "If they kill me," said Archbishop Oscar Romero shortly before his assassination in El Salvador, "I will rise again in the Salvadoran people."

Liberation movements seem to require martyrs, men and women, young and old, who stand for justice with such courage and commitment that their enemies cannot afford to let them live. Do you ever wonder why there are so few of them around today? Hermann Hagedorn, a historian and poet, asked why the world is short on martyrs in his classic poem *The Bomb That Fell on America*:[25]

"I stood in a desert," he wrote, "and there was a Cross in the desert and a Man on the Cross. 'Look at Him,'" said the Voice, "and look at yourself. Look at Him, and be still, look at yourself and be honest. How do you appear to yourself beside Him?"

I looked, and it seemed as though the earth dropped from under my feet, and I was hanging in space between currents that pressed me down and currents that pushed me up. "What do you see?" said the Voice. "I have never been crucified" I said. "No," said the Voice, "you have never been crucified. Do you know why?"

I felt suddenly ashamed. "I have never made people angry enough."

"The Voice was still for a long time and when it spoke again it seemed to come from mountains, afar off. 'The world is sick,'" said the Voice, 'for dearth of crucifixions.'"

In *Why We Can't Wait*, Martin Luther King, Jr., describes

the 1963 struggle for civil rights (Albany, Birmingham, and the March on Washington) that made his enemies angry enough to kill him. The young African-Americans who followed King found themselves facing that same kind of deadly anger when they decided it was time to take it to the streets. These are similar times. Dr. King's book might have been titled *Why We Didn't Wait*, for he describes the "disappointments" that drove African-Americans into the streets—"disappointments" that gay and lesbian Americans know all too well.

We, too, are disappointed in the Congress and the courts; disappointed in both political parties and their leadership; disappointed in the lack of change in the United States when liberation is happening in other nations. We, too, are tired of slow change and token changes, tired of defending ourselves against the claims of moral inferiority, tired of being victims of public laws and private humiliations, tired of intolerance and inequality, tired of suffering and dying just because we are different.

The historic civil rights legislation of 1964 came just eight years after Rosa Parks and the Montgomery bus boycott. It's been more than thirty years since this latest season of protest began at the Stonewall Bar in New York City, and with all the changes we can celebrate, the real problem remains the same: the antigay religious teachings and actions that support intolerance and discrimination are still powerfully in place in our Protestant and Catholic churches.

These antigay, religion-based teachings and actions have become the primary source of misinformation against sexual and gender minorities, misinformation that leads to suffering and death. Most antigay initiatives and antigay court decisions (local, statewide, and national) flow out of those same religious teachings. Instead of changing minds and hearts, the thirty-five-year war of words has seen those antigay religious teachings harden into place. When will we realize that the antigay teachings cannot be "studied" or "debated" or simply "voted" away? When will we understand injustice will prevail until we mobilize another nonviolent civil rights movement to end it? For decades we've tried to negotiate with fundamentalists to end their antihomosexual campaign. They've refused. It's time to take the next step. Agape love demands it.

Love demands that we refuse to participate in church studies and debates any longer. We must not allow ourselves to be examined and discussed like lab rats or exotic insects by clergy or laity who act as though we aren't even in the room. To accept the role of a "specimen," to have our humanity researched and analyzed like a virus or rare fungi, is the ultimate act of self-denigration. We must boycott and protest those events where our dignity is debated and our integrity impugned. To sit patiently through another vote (let alone be silent when another "study" is called for) is another proof of our internalized homophobia. To play along with this game of studying, debating, and discussing if we are worthy of our civil rights is to help postpone justice and support the structures of religion-based bigotry.

Love demands that we quit cooperating with those who oppress us by their actions or with those who oppress us by refusing to act. It is time to begin a campaign of relentless nonviolent resistance that will convince church leaders to do justice at last. They have assumed that we are infinitely patient or too comfortable in our closets to call for revolution. For their sake, and for the sake of the nation, we must prove them wrong.

Love demands (in Gandhi's words) that it is "as much our moral obligation NOT to cooperate with evil as it is to cooperate with good." If a local congregation refuses to accept us without reservation, we must lovingly express our concerns, demonstrate our case, and if full acceptance is not forthcoming, discontinue our support. If a local clergyman or woman refuses to marry us or help us get ordained, we must lovingly express our concerns, demonstrate our case, and if full participation in the rites of the church is not forthcoming, discontinue our support. When we withhold tithes and offerings (or time and energy) from a local church or denomination that refuses to welcome us without reservation, we are doing justice and at the same time ending the support of our own oppression.

Love demands that we begin serious efforts to recruit, train, and organize around the principles of relentless nonviolent resistance. We must help our own sisters and brothers understand the importance of leaving their closets to join us. We must convince gay and lesbian people who are safely "out" that checkbook activism is important but not enough. We need them on the front lines with us. We must reach out to other oppressed communities, experience their suffering, and build a network of cooperating organizations committed to helping cut their suffering at its source, as well.

Love demands that we conduct massive and relentless nonviolent direct actions to confront the injustice and end the untruth. Our faithful friends who are working from inside to change the Catholic and Protestant churches cannot do it alone. And our sisters and brothers who are lobbying government to defeat laws that are unjust and to pass just laws need pressure from the outside to help support their negotiation efforts.

Love demands we take it to the streets. It's time for boycotts, picket lines, mass vigils, serious fasts, candlelight marches, pray-ins, sit-ins, kneel-ins, and acts of nonviolent civil disobedience (spiritual obedience). We need to mount permanent protests, massive nonviolent vigils, and acts of civil disobedience at the headquarters of Dobson's Focus on the Family and Robertson's Christian Broadcasting Network; at the Southern Baptist Convention offices in Nashville; the Latter-Day Saints' headquarters in Salt Lake City; at the Vatican Embassy in Washington, D.C., and in St. Peter's Square. We must stage powerful and long-term direct actions against local churches and local pastors who are the primary source of the antigay propaganda in our communities...even if it means risking our jobs or even going to jail. We must recruit, train, plan, and act carefully, relentlessly, nonviolently. There is no way to know exactly how our "Salt March," our Montgomery, or our Birmingham will take shape. Gandhi said, "Just take the first step and see." The rest is in God's hands and the hands of our adversaries.

While writing the biography of Ninoy and Cory Aquino, Cory told me an amazing story about how her husband, the youngest mayor, governor, and senator in Philippine history, discovered the power of love in prison. After living in exile and teaching at Harvard, he returned to his country to become the first legally elected president of a truly democratic nation. Ferdinand Marcos, the tyrant who ruled the Philippines with U.S. support, was so threatened by Ninoy's return that he had him shot and killed on the runway at Manila's International Airport. Nino's death ignited a nonviolent revolution that swept Ferdinand and Imelda Marcos out of the country and Corazon Aquino, Ninoy's wife, into Malacañang, the presidential residence.[26]

On the fifth anniversary of her husband's death, August 21, 1988, Cory Aquino stood on the runway exactly where her husband died and addressed a million supporters who had gathered to honor his memory. "On this day," she said, "I wish to honor not just my husband, Ninoy, but his beloved friend who showed him the way." Cory went on to describe this mysterious friend as someone "Ninoy" had known from childhood. Unfortunately, distance had grown between Ninoy and his friend "with every increase of Nino's fame, power and responsibility."

It was during Ninoy's last imprisonment that "their friendship began to flower again."

Cory told how Ninoy's friend had been "a regular visitor to Ninoy's lonely cell." She explained how neither guards nor high walls could keep him out once Ninoy had let him in. "That friend," Cory said quietly, "came day after day, night after night, more faithful than any other."

When Ninoy's captors, seeking to break his defiance, threw him into a box, "unknown to them, his friend had slipped in with him. And there, in the utmost solitude and utter darkness of despair, Ninoy saw more vividly than in the full light of his days of freedom the true face of Jesus."

"He stood me face to face with myself," Ninoy later wrote, "and forced me to look at my emptiness and nothingness, and then he helped me discover Him who has never really left my side; but because pride shielded my eyes, and lust for earthly and temporal power, honor and joys drugged my mind, I failed to notice Him."

"In the moment of recognition," Cory reminded them, "friendship turned to the love that never left Ninoy. Together they embarked upon that long journey which ended on this day of the week, five years ago. He would face many more dangers and difficulties and suffering," Cory said, "but this time Ninoy had strength beyond his own. He was not alone!"

Moments later, while recalling her husband's assassination, Cory said, "When a bullet strikes you in the back of the head, the tendency is for the head to jerk back. So the last thing that Ninoy saw, before his face slammed on the tarmac and the blood began to form in a pool around his head, was the sky, and the face of his Friend who had come to take him home."

Active love creates a force in the world that overthrows tyrants and defeats injustice. "Soul force" is born in the hearts of men and women who put love into action, who finally decide to do something about injustice guided by the principles of relentless nonviolent resistance. "Soul force" enabled Cory Aquino, a housewife who never wanted to be president, to inspire and sustain the People Power Revolution. "Soul force" empowered her husband, Senator Ninoy Aquino, to face arrest, torture, and assassination. Here's the irony. The person who benefits most from demanding justice is the person who demands it. The main reason for insisting that the fundamentalist leaders meet with us is not to change them, but to change us. Win or lose, we take it to the streets because just being there enriches and empowers our lives. When we help those who suffer, we are the ones who benefit most. When we volunteer to help cut off the suffering at its source, our lives are given new meaning and new power. Our Creator is not in church or synagogue, temple or mosque. Our Creator is on the front lines where people are suffering injustice, and when we join her there we discover what it means to be a son or daughter of God, what it means to be truly human.

NOTES

PREFACE

1. Although the tape of Matthew Williams's conversation with his mother has not been released to the public, a summary of his reasons for killing the gay men can be found at Affirmation General Conference News Letter, May 8, 2000, http://www.umaffirm.org/tm0508.html. That summary is pieced together from articles written by reporters who actually heard the tape replayed and quoted from it. Those articles include: Maline Hazle, a reporter for the Record Searchlight, Redding, California, who covered the story extensively at www.redding.com; and reporters from the Sacramento Bee at http:///www.sacbee.com; http://www.salon.com/news/feature/1999/10/06/redding; http://gaypeopleschronicle.com/stories/00Mar24.htm; http://www.pbs.org/niot/citizens_respond/redding.html; http://www.rickross.com/reference/supremacists/supremacists102.html;

2. Eric Resnick, "Williams admits killing couple; says he 'obeyed God's law,'" Gay People's Chronicle, November 12, 1999, http://www.gaypeopleschronicle.com/stories/99nov12.htm

3. Ibid.

4. http://search.aol.com/aol/search?query=tea+party+and +the+Christian+rights&s_it=client95_searchbox MSNBC

5. Public Religion Research Institute

6. http://abcnews.go.com/Politics/sarah-palin-sparks-church-state-separation-debate/story?id=10419289&page=2

7. http://theweek.com/article/index/202838/sarah-palin-base-law-on-the-bible

8. http://www.thelangreport.com/political-commentary/ sarah-palin-creationism-god-and-country-pt2/

9. http://newsweek.washingtonpost.com/onfaith/ panelists/robert_parham/2010/08/glenn_becks_generic_god. html

10. Falwell, Listen, America! (Doubleday 1980:244)

11. http://newsweek.washingtonpost.com/onfaith/ panelists/robert_parham/2010/08/glenn_becks_generic_god. html

12. http://blogs.alternet.org/speakeasy/2010/09/07/16-anti-gay-extremists-in-glenn-becks-creepy-christian-army/

13. http://santitafarella.wordpress.com/2010/12/28/dadt-meltdown-watch-baptist-ethicist-richard-land-warns-of-gods-judgment-on-america/

14. http://www.huffingtonpost.com/max-blumenthal/ pastor-hagee-the-antichri_b_104608.html

15. http://mediamatters.org/mmtv/201004190043

16. From Falwell's November 21 televised sermon, broadcast from his Thomas Road Baptist Church, http:// mediamatters.org/research/200411240002

17. http://query.nytimes.com/gst/fullpage.html?res=9A0D E1DC1F3DF936A15755C0A962958260&sec=&spon=&page wanted=all

18. Ibid.

19. http://en.wikiquote.org/wiki/Rush_Limbaugh

20. http://blog.zap2it.com/pop2it/2010/05/rush-limbaugh-oil-spills-are-part-of-gods-plan-no-need-to-clean.html

21. http://www.jesusneedsnewpr.net/rush-limbaugh-says-that-god-hates-our-new-health-care-bill/

22. http://mediamatters.org/research/200411090003, Rush Limbaugh Show, November 5, 2005

23. http://blog.seattlepi.com/seattlepolitics/archives/217316.asp, Rush Limbaugh Show, August 8, 2010

24. http://glaadblog.org/2009/01/09/rush-limbaugh-directs-juvenile-anti-gay-joke-at-rep-barney-frank/

25. http://blogs.seattleweekly.com/dailyweekly/2010/06/rush_limbaugh_married_by_anti-.php

26. http://iowaindependent.com/44775/second-iowa-pastor-takes-aim-at-judges

27. Ibid.

28. http://iowaindependent.com/53431/ralph-reed-marriage-rights-will-not-be-deciding-factor-in-2012

29. http://www.snopes.com/politics/quotes/raskin.asp (This is an edited but accurate version of the actual exchange as reported in the Baltimore Sun, March 1, 2006.)

CHAPTER 1. THE CALL TO WAR: BILLY GRAHAM, FRANCIS SCHAEFFER, AND W. A. CRISWELL

1. Although Jerry Falwell described fundamentalism with these words in a sermon I heard at Thomas Road Baptist Church, it is actually borrowed from George M. Marsden, author of Fundamentalism and American Culture, in a description of that book online at Oxford University Press: http://www.us.oup.com/us/catalog/general/ subject/ReligionTheology/HistoryofChristianity/American/?view=usa&ci=9780195300475.

2. Sir Jonathan Sacks, chief rabbi, "The Children of Abraham," episode 3, Ten Alps Communications PLC, History Channel,

3. Karen Armstrong, *The Battle for God* (New York: Knopf, 2000), p. ix.

4. John Shelby Spong, *Rescuing the Bible from Fundamentalism* (HarperSanFrancisco, 1991), p. 3.

5. Edward John Carnell, The Case for Orthodoxy (Philadelphia: Westminster Press, 1959), Chapter VIII, "Perils."

6. Bill Moyers, "Armageddon and the Environment," published Dec. 6, 2004, at Com mon Dreams.org.

7. Bill Moyers's speech to the National Conference for Media Reform, May 15, 2005, convened by Free Press, online at http://www.freepress.net/news/8120.

8. Billy Graham and the Billy Graham Evangelistic Association Archives, Billy Graham Center at Wheaton College, http://wwwwheaton.edu/bec/archives/bio.html.

9. Harry Truman quoted in *Time* magazine, June 14, 1999.

10. Martin Luther King, Jr., "Pilgrimage to Nonviolence;' in *A Testament of Hope: The Essential Writings and Speeches of Martin Luther King, Jr.*, James M. Washington, ed. (San Francisco: HarperSanFrancisco, 1986), pp. 37-38.

11. William Sloan Coffin, *Credo* (Westminster: John Knox Press, 2004), p. 51.

12. For the typical fundamentalist critique of Billy Graham and dozens of other Christian leaders, see Rick Miesel's Biblical Discernment Ministries, www.rapidnet.com/ —jbeard/bdm/ exposes.

13. Billy Graham in the *Los Angeles Herald-Examiner*, July 22, 1985, from David Cloud's Fundamental Baptist Information Service, fbns@wayoflife.org.

14. Billy Graham in a 1978 issue of *McCall's* on Rick Miesel's Biblical Discernment Ministries Web page, http://

www.rapidnet.com/—jbeard/bdm/exposes/graham/ general.
htm.

15. Attributed to Billy Graham in *Newsweek* magazine,
April 26, 1982, by Rick Miesel.

16. Billy Graham on NBC's *Today* show, March 5, 1998.

17. Billy Graham in *TV Guide*, August 6, 1984.

18. Billy Graham on *Good Morning America*, September 5,
1991.

19. Billy Graham in a *20/20* television interview, May 2,
1997.

20. Billy Graham in *The Statesman Journal*, Salem, OR,
September 22, 1992.

21. Billy Graham in the *Los Angeles Herald-Examiner*, July
22, 1985.

22. http://www.io.com/gibbonsb/mencken.

23. http://www.english.ilstu.edu/separry/sindairlewis/
thejob.html.

24. Francis A. Schaeffer, "A Christian Manifesto." This
sermon was delivered by the late Dr. Schaeffer in 1982 at the
Coral Ridge Presbyterian Church, Fort Lauderdale, Florida. It
is based on one of his books, which bears the same title. It is
available online at: http://www.peopleforlife.org/francis.html.

25. Excerpted from. Letters of Francis A. Schaeffer, Lane T.
Dennis, ed. (Westchester, IL: Crossway Books, 1985).

26. Francis Schaeffer, "A Christian Manifesto," 1982, a
sermon delivered at the Coral Ridge Presbyterian Church.

27. W. A. Criswell, "The Infallible Word of God," a sermon
preached June 9, 1985, in the Criswell Sermon Library, www.
wacrisell.org.

28. Ibid.

29. "Jimmy Carter says he can 'no longer be associated'
with the SBC." Greg Warner, Associated Baptist Press, October
23, 2000, http://www.baptiststandard.com/2000/ 10_23/pages/
carter.html.

30. "Why I became a Pre-Millennialist," sermon by W. A. Criswell, March 29, 1988, found in the Criswell Sermon Archives.

31. Reported by Timothy George, dean of Beeson Divinity School at Samford University and an executive editor of *Christianity Today*, in an issue of that magazine, March 11, 2002.

32. The Reverend Nancy Wilson, *OUR TRIBE: Queer Folks, God, Jesus, and the Bible* (New York: HarperCollins, 1989), pp. 148-53.

33. Paul Varnell, "Sodom: A Visitor's Guide," *Chicago Free Press*, April 19, 2000, http:// www.indegayforum.org/authors/varnell/varnell33.html.

34. W. A. Criswell, "LOT: LIVING WITH HOMOSEXUALS (Genesis 19:1-11)," September 21, 1980, http://www.wacriswell.com/index.cfm/FuseAction/Search. Transcripts/sermon/864.cfm.

CHAPTER 2. THE WARRIORS: JERRY FALWELL AND PAT ROBERTSON

1. World Census of Religious Activities, United Nations Information Center, New York, 1989, found online at http:// www.bringyou.to/apologetics/al20.htm.

2. Jerry Falwell, Strength for the Journey (New York: Simon & Schuster, 1987), p. 361.

3. Ibid.

4. Quote from review of MarkTaylor Dalhouse, *An Island in the Lake of Fire: Bob Jones University, Fundamentalism & the Separatist Movement in Kirkus Reviews*, at www.barnesandnoble.com.

5. Ibid., p. 362.

6. In 1999, Cal Thomas and his cowriter, Ed Dodson,

released *Blinded by Might: Why the Religious Right Can't Save America*. In the book, Thomas clearly disassociates himself from Falwell and the Moral Majority and gives his take on what went wrong with the religious right.

7. NEWS BRIEF: "Religious right finds its center in Oval Office: Bush emerges as movement's leader after Robertson leaves Christian Coalition," by Dana Milbank, Washington Post staff writer, Monday, December 24, 2001, p. A02, http://www.washingtonpost.com/wp-dyn/articles/A1 9253-2001 Dec23.html.

8. I recommend Pat Robertson's *America's Dates with Destiny* (Nashville, TN: Thomas Nelson Publishers, 1986). These thoughts about Finney and his friends were inspired by rereading from that book the chapter "Charles Finney's Sermon at Utica (America's Second Great Awakening)," pp. 129-59.

9. 102 Cong. Rec. 4515-16 (1956).

10. Pat Robertson's biography on CBN.com.

11. Sara Diamond, `Pat Robertson's Central America Connection," Guardian, September 17, 1986.

12. John J. Fiaka and Ellen Hume, "TV Preacher, Possibly Eyeing the Presidency, Is Polishing His Image;' *Wall Street Journal*, October 17, 1985.

13. For Jerry Falwell's own history of the Moral Majority, refer to his autobiography, *Strength for the Journey* (New York: Simon & Schuster, 1987).

14. Press release, Media Matters for America (a Web-based, not-for-profit, progressive research and information center dedicated to comprehensively monitoring, analyzing, and correcting conservative misinformation in the US. media), August 28, 2005, www.mediamatters.org/items/200508230005.

15. David Brock, president and CEO, Media Matters for America, ibid.

16. Norfolk Virginian-*Pilot*, November 9, 1991.

17. "Who to Challenge on the Theocratic Right." 1995, PublicEye.Org, Political Research Associates, data compiled by Institute of First Amendment Studies, http:// www.publiceye. org/research/directories/theo_top.html.

18. Peter Hardin, Washington correspondent, Times-Dispatch, Richmond, VA, November 4, 2005, http://www. timesdispatch.com/servlet/Satellite?pagename=RTD%2FMG Article%2FRTD_BasicArticle&c=MGArtide&cid=112876793 9316&path=!new sipolitics&s=1045855935264.

19. "Guards Don Gloves as Gay Officials Visit White House," Al Kamen, Washington Post, June 15, 1995, p. Al.

20. Colbert King, "Pat Robertson and His Business Buddies," Washington Post, November 10, 2001, p. A27.

CHAPTER 3. THE SPOILS OF WAR: JAMES DOBSON (THE ENFORCER) AND D. JAMES KENNEDY (THE EXTREMIST)

1. From Dr. Dobson's Newsletter, May 2003, "Change Is in the Air." http:// www.family.org/docstudy/newsletters/ a0025678.cfm.

2. James Dobson, Focus on the Family and Homosexuality: An Open Letter from Dr. James C. Dobson, president, Focus on the Family, to the Reverend Mel White, *Gazette Telegraph*, July 17, 1994 (a paid advertisement).

3. During our seven-day "Fast for Understanding" in front of Dobson's world headquarters, a newspaper reporter made the mistake of including Dobson in the list of fundamentalist leaders I had served. The reporter made a public apology, but to this day Dobson daims that I lied about our relationship.

4. "Portraits in Power." Boston Globe, "Dobson spiritual empire wields political clout," Brian MacQuarrie, *Globe* staff, October 9, 2005, http://www.boston.com/news/

nation/articles/2005/ 10/09/dobson_spiritual_empire_wields _____ clout/.

5. Howard Fineman, MSNBC Web page, May 4, 2005, http://msnbc.msn.com/id/7723798/.

6. "US right attacks SpongeBob video," BBC Web page, Thursday, January 20, 2005, 11:32 GMT, http://news.bbc.co.uk/2/hi/americas/4190699.stm.

7. Ibid.

8. 8,http://headlines.agapepress.org/archive/1/afa/102005a.asp.

9. The Reverend John Thomas quoted in a column by J. Bennett Guess, "SpongeBob receives 'unequivocal welcome' from United Church of Christ," *United Church News*, Jan. 24, 2005, http://www.ucc.org/news/r012405.htm.

10. Ibid.

11. J. Bennett Guess, "Sponge Bob."

12. Dobson's endorsement letter can be found online at http://www.agapepress.org/ JDobsonLtr.jpg.

13. Mark Kittel, "Another Trip Through Fundamentalist Politics," Moderate Republicans.Net, Commentaries, April 2004, http://moderaterepublican.net/idl4.html.

14. Vonette Bright, quoted in "Interfaith Day of Reflection and Prayer, 2004," http:// www.milpagan.org/PC/May_7_2004.html.

15. "Religion: Evangelicals Exploit Air Force Academy: Military Officials Interlocked with Local Activists." Devlin Buckley, contributing writer, Online Journal, April 2005, http://www.onlinejournal.com/artman/publish/printer_363.shtml.

16. T. R. Reid, "Air Force Removes Chaplain from Post: Officer Decried Evangelicals' Influence," *Washington Post*, May 13, 2005, p. A04, http://www.washingtonpost. com/wp-dyn/content/article/2005/05/12/AR200505 1201 740_2.html.

17. Bill Berkowitz, "Heathens' need not apply,"

WorkingForChange, June 23, 2005, http://www. workingforchange.com/printitem.cfm?itemid=19250.

18. Howard Fineman, MSNBC Web page.

19. http://www.familyfoundation.org/.

20. Ibid.

21. *New York Times*, May 13, 2004, from Dr. Dobson's *Action Newsletter*, July 2004.

22. "The fundraising success of a new James Dobson group spurs debate on the rules," by Eric Gorski, *Denver Post* staff writer, June 3, 2005, at DenverPost.com, or http:// www. theocracywatch.org/focus_money_denverpost_june3_05.htm.

23. Dobson letter to the Florida Family Policy Council (no date given), http:// www.flfamily.org/Dobson%20note%20 for%20FPCs%20-%20on%2OLtrhead.pdf.

24. Ibid.

25. Michael Crowley in Slate, an Internet magazine, Taking Stock of People in the News, "James Dobson: The religious right's new kingmaker." Posted November 12, 2004.

26. "The Futile Crusade," Kay S. Hymowitz, City Journal, Spring 1993, http:// www.city-journal.org/artide0 1 .php?aid=1495.

27. Focus on the Family Web page, December 1, 2005, http://vvww.family.org/welcome/ press/a0038760.cfm.

28. Focus on the Family, December 1, 2005.

29. "Focus on the Family and Homosexuality: An Open Letter from Dr. James C. Dobson, president, Focus on the Family, to the Reverend Mel White," *Gazette Telegraph*, July 17, 1994.

30. "A False Focus on My Family: Why every person of faith should be deeply troubled by Dr. James Dobson's dangerous and misleading words about the lesbian, gay, bisexual, and transgender community," by Jeff Lutes, MS, LPC, foreword by Mary Barber, MD, president of the Association of Gay and

Lesbian Psychiatrists, available to download online at http://www.soulforce.org/artide/false-focus-family.

31. "Dear Dr. Dobson: An Open Video Letter to Focus on the Family," produced by Jeff Lutes, MS, LPC, available online at www.soulforce.org (29-minute DVD or video).

32. Alan Sears and Craig Osten, *The Homosexual Agenda: Exposing the Principal Threat to Religious Freedom Today* (Broadman & Holman), available through FOF.

33. Joseph Nicolosi, Focus on the Family's "Love Won Out" Conference, Oklahoma City, 2003.

34. Ibid.

35. Ibid.

36. Ibid.

37. Ibid.

38. Dr. James Dobson, "Marriage Under Fire" (Sisters, OR: Multnomah Publishers, 2004), p. 68.

39. America's primary mental health organizations all condemn the ex-gay "reparative" and "transformational" therapies recommended by Dobson and his staff. See "Just the Facts: Sexual Orientation and Youth, A Primer for Principals, Educators, and School Personnel" online at http://www.apa.org/pi/lgbc/facts.pclf.

40. Dr. James Dobson, Straight Answers: Exposing the Myths and Facts About Homosexuality, October 8, 2003 (updated November 30, 2004), http://www.family.org/ cforum/ fosi/homosexuality/maf/a0028248.cfm.

41. Available to download online without cost at http://www.soulforce.org/article/ homosexuality-bible. Printed copies of the thirty-two-page booklet are also available to purchase at https://www.soulforce.org/store.

42. Dr. James Dobson, Focus on the Family Newsletter, April 2004 (mailed to an estimated two million people and read aloud on his March 24, 2004, radio broadcast).

43. Ibid.

44. Ibid.

45. Ibid.

46. Ibid.

47. Ibid.

48. 48, Ibid.

49. Coral Ridge Presbyterian Web page: www.crpc.org.

50. *A Manifesto for the Christian Church*, original document posted on the official Council on Revival Web page: http://wwwreformation.net/COR/cordocs/Manifesto.pdf.

51. Ibid., p. 9.

52. *The Lynchburg News &Advance*, January 13, 2006, p. Al, vol. 141, no. 13.

53. Senator George J. Mitchell from the George J. Mitchell Papers, Bowdoin, http:// library.bowdoin.edu/arch/mitchell/research/bio.htm.

54. http://www.coralridge.org/.

CHAPTER 4. THE SECRET MEETING AT GLEN EYRIE: DECLARING WAR ON HOMOSEXUALS

1. Other states represented were: Arkansas, California, Florida, Hawaii, Kansas, Kentucky, Michigan, Missouri, New Mexico, New York, Ohio, Oregon, Rhode Island, Texas, Virginia, and Washington.

2. *Washington Times*, May 19, 1994, section: A NATION, edition 2, p. A3.

3. National Gay and Lesbian Task Force, www.ngltf.org.

4. Thanks to Skip Porteus and his Institute of First Amendment Studies, we have a complete record of the Glen Eyrie meeting on audiotape. Mr. Porteus founded the Institute in the late 1980s "to keep watch on the religious right." And

though he had to dose down the Institute for lack of support from progressive individuals and organizations, the archives he collected remain a priceless record of the fundamentalist Christian rise to power in the 1980s and 1990s. Mr. Porteus donated his collection to the Tuft University Library, and it is catalogued online at http://nils.lib.tufts.edu/cgi-bin/ptext?do c=Perseus:text:4000.08.0031. Mr. Porteus gave permission to transcribe and quote from the Glen Eyrie tapes.

5. In fact, Will Perkins's Amendment 2 was the first attempt by fundamentalist Christians to withhold all civil rights and protections from lesbian, gay, bisexual, and transgender Americans, and it still frightens me to think that as I write, the uneasy balance in the U.S. Supreme Court is about to be undone by newly appointed justices who may agree wholeheartedly with that fundamentalist Christian agenda for sexual and gender minorities.

6. http://www.constitution.org/primarysources/franldin. hard.

7. http://www.fordham.edu/halsall/pwh/swiftl.html.

8. David Bianco, "First Sodomy Laws in the American Colonies," http://www.planetout.com/news/history/archive/06071999.html.

9. Rictor Norton, "Queen James and His Courtiers," The Great Queens of History, updated 8 Jan. 2000, <http://www.infopt.demon.co.uk/jamesi.htm>.

10. Ibid.

11. Ibid.

12. http://thewitness.org/agw/monroe.jan2001.html.

13. Roman Catholicism (and Homosexuality), Claude J. Summers, p. 1, GLBTQ: An Encyclopedia of Gay, Lesbian, Bisexual, Transgender, Queer Culture, online at http://www.glbtq.com/social-sciences/roman_catholicism.html.

14. Bianco, "First Sodomy Laws."

15. Ibid.

16. H. R. McIlwaine, ed., Minutes of the Council and General Court of Colonial Virginia 1622-1632, 1670-1676... (Richmond: Colonial Press, 1924), pp. 34, 42, 78, 81, 83, 85, cited online at http://www.claytoncrarner.com/primary.html.

17. http://www.sodomylaws.org/sensibilities/Virginia. htm#fn27#fn27.

18. http://www.religioustolerance.org/homscotus.htm.

19. Ibid.

CHAPTER 5. THE GLEN EYRIE PROTOCOL: HOW THE WAR WILL BE WAGED

1. John Eldredge, keynote address, Glen Eyrie Conference, May 1994. (Transcripts available through Soulforce, P.O. Box 3195, Lynchburg, VA 24503).

2. A thorough introduction to the life and work of Paul Cameron can be found at "Sexual Orientation: Science, Education, Policy," by Dr. Gregory Herick, professor of psychology at the University of California Davis, online at http://psychology. ucdavis.edu/rainbow/html/facts_cameron. html.

3. *Notice: Persons dropped from membership in the American Psychological Association* (1984). Internal communication from APA to all members.

4. Nebraska Psychological Association (October 19, 1984). Resolution. *Minutes of the Nebraska Psychological Association*, Omaha.

5. ASA Footnotes, February 1987, p. 14. Available from the American Sociological Association, Committee on the Status of Homosexuals in Sociology, 1722 N Street, NW Washington, D.C. 20036,

6. C. Everett Koop, KOOP: The Memories of America's Family Doctor (New York: Random House, 1991), pp. 208, 230.

7. "Hate on Tape: The Video Strategy of the Fundamentalist Right;' by Laura Flanders, on PublicEye.Org, the Web site of Political Research Associates, 1310 Broadway, Suite 201, Somerville, MA 02144, http://www.publiceye.org/eyes/hatetape.html.

8. Ibid.

9. "Medical Consequences of What Homosexuals Do;' by Paul Cameron, Ph.D., chairman of the Family Research Institute, PO Box 62640, Colorado Springs, CO 80962, USA, available online at http://www.familyresearchinst.org/FRI_EduPamphlet3.html.

10. "Homosexuality and Child Molestation," by Paul Cameron, Ph.D., published by Family Research Institute, availble online at www.familyresearchinst.org.

11. "What Causes Homosexual Desire and Can It Be Changed?" by Paul Cameron, Ph.D., published by Family Research Institute, available online at www.familyresearchinst.org.

12. "Same Sex Marriage: Til Death Do Us Part?" by Paul Cameron, Ph.D., published by Family Research Institute, available online at www.familyresearchinst.org.

13. http://www.affirmation.org/suicides/.

14. "Don't Forsake Homosexuals Who Want Help," by Charles Socarides, Benjamin Kaufman, Joseph Nicolosi, Jeffrey Satinover, and Richard Fitzgibbons, reprinted from Letters to the Editor, Wall Street Journal, January 9, 1997. Reprinted on the NARTH Web page: www.NARTH.com.

15. http://www.pathinfo.org/.

16. http://www.pfox.org/.

17. "Instruction Concerning the Criteria of Vocational Discernment," Vatican, November 2005.

18. "A Survey on Homosexuality and Religion," by the Princeton Survey Research Associates for the Pew Forum on Religion and Public Life. The information was gathered during telephone interviews with more than 1,500 people. http://pewforum.org/publications/surveys/religion-homosexuality.pdf.

19. John Eldredge, keynote address, Glen Eyrie Conference, May 1994.

20. John Eldredge quoting C. S. Lewis from an article by C. S. Lewis, "We Have No Right to Happiness," *Saturday Evening Post*, December 1963.

21. John Eldredge, op. cit.

22. "Foundation Principles," a worksheet distributed to every Glen Eyrie delegate, May 1994.

23. John Eldredge, op. cit. and in "Foundation Principles" (induded in delegate package).

24. Alan Turing is described by Andrew Hodges, author of *Alan Turing: The Enigma*, as "...the founder of computer science, mathematician, philosopher, codebreaker, strange visionary and a gay man before his time." Turing, a mathematical genius, was instrumental in changing the course of World War II when he cracked the Germans' Enigma code. In 1952, arrested for being a homosexual, Turing lost his security clearance, ending his important work in biology and physics. In 1954 Turing committed suicide by cyanide poisoning. http://www.turing.org.uk/turing/.

25. Mark E. Pietrzyk, *News-Telegraph*, March 10, 1995, on-line at http://www.hatecrime.org/subpages/hatespeech/cameron.html. Reiterated on the Southern Poverty Law Center's intelligence report, The Thirty Years' War—A Timeline on the antigay movement: http://www.splcenter.org/intel/ intel-report/article.jsp?aid=523. Original article: Mark E. Pietrzyk, "Paul Cameron, Professional Sham—QUEER SCIENCE,"

The New Republic, October, 1994.Note: In a letter to the editor of *The New Republic*, Cameron replies to this charge: "I have never proposed extermination of homosexual males"; see www. familyresearchinst.org/New Republic100394_pietrzyk. html#correspondence. In his response, Mark E. Pietrzyk wrote: "In the early years of the AIDS crisis while Cameron was lobbying for the forcible tattooing and quarantine of AIDS patients, Cameron stated in an interview with *Penthouse* magazine, "It would probably be a lot cheaper to just exterminate male homosexuals." Pietrzyk also responds: "...that according to Surgeon General Koop, Cameron was calling for exterminating homosexuals as early as 1983."

26. Ibid.

27. Paul Cameron, Ph.D., "Violence and Homosexuality," available through the Family Research Institute, PO Box 62640, Colorado Springs, CO 80962, http:// www.familyresearchinst. org/FRI_EduPamphlet4.html.

28. Paul Cameron, "Child Molestation and Homosexuality," available through the Family Research Institute, PO Box 62640, Colorado Springs, CO 80962, http:// www.familyresearchinst. org/FRI_EduPamphlet2.html.

29. Ibid.

30. Ibid.

31. Ibid.

CHAPTER 6. IDOLATRY: THE RELIGION OF FUNDAMENTALISM

1. James Finley, *Christian Meditation: Experiencing the Presence of God* (HarperSanFrancisco, 2004), p. 82.

2. E. John Carnell, *The Case for Orthodox Theology* (Philadelphia: Westminster Press, 1959), chapter VII, "Perils," p. 5.

3. "Gods and Mythology of Ancient Egypt," author unknown, one of many fascinating articles on Egyptian history provided by the Egyptian government at http:// touregypt.net/ godsofegypt/.

4. Pat Robertson's biography on CBN.com.

5. S. Pat Robertson, *Answers to 200 of Life's Most Probing Questions* (Nashville, TN: Thomas Nelson Publishers, 1984), pp. 265-66.

6. Ibid., pp. 268-69.

7. Ibid., pp. 260-62.

8. Pat Robertson in The Rhetoric of Intolerance: An Open-Letter Video to Pat Robertson from Dr. Mel White, a Soulforce Production available online at www.soulforce.org, or by mail at Soulforce, PO Box 3195, Lynchburg, VA 24503.

9. Guigo II, *The Ladder of Monks*, translated by Edmund College and James Walsh, in James Finley's *Christian Meditation* (San Francisco: HarperSanFrancisco, 2004), p. 80.

10. Thomas a Kempis, *Of the Imitation of Christ* (Old Tappan, NJ: Fleming H. Revell, 1953), p. 9.

11. D. James Kennedy, As the Family Goes, quoted in an ad announcing the new book on Kennedy's Web page: http://www.coralridge.org/CRMResCtrdetaiLasp?cat= booklet&pc=102056.

12. Jerry Falwell, fund-raising enclosure, "Same-Sex Marriage: Destroying the Family and America," March 1999, on file.

13. "Christians are more likely to experience divorce than are non-Christians," Barna Research Group, December 21, 1999, at http://www.barna.org/cgi-bin.

14. Robert Skolrood, second keynote speaker, Glen Eyrie Conference, May 1994.

15. Rick Warren quoted by the Reverend Dr. James Armstrong, United Methodist bishop (retired), in "Who Is

Rick Warren?" Viewpoint, Zion's Herald: An Open Forum for People of Faith, November/December 2005, pp. 37-38.

16. American Academy of Child and Adolescent Psychiatry, "Gay, Lesbian, and Bisexual Parents," June 1999.

17. American Psychiatric Association, "Adoption and Co-parenting of Children by Same-Sex Couples," approved by the Board of Trustees and by the Assembly, November 2002.

18. American Psychological Association, "Answers to Your Questions about Sexual Orientation and Homosexuality," www.apa.org/publicinfo/answers.html.

19. *Family News* from Dr. James Dobson, September 2003, p. 3.

20. American Anthropological Association, *Statement on Marriage and Famiy*, February 25, 2004.

21. http://wvvw.constitutioncenter.org/timeline/html/cw10_12239.html.

22. Suzanne Pharr, *Homophobia: A Weapon of Sexism* (Oakland, CA: Chardon Press, 1988), p. 7, available through The Women's Project, 2224 Main, Little Rock, AR 72206.

23. I am in debt to the Ontario Consultants on Religious Tolerance for their excellent summary "Eight Types of Marriages and Families in the Bible, As Compared to Today's Practices," no author listed, online at http://wwwreligioustolerance.org/mar_bibl.htm.

24. "Ward and June Cleaver: The True Story of Despotism and Discontent," by Karen De Coster for LewRockwell.com at http://www.lewrockwell.com/decoster/decoster29.html.

25. Stephanie Coontz, *The Way We Never Were: American Families and the Nostalgia Trap*, online at http://www.amazon.com/gp/product/0465090974/gid=1136373817/sr=82/ref=pd_bbs_2/002-9338054-2516006?n=507846&s=books&v=glance.

26. Pat Robertson, *700 Club*, October 14, 2003,

27. D. James Kennedy, "Spiritual State of the Union," 1995, fund-raising enclosure, on file.

28. Robert Linden, first keynote speaker, Glen Eyrie Conference, May 1994,

29. Robert Skolrood, second keynote speaker, Glen Eyrie Conference, May 1994.

30. Jane Lampman, "For evangelicals, a bid to `reclaim America." For the faithful who gathered in Florida last month, the goal is not just to convert individuals—but to reshape US society;' *Christian Science Monitor*, March 16, 2005, http://www. csmonitor. com/2005/0316/p 1 6s01 -lire.html.

31. D. James Kennedy, May 1, 1995, fund-raising letter to establish his Center for Christian Statesmanship in Washington, D.C.

32. D. James Kennedy quoting C. S. Lewis, referenced by Skipp Porteous in "D. James Kennedy: Reclaiming America for Christ." Institute for First Amendment Studies, Freedom Writer, March/April 1997, http://www.publiceye.org/ifas/ fw/9703/ quotes.html.

33. D. James Kennedy, fund-raising letter, undated, on file in Daryl Lach/Soulforce Archives,

34. D. James Kennedy, sermon "Christian Offensive," 1980, quoted by Skipp Porteous in "D. James Kennedy: Reclaiming America for Christ." Institute for First Amendment Studies, *Freedom Writer*, March/April 1997, http://www.publiceye.org/ ifas/ fw/9703/quotes.html.

35. D. James Kennedy, quoted by Skipp Porteous in "D. James Kennedy: Reclaiming America for Christ," Institute for First Amendment Studies, Freedom Writer, March/ April 1997, http://www.publiceye.org/ifas/fw/9703/quotes.html.

36. D. James Kennedy, fund-raising letter "Stop Judicial Tyranny!" September 11, 1997.

37. D. James Kennedy, Coral Ridge Ministries: Alert Bulletin, undated.

38. D. James Kennedy, fund-raising letter, October 23, 1998.

39. D. James Kennedy, fund-raising letter, July 29, 1998.

40. D. James Kennedy, fund-raising letter, undated, in Daryl Lach/Soulforce Archives.

41. D. James Kennedy, Mother's Day sermon, *Coral Ridge Hour*, May 8, 1994.

42. D. James Kennedy, fund-raising letter, June 1995.

43. D. James Kennedy, "Today's Unpardonable Sin," commentary from Dr. Kennedy, *Impact Magazine*, Coral Ridge Ministries, Fort Lauderdale, Florida, February 1999.

44. D. James Kennedy, "Spiritual State of the Union '93," sermon preached at Coral Ridge Presbyterian Church.

45. Narrator, "The Children of Abraham," episode 3, Ten Alps Communications PLC, History Channel.

46. Paul Tillich, *The Dynamics of Faith* (New York: Perennial Classics, HarperCollins, 1989), p. 20.

CHAPTER 7. FASCISM: THE POLITICS OF FUNDAMENTALISM

1. Mel White, *Stranger at the Gate* (New York: Plume/Penguin, 1995), pp. 245-46.

2. "Public Lives: Warning from a Student of Democracy's Collapse," by Chris Hedges, *New York Times*, January 6, 2005, Metropolitan Desk, Late Edition—Final, section B, p. 2, http://select.nytimes.com/gst/abstract.html?res=F50613FC3B5DOC758CD DA80894DD404482.

3. Henry A. Giroux, *The Terror of Neoliberalism: Authoritarianism and the Eclipse of Democracy* (Boulder/London: Pardigm Publishers, 2004), p. 14.

4. Umberto Eco, "Eternal Fascism: Fourteen Ways of Looking at a Blackshirt," *New York Review of Books* (November/December 1995), quoted in Henry A. Giroux, p. 15.

5. Davidson Loehr, *America Fascism + God* (White River

Junction, VT: Chelsea Green Publishing Company, 2005), p. 76, from the sermon "Living Under Fascism," preached on Nov. 7, 2004.

6. Jerry Falwell, fund-raising letter, January 1999.

7. D. James Kennedy in a fund-raising letter headlined "Are You Dangerous?," January 30, 1999.

8. D. James Kennedy quoted in "Reclaiming America for Christ," by Skipp Porteous, Freedom Writer, March/April 1997, http://www.publiceye.org/ifas/fw/9703/ kennedy.html.

9. Pat Robertson, *The 700 Club*, March 15, 1999.

10. Pat Robertson, *The 700 Club*, October 9, 2003.

11. Pat Robertson, *The 700 Club*, August 22, 2005.

12. Pat Robertson, *The 700 Club*, August 27, 2005.

13. Pat Robertson, *The 700 Club*, January 3, 2005.

14. Bill Moyers, "Armageddon & the Environment," published December 6, 2004, by CommonDreams.org.

15. Laurence W Britt, "Fascism Anyone?" in *Free Inquiry magazine*, 2003, vol. 23, no. 2, http://www secularhumanism. org/index.php?section=library&page=britt_23_2.

16. Ibid.

17. Davidson Loehr, p. 81.

18. Adorno, et al, *The Authoritarian Personality* (New York: Harper and Brothers, 1950).

19. I was present and wrote down the words as Jerry Falwell spoke them on Sunday, October 30, 2004, from the pulpit of the Thomas Road Baptist Church.

20. Adorno, et al, pp. 231, 228.

21. Ibid., pp. 102, 228.

22. Ibid., pp. 107-109.

23. Ibid., pp. 228, 235, 236.

24. Joseph Berger, "At Holocaust Museum: Turning a Number into a Name," *New York Times*, November 21, 2004.

25. Adorno, et al, pp. 236, 235.

26. Ibid., pp. 232-34, 148.

27. Ibid., pp. 219, 220,

28. Thom Hartmann, "The Ghost of Vice President Wallace Warns: 'It Can Happen Here'" at CommonDreams. org, published July 19, 2004. I am grateful to the author for leading me to the discovery of the vice president's prophetic stance. http://www.commondreams.org/views04/0719-1 5.htm.

29. Henry Wallace, "Wallace Defines American Fascism:" *New York Times*, April 9, 1944, available at ProQuest Historical Newspapers, New York Times (1851-2002), p. SM7.

30. Ibid. While serving as Roosevelt's vice president, Henry A. Wallace was being investigated secretly by the FBI for his "leftist leanings.' In a speech Wallace made in 1948, he explained why he didn't defend himself against the charges that he was a "Communist sympathizer." "If I fail to cry out that I am anti-Communist," Wallace said, "it is not because I am friendly to Communism, but because at this time of growing intolerance I refuse to join even the outer circle of that band of men who stir the steaming cauldron of hate and fear." At http://www. christers.net/veeps/ henry-wallace.html.

31. Quoted in "Public Lives...."

32. Richard Plant, *The Pink Triangle* (New York: Holt, 1986), pp. 21-29.

33. Ibid., p. 26.

34. "Nazi Anti-Jewish Speech vs. Religious Right Anti-Gay Speech," Matthew Shepard Online Resources, http:// www.hatecrime.org/subpages/hider/hitler.html. John Aravosis, founder of hatecrime.org and AMERICABIog, continues to be a primary resource for information about "the religious right." His online chart comparing right-wing attacks on homosexual Americans with attacks on Jews in the Nazi propaganda film *The Eternal Jews* documents the similarity in detail.

35. The Holocaust History Project, "Still Images (with

transcript of narration) from *Der ewige Jude* (The Eternal Jew),"
commentary by Stig Hornshoj/Moller, http:// www.holocaust-
history.org/der-ewige-jude. Once again, I thank John Aravosis
for discovering this very important film and its critique online.

36. Pat Robertson, *The 700 Club*, May 6, 1982 (source:
People for the American Way Foundation), http://www.
hatecrime.org/subpages/hatespeech/robertson.html.

37. D. James Kennedy, Coral Ridge Ministries Special
Report, fund-raising letter enclosure, undated, on file.

38. Jerry Falwell, fund-raising letter, January 1999, on file.

39. Pat Robertson *The 700 Club*, June 6, 1988 (source: People
for the American Way Foundation), http://www.hatecrime.org/
subpages/hatespeech/robertson.html.

40. James Dobson, *Bringing Up Boys*, chapter 9, "The
Origins of Homosexuality" (Wheaton, IL:Tyndale Publishing),
p. 127, in "A False Focus on My Family," a soul-force publication
available at www.soulforce.org.

41. Jerry Falwell, fund-raising letter, undated (1995?), on
file.

42. James Dobson, Focus on the Family fund-raising letter,
April 2004, in "A False Focus on My Family," a Soulforce
publication available at www.soulforce.org.

43. D. James Kennedy, fund-raising letter, August 31, 1995,
on file.

44. *The 700 Club*, September 17, 1992 (source: People for
the American Way Foundation), http://www.hatecrime.org/
subpages/hatespeech/robertson.html.

45. D. James Kennedy, ad for video "Gay Rights. Special
Rights," fund-raising letter enclosure, undated, on file.

46. James Dobson, "Family News from Dr. Dobson," a
Focus on the Family fundraising letter, September 2003, on file.

47. Jerry Falwell, fund-raising letter, March 1999, on file.

48. Pat Robertson, fund-raising letter, May 24, 1994, on file.

49. D. James Kennedy, fund-raising letter, undated, on file.

50. Jerry Falwell, fund-raising letter, received April 20, 1993, on file.

51. Pat Robertson, The 700 Club, October 14, 2003, on file.

52. D. James Kennedy, "Why It Matters: Q&A About Free Speech, the Homosexual Agenda," and "Truth in Love," a fund-raising letter enclosure, undated, on file.

53. James Dobson, Focus on the Family newsletter, April 2004,

54. Jerry Falwell, fund-raising letter, received April 20, 1993, on file.

55. Pat Robertson, 1993 Interview with Molly Ivins, at http://www.geocities.com/ CapitolHill/7027/quotes.html.

56. Jerry Falwell, fund-raising letter, March 1999, on file.

57. Jerry Falwell, fund-raising letter, undated (1995?), on file.

58. D. James Kennedy, "Why It Matters: Q&A About Free Speech, the Homosexual Agenda," and "Truth in Love," a fund-raising letter enclosure, undated, on file.

59. James Dobson, fund-raising letter, "Marriage Under Fire," excerpt from *Marriage Un derfire: Why We Must Win this Battle* (Sisters, OR: Multnomah Press, 2004).

60. D. James Kennedy, fund-raising letter, August 31, 1995, on file.

61. D. James Kennedy, "Spiritual State of the Union '93," a published sermon, on file.

62. Jerry Falwell, "Faith Partner" letter, December 1998, on file.

63. Pat Robertson, *The 700 Club*, January 21, 1993.

64. 64, Jerry Falwell, fund-raising letter, received April 20, 1993, on file.

65. Jerry Falwell, fund-raising letter, October 1993, on file.

66. James Dobson, "Marriage Under Fire: The State of Our

Union," Focus on the Family Web site.

67. D. James Kennedy, fund-raising letter, undated, on file.

68. Pat Robertson, *New York magazine*, August 18, 1986, at http://www.geocities.com/ CapitolHill/7027/quotes.html.

69. Abraham Heschel quoted in Taylor Branch, *Pillars of Fire: America in the King Years* (1963-1965) (New York: Simon & Schuster, 1998), p. 23.

70. Ibid.

71. 71, David D. Kirkpatrick, "The 2004 Campaign: The Conservatives; Club of the Most Powerful Gathers in Strictest Privacy," New York Times, August 28, 2004, the National Desk.

72. Ibid.

73. Ibid.

74. Mel White, p. 159.

CHAPTER 8. RECLAIMING OUR PROGRESSIVE POLITICAL VALUES

1. "The Price in Blood: Casualties in the Civil War," http://www.civilwarhome.com/ casualties.htm.

2. *A Manifesto for the Christian Church*, pp. 4-5, www. reformation.net/COR/cordocs/ Manifesto.pdf.

3. U.S. Constitution, Article III, Section 3.

4. *A Manifesto for the Christian Church*, original document posted on the official Council on Revival Web page: http://www.reformation.net/COR/cordocs/Manifesto.pdf.

5. Tom Strode, "Land, others push Bush to support marriage amendment," January 15, 2004, Baptist Press.

6. Ibid.

7. Ibid.

8. White House, Office of the Press Secretary, February 24, 2004.

9. The Southern Manifesto is available online at http://www.cviog.uga.edu/Projects/ gainfo/manifesto.htm.

10. The response is attributed to Benjamin Franklin—at the close of the Constitutional Convention of 1787, when queried as he left Independence Hall on the final day of deliberation—in the notes of Dr. James McHenry, one of Maryland's delegates to the convention, http://www.bartleby.com/73/1593.html.

11. http://www.usconstitution.net/const.html.

12. Leon Jaworski, *The Right and the Power* (Houston, TX: Gulf Publishing, 1976), p. 279.

13. Pat Robertson, *The 700 Club*, undated, in "The Rhetoric of Intolerance: An Open Letter Video to Pat Robertson," a Soulforce video/DVD available online or order at www.soulforce.org/store.

14. The Avalon Project at Yale Law School, "The Barbary Treaties: Treaty of Peace and Friendship Signed at Tripoli," November 4, 1796, http://www.yale.edu/lawweb/avalon/diplo-macy/barbary/bar1796t.htm.

15. Francis Schaeffer, "A Christian Manifesto," a sermon preached in 1982 at the Coral Ridge Presbyterian Church, Fort Lauderdale, Florida. The sermon is based on his book *A Christian Manifrsto*. The sermon is available online at http://www.peopleforlife. org/francis.html.

16. Thomas Jefferson, "The Virginia Act for Establishing Religious Freedom," 1786, document available online at "The Religious Freedom Page," http://religiousfreedom. lib.virginia. edu/sacred/vaact.html.

17. This is a paraphrase of Joseph Goebbels's most famous quote: "If you tell a lie big enough and keep repeating it, people will eventually come to believe it. The lie can be maintained only for such time as the State can shield the people from the political, economic and/or military consequences of the lie. It thus becomes vitally important for the State to use all of its

powers to repress dissent, for the truth is the mortal enemy of the lie, and thus by extension, the truth is the greatest enemy of the State." http://en.thinkexist.com/quotes/joseph_goebbels/.

18. http://en.thinkexist.com/quotes/josepLgoebbels/.

19. Pat Robertson, *The 700 Club*, in "The Rhetoric of Intolerance," a Soulforce Production available at www.soulforce. org.

20. James Kennedy with Gary Newcombe, *What If America Were Christian Once Again* (Thomas Nelson Publishers, 2003), pp. 4-5, http://nonprophet.typepad.com/ nonprophet/2005/04/ focus_on_the_fa.html.

21. James Dobson, "Restoring the Foundations: Repealing Judicial Tyranny," Focus on the Family's Family.Org, http:// wwwfamily.org/finedia/misc/a0027564.cfin.

22. Quoted on the Americans United Web page in "Americans United Responds to Falwell, Robertson Statements About Terrorist Attacks on America," http://www. refuseandresist.org/normalcy/091901 aufscs.html.

23. This collection of quotes is lifted verbatim from "The Rise of the Religious Right in the Republican Party," a public information project from TheocracyWatch.org, http://www. theocracywatch.org/separation_church_state2.htm.

24. Ibid.

25. Jerry Falwell, sermon, July 4, 1976, http://www. ethicalatheist.com/docs/separation_ church_state.html.

26. I was present and wrote down the words as Jerry Falwell spoke them on Sunday, October 30, 2004, in the Thomas Road Baptist Church.

27. E. J. Dionne, Jr., "Faith-Based Hypocrisy," *Washington Post*, October 7, 2005, p. A23, http://www.washingtonpost.com/ wp-dyn/content/article/2005/ 10/06/AR2005 100601584.html.

28. James Dobson, "Transcript of Dobson Comments on Miers/Rove," family.org, Press Room, October 11, 2005, http://

www.family.org/welcome/press/a00382 14.cfm.

29. Amasa Mason Eaton, "Roger Williams, the Founder of Providence—the Pioneer of Religious Liberty;' Providence: E. L. Freeman, 1908 (microfilm), quoted in a brief but incisive and very helpful essay by Ronald Bruce Meyer, "Roger Williams Banished (1635): Separation of Church and State," on his Web page: http:// www.ronaldbrucemeyer.com/rants/0913almanac. htm.

30. Roger Williams in "Mr. Cotton's Letter Lately Printed, Examined and Answered," London, 1644, in Reuben Aldridge Guild, ed., *The Complete Writings of Roger Williams* (New York: Russell & Russell, 1963), vol. 1, p. 108 (1644), http://history. missouristate.edu/FTMiller/Docs/wall.htm.

31. Thomas Jefferson, *Jefferson Writings*, Merrill D. Peterson, ed. (NewYork: Literary Classics of the United States, 1984), p. 510, January 1, 1802.

32. James Madison, "Memorial and Remonstrance Against Religious Assessments," 1785, "The Religious Freedom Page,"http://religiousfreedom.lib.virginia.edu/sacred/ madison_m&r_1785.html.

33. "Christianity and Slavery: The Final Abolition of Slavery in Christian Lands," ReligiousTolerance.org, maintained by the Ontario Consultants on Religious Intolerance, online at http:// www.religioustolerance.org/chr_slav2.htm.

34. South. http://home.att.net/—rjnorton/Lincoln72.html.

35. *The Collected Works of Abraham Lincoln*, Roy P. Basler, ed., Abraham Lincoln Association, available online at http:// showcase.netins.net/web/creative/lincoln/speeches/inaug2. htm.

36. Ibid.

CHAPTER 9. RECLAIMING OUR PROGRESSIVE MORAL VALUES

1. This quotation and the three that follow can be found in Henry H. Haley, *Haley's Bible Handbook* (Michigan: Zondervan, 1965), pp. 18-19, http://www.bible-history.com/quotes/henry_h_haley_l.htrril.

2. BillMcKibben,"TheChristianParadox,"Harper's,August 2005, http://www. harpers.org/ExcerptTheChristianParadox. html.

3. Ibid.

4. Ibid.

5. Peter Gomes, *The Good Book* (New York: Morrow, 1996), p. 5.

6. Bill McKibben, "Christian Paradox."

7. "English Bible History Artide and Time Line," John L. Jeffcoat III, ed., with Dr. Craig H. Lampe, http://WWW. GREATSITE.COM/timeline-english-biblehistory/.

8. http://www.characterbuildingforfamilies.com/names. html.

9. Billy Graham in the *Los Angeles Herald-Examiner*, July 22, 1985, from David Cloud's Fundamental Baptist Information Service, fbns@wayoflife.org.

10. E. Stanley Jones, *Mahatma Gandhi: An Interpretation* (New York: Abingdon-Cokesbury, 1948), p. 8.

11. M. K.Gandhi in E. Stanley Jones, Mahatma Gandhi: An Interpretation, pp. 51-52.

12. Stanley Fish, "Our Faith in Letting It All Hang Out," New York Times op-ed, Week in Review, Feb. 12, 2006, p. 15.

13. M. K. Gandhi, *Autobiography*, Vol. 1, p. 7, in Gopinath Dhawan, *The Political Philsophy of Mahatma Gandhi*, Navajivan Publishing House, India, pp. 41-42. Gandhi's comments about God that follow were assembled from Gandhi's writings by his

student, G. N. Dhawan, for his Ph.D. dissertation, 1939-1941, Lucknow University.

14. Gandhi's letter quoted in Diary I, p. 135, in Dhawan, pp. 38-52.

15. *Young India*, Vol. III, p. 143, in Dhawan, op. cit.

16. Autobiography, II, p. 432, in Dhawan, op. cit.

17. Harijan, May 6, 1933, in Dhawan, op. cit.

18. *Young India*, vol. I, p. 720, in Dhawan, op. cit.

19. Harijan, June 25, 1938, p. 163, in Dhawan, op. cit.

20. Harijan, August 24, 1947, p. 285, in Dhawan, op. cit.

21. Harijan, July 20, 1947, p. 240, in Dhawan, op. cit.

22. Harijan, July 20, 1947, p. 240, in Dhawan, op. cit.

23. Harijan, October 13, 1940, p. 319, in Dhawan, op. cit.

24. Harijan, October 13, 1940, p. 318, in Dhawan, op. cit.

25. Harijan, August 22, 1936, p. 220, in Dhawan, op. cit.

26. Martin Luther King, Jr., "Eulogy for the Martyred Children," in *A Testament of Hope: The Essential Writings and Speeches of Martin Luther King, Jr.*, James Melvin Washington, ed. (San Francisco: HarperSanFrancisco, 1986), pp. 221-22.

27. Martin Luther King, Jr., "A Time to Break Silence," in *A Testament of Hope*, p. 242.

28. Martin Luther King, Jr., "A Christmas Sermon on Peace," in *A Testament of Hope*, p. 255.

29. Martin Luther King, Jr., "I See the Promised Land," in *A Testament of Hope*, p. 286.

30. Paul Johnson, History of the Jews, online at SimpletoRemember: Judaism on Line, "Jewish Quotes," http://www.simpletoremember.com/vitals/quotes.htm.

31. Attributed to Bonhoeffer in many publications but unable to find the reference.

32. Read the verse in John 21:20 and tell me exactly what you picture when the writer says, "Then, Peter, turning about, saw the disciple whom Jesus loved following; which also leaned

on his breast at supper...." *The New Oxford Bible* panics and translates that phrase as "...reclined next to Jesus after dinner." I don't think so. The New English Bible also tries to censor the passage with "...leaned back close to him." Oh, please. And the Revised Standard Version gets spooked by the picture and mumbles, "...who had lain close to his breast." What a bunch of cowards. Go through the various translations and see what they do to avoid what is plainly written in the Greek "...on the breast." Our GLBT Bible stories have been taken from us by homophobic translators, and it's time we take them back. The "beloved disciple" was either in Jesus' lap looking up at him or lying between his legs leaning up against his chest, or if Jesus was reclined on one elbow, the disciple could have used Jesus as a pillow. I'm not inferring anything about Jesus' sexuality. I'm glad the biblical authors leave that ambiguous so we all can claim him. But the point is that Jesus is not afraid of intimate physical contact with another man.

CHAPTER 10. DISCOVERING SOUL FORCE

1. James Melvin Washington, ed., *Testament of Hope: The Essential Writings and Speeches of Martin Luther King, Jr* (San Franscisco: HarperSanFranscisco, 1986), p. 16.

2. Ibid., p. 570.

3. Ibid., p. 571.

4. Matthew 5:44.

5. John 15:17.

6. *Young India II*, p. 1054 in Gopinath Dhawan, op. cit., p. 128.

7. Gopinath Dahwan, op. cit., p. 27.

8. Martin Luther King, Jr., "An Experiment in Love," in *A Testament of Hope*, pp. 16-17.

9. M. K. Gandhi paraphrased by his student Gopinath Dhawan, in *The Political Philosophy of Mahatma Gandhi* (Ahmedabad-14: Navajivan Publishing House, 1946), p. 66.

10. Martin Luther King, Jr., "An Experiment in Love," p. 16.

11. Martin Duberman, *Stonewall* (New York: Dutton, 1993).

12. Donn Teal, *The Gay Militants: How Gay Liberation Began in America*, 1969-1971 (New York: St. Martin's Press, 1971), p. 55.

13. Urvashi Vaid, *Virtual Equality: The Mainstreaming of Gay and Lesbian Liberation* (New York: Anchor Books-Doubleday, 1995), p. 361.

14. King, pp. 16-17.

15. King, p. 23.

16. King, p. 38.

17. M. K. Gandhi, *Satyagraha in South Africa* (Ahmedabad, India: Navajivan Trust, 1928), pp. 104-5.

18. M. K. Gandhi, *An Autobiography or The Story of My Experiment with Truth* (Ahmedabad, India: Navajivan Trust, 1927), p. 58.

19. Martin Luther King, Jr., "Advance 150" (February 28, 1958): 14ff, in *Testament of Hope*, pp. 85-88.

20. Martin Luther King, Jr., "An Address to the National Press Club," July 19, 1962, in *Testament of Hope*, p. 103.

21. Martin Luther King, Jr., "Letter from a Birmingham Jail," in *Testament of Hope*, p. 292.

22. King, p. 291.

23. Martin Luther King, Jr., "Suffering and Faith," in *A Testament of Hope*, p. 41.

24. http://groups.yahoo.com/group/bonhoefferscell/message/769.

25. Hermann Hagedorn, *The Bomb That Fell on America* (Santa Barbara, CA: Pacific Coast Publishing, 1946), p. 43.

26. Mel White, *Aquino: The Untold Story! Ninoy and Cory Aquino's Journey of Faith* (Waco, TX: Word Publishing, 1989), pp. 240-41.

ACKNOWLEDGMENTS

In twenty-five years, Gary Nixon has never failed to love, forgive, encourage, inspire, and support me. And that has made everything possible.

I also thank Daryl Lach, a registered nurse working with ventilator-dependent children, who has volunteered for more than a decade to help us monitor the toxic, antigay rhetoric of fundamentalist Christian leaders, Protestant and Catholic alike.

The examples I use to illustrate the half-truths, hyperbole, and lies used by fundamentalists to demean, dehumanize, and demonize homosexuals are only a small sample of the vast and valuable collection of materials in the Daryl Lach/Soulforce Archives.

Daryl, who has served this project as archivist, research assistant, and untiring creative resource, is also a skilled writer, humorist, and sometimes stand-up comic. There is no way to thank adequately other friends who have read the manuscript and/or given me their frank and helpful suggestions: Rodney Powell, Jack Rogers, Jim Wright, Ken Martin, Kerry Sieh, Chuck Phelan, Jimmy Creech, Mitchell Gold, Elizabeth "Babs" Conant, Randi and Phil Reitan, Corey Hidlebaugh, Jeff Lutes, our new executive director, Kara Speltz, my personal assistant, and the other board members and staff of Soulforce who persuaded me to "keep at it" and then took on extra responsibilities to make it happen.

I want to thank my pastor, Tim Hessel-Robinson, and the people of First Christian Church in Lynchburg for their unqualified welcome and spiritual support; my counselor and friend J. Michael Bostwick; and my extended family: Lyla, Mike, Erinn, my son-in-law, Terry Rich, my bright and beautiful granddaughter, Katie, my new grandson, Sean, my brother, Marshall, and Bunny, his wife, my sister, Judy, and her husband, Ed, and of course Carl, my wonderful, ninety-three year-old father. Like Gary, in spite of my long periods of preoccupation and absence, they never stop loving me, giving me "the guilts" only on rare and appropriate occasions.

I am also indebted to Jake Reitan, our Soulforce Young Adult organizer, and my godson, for encouraging me to continue my research and writing during the year he lived with us in Lynchburg working on his historic Soulforce Equality Ride. Follow Jake's latest Soulforce adventures at: www.soulforce.org. Special thanks to my agent, Matthew Carnicelli, who believed in this book from the beginning, and demonstrated his skills as manager, editor, and counselor all along the way; and to my new friends at Jeremy P. Tarcher/Penguin, especially Joel Fotinos, publisher, and Mitch Horowitz, executive editor.

Please don't blame any of the people mentioned above if I have failed to persuade you that the hidden dangers from the Christian right are real and must be taken seriously. That failure would be mine alone. And if I've succeeded in any small way in overcoming my own anger and speaking truth in love about my fundamentalist Christian sisters and brothers, I thank God, who created us all, loves us all, and wants more than anything for us to love each other.

ABOUT THE AUTHOR

For almost forty years, Mel White served the evangelical Christian community as pastor, professor, author, filmmaker, and ghostwriter to some of the nation's most powerful religious figures. After a thirty-year struggle to "overcome" his homosexuality, White finally accepted his sexual orientation as "a gift from God," and came out to the nation in his best-selling autobiography, *Stranger at the Gate: To Be Gay and Christian in America.*

Ignored or rejected by all his famous clients, White began a campaign to oppose the antihomosexual teachings of Protestant and Catholic church leaders. In 1998, he and his partner, Gary Nixon, founded Soulforce, a movement inspired by the principles of relentless nonviolent resistance of Gandhi and King, to protest religion-based bigotry and oppression. Since that time, more than ten thousand Soulforce volunteers have been trained to participate in nonviolent direct actions against religion-based intolerance. At least a thousand volunteers—including White, several times—have been arrested, fined, and jailed for their Soulforce protests.

In 1997, White received the ACLU's National Civil Liberties Award. You can visit Soulforce online at: www.soulforce.org.

Dr. Mel White

Co-Founder, **Soulforce**
Author, *Stranger at the Gate:
To be Gay and Christian in America*
and
*Holy Terror: Lies the Christian Right
Tells Us to Deny Gay Equality*

**AVAILABLE NOW TO SPEAK
ON YOUR CAMPUS, IN YOUR
CHURCH, OR AT YOUR
SPECIAL EVENT**

For 25 years, Mel White, and his partner, Gary Nixon, have worked to end policies that discriminate against homosexuals and to bring understanding to people on all sides of the issue. Don't miss this rare opportunity to invite Dr. White to speak on your campus, in your church, or for your special event. Mel is "articulate," "funny," "insightful," and "genuine." "He handles controversy calmly and with integrity." "He is skilled at confronting hatred and ignorance." "He is one of a kind." (*Feedback from college, church, and convention appearances.*)

CREATE A FULL-DAY EVENT

- A major address with plenty of time for Q&A with Dr. White
- A visit to a class, a gay-straight alliance, or other special groups
- A meal with your host committee
- A session with staff or faculty to discuss your specific concerns
- Interviews with local media before and during your event

When you call to inquire about booking Dr. White, you will be sent a press packet including a resume, a DVD, and a copy of Mel's "What the Bible Says and Doesn't Say about Homosexuality."

"*Mel White is one of the prophetic voices of our time. He embodies everything that is good about the Christian faith, compassion, forgiveness, love and a bedrock commitment to justice for all of God's children. His voice is a unique and important one in American Christianity. I have been enriched and blessed by it.*"
—CHRIS HEDGES, AUTHOR, ACTIVIST, PULITZER PRIZE WINNING JOURNALIST

Mel and his partner, Gary

***Contact Gary Nixon for information about a booking, photos, and a resume.**
Phone: (434) 384-7696 • www.melwhite.org • Email: infomelwhite@aol.com*